"Conservatives worry about government bureaucracy. Liberals worry about government spy agencies. But the red tape and the black ops got together and had a bastard child, the CIA. Lindsay Moran's book will worry everyone—but in the most likable, readable, and funny way. . . . *Blowing My Cover* is better than *Top Secret*, it's true."

P. J. O'Rourke, author of
Peace Kills and *Give War a Chance*

"We've all read of the follies of war. Now, thanks to the sharp and fun *Blowing My Cover*, we're privy to the follies of real-life American espionage. As they shadow, buck, and fight for one another, Lindsay Moran and her fellow CIA recruits explode not only bombs and cars, but myths, for, unlike James Bond, the spies here are by turns weepy, cool, klutzy, and noble. Don't miss the finale, where Moran herself acts (as she writes) in that most American of ways: with fierce, inspiring independence."

—David Schickler, author of
Sweet and Vicious and *Kissing in Manhattan*

"In this fascinating book, Lindsay Moran drops her cloak to offer a rare first-person account of the life of a street-level CIA clandestine officer. From her secret training at 'The Farm' to undercover assignments overseas, she uses a great amount of wit, candor, and keen insight to show that the 'real' life of a CIA spy is far from that portrayed by Hollywood."

—James Bamford, bestselling author of
Body of Secrets, The Puzzle Palace,
and *A Pretext for War: 9/11, Iraq,*
and the Abuse of America's Intelligence Agencies

Blowing
My Cover

MY LIFE AS A CIA SPY

Lindsay Moran

BERKLEY BOOKS

New York

THE BERKLEY PUBLISHING GROUP
Published by the Penguin Group
Penguin Group (USA) Inc.
375 Hudson Street, New York, New York 10014, USA
Penguin Group (Canada), 90 Eglinton Avenue East, Suite 700, Toronto, Ontario M4P 2Y3, Canada
(a division of Pearson Penguin Canada Inc.)
Penguin Books Ltd., 80 Strand, London WC2R 0RL, England
Penguin Group Ireland, 25 St. Stephen's Green, Dublin 2, Ireland (a division of Penguin Books Ltd.)
Penguin Group (Australia), 250 Camberwell Road, Camberwell, Victoria 3124, Australia
(a division of Pearson Australia Group Pty. Ltd.)
Penguin Books India Pvt. Ltd., 11 Community Centre, Panchsheel Park, New Delhi—110 017, India
Penguin Group (NZ), Cnr. Airborne and Rosedale Roads, Albany, Auckland 1310 New Zealand
(a division of Pearson New Zealand Ltd.)
Penguin Books (South Africa) (Pty.) Ltd., 24 Sturdee Avenue, Rosebank, Johannesburg 2196,
South Africa

Penguin Books Ltd., Registered Offices: 80 Strand, London WC2R 0RL, England

The material in this book has been reviewed and approved by the CIA. That review neither constitutes
CIA authentication of information nor implies CIA endorsement of the author's views.

Some names of individuals have been changed by the author.

Copyright © 2005 by Lindsay Moran Kegley
Cover design © 2004 Raquel Jaramillo
Author photo © James Kegley
Book design by Amanda Dewey

All rights reserved.
No part of this book may be reproduced, scanned, or distributed in any printed or electronic form without
permission. Please do not participate in or encourage piracy of copyrighted materials in violation of the
author's rights. Purchase only authorized editions.
BERKLEY is a registered trademark of Penguin Group (USA) Inc.
The "B" design is a trademark belonging to Penguin Group (USA) Inc.

PRINTING HISTORY
G. P. Putnam's Sons hardcover edition / January 2005
Berkley trade paperback edition / November 2005

Berkley trade paperback ISBN: 0-425-20562-2

The Library of Congress has catalogued the G. P. Putnam's Sons hardcover edition as follows:

Moran, Lindsay.
Blowing my cover: my life as a C.I.A. spy / Lindsay Moran.
p.   cm.
ISBN 0-399-15239-3
1. Moran, Lindsay.   2. Intelligence agents—United States—Biography.
3. United States. Central Intelligence Agency.   I. Title.
UB271.U52M67   2005   2004054461
327.1273'0092—dc22
[B]

Printed in the United States of America

10   9   8   7   6   5   4   3

*For all the men and women of the CIA, who continue
to strive for excellence and to serve our country,
despite the obstacles placed in their way*

ONE

I am in a medical laboratory at the Central Intelligence Agency, waiting to pee in a cup. The sterility of the atmosphere here—everything is white—chills me to the bone. I am slightly humiliated by the prospect of a drug test, but I want this job badly enough that I'm willing to submit to it.

I've just finished another test in a soundproof chamber, raising my right hand every time I hear a shrill high-pitched sound, not unlike a dog whistle. One among the many things I must prove over the next few days is that I am not deaf. The sight and hearing exams provide me a surging sense of pride—perhaps, like one of the pioneer astronauts, I possess "The Right Stuff." The drug test, on the other hand, just makes me feel like a derelict.

"Why would you want to work for an organization that doesn't

trust you from the get-go?" my boyfriend had asked me about the
week of screening required in my quest to be hired by the CIA.

"Drug tests are normal for any number of jobs," I pointed out.

"Yeah, but a lie-detector test is not," he said, referring to the
polygraph, which will follow in the coming days.

"Be sure to provide enough urine to reach the designated spot."
A Nurse Ratchet look-alike with eyes the color of a corpse hands
me a plastic cup whose side has been marked halfway up with a
thick black slash.

I take the cup and head into the restroom. My eyes dart about
the tiny chamber as I wonder if the mirror is made of two-way
glass. If not, where is the hidden camera? I sit on the toilet, plastic
cup in hand, and think about how I got here in the first place.

Five years earlier, I'd given the commencement speech at
my college graduation. I had concluded my—in retrospect—
sanctimonious talk by saying, "It is my hope that each of us
will influence a particular community, and that we will do so
not by shouldering the expectations of others but by remaining faithful, foremost, to ourselves."

The day after I made this speech, I sent my résumé to the
Central Intelligence Agency. At the age of twenty-one, this
was my personal act of faithfulness.

My father, who worked for the Defense Department his entire life, was certain the CIA would never take me. "You're not
their type," he said. "They look for people who've been the
president of the Young Republicans Club."

Maybe my father's doubt impelled me to approach the CIA in the first place. I was intent on proving him wrong. Aside from that, I'd always wanted to be a spy and felt as if I'd spent my entire life in training. In childhood, my favorite books, which I would read over and over again, starred Harriet the Spy. When I'd been naughty and was sent to my room as punishment, I used the opportunity to monitor the movements of our next-door neighbors, the McCormicks. I routinely communicated in secret code, using a flashlight, with my best friend, who lived two doors down. I was expert at rifling through drawers or ferreting around the attic to find the Christmas presents, which I would open in advance and then undetectably rewrap. I also seemed to have no problem lying, especially to my parents.

Once, when my father confronted my brother and me about who had defiled the living room walls with green crayon, and neither one of us would fess up, he finally said, "Okay, Lindsay, I know it was you."

"Me?!" I wailed, injured by and indignant over his accusation. "How do you know it was me?!"

"First of all, your brother would not graffiti the walls," my father said. And then, with somewhat more gravity: "Second of all, your brother would not lie."

I couldn't really argue. I was naturally subversive, and always had been. During my teenage years, my albeit mild acts of sedition included skipping school, forging excuse notes, sneaking out of the house, and raiding my father's liquor cabinet. Throughout my liberal arts education—when I at least excelled academically and everybody was telling me that I should be a writer, or a lawyer, or go into politics—I always thought, *What I really want to be . . . is a spy.*

My fascination with all things espionage was consummate. I devoured spy novels and CIA memoirs, and delighted in the occasional James Bond triple feature at the cheap movie theater in Boston. I wasn't naive enough to think that the life of a CIA agent was all Hollywood glamour, but I was pretty sure I'd be good at it.

Also, I harbored what I now realize was a delusion: that espionage was something of a family legacy, and therefore my destiny. While Dad always had maintained that he worked at "the lab," his inability to talk about top secret projects, coupled with his frequent travel and late-night comings and goings, had me convinced that he must be a spy. I used to go on business trips with him and keep an eye out for possible surveillants. Or I would pack my own luggage in a particular, persnickety way so that I could detect if someone had tampered with it. Even after I realized Dad was unlikely a covert operative—and that he probably *was* the naval architect he claimed to be—I remained equally suspicious about *his* dad, my grandfather.

Boompah had lived all over the world, supposedly as a U.S. Army engineer. It seemed coincidental, to say the least, that during each of his overseas postings, an unexpected coup toppled the government of the country where he was stationed. Boompah died before I got a chance to question him, but a part of me suspected I would find out the truth if only I could get inside the CIA. In doing so, I also would fulfill my cloak-and-dagger birthright.

I proved my father wrong early on. Within one month of sending off my résumé, I was invited, by way of a succinct letter, to an informational CIA meeting in Washington, D.C.

And so, at the tail end of a long, hot summer, I traveled by train from my postcollege home of Boston, joining a group of about twenty other slightly anxious-looking young men and women in a banquet room at a Holiday Inn. The CIA representatives who greeted us were somewhat disappointing: a dowdy, middle-aged woman with thick glasses and orthopedic shoes, and a paunchy, balding guy who had the aura of someone just completing a messy divorce.

They explained to us that the CIA had four primary components. In addition to Directorates for Science and Technology (DS&T) and Administration (DA), there were two others that the CIA particularly hoped would interest us: the Directorate of Intelligence (DI), composed of *overt* "information analysts," and the Directorate of Operations (DO). This last, the bald guy said, was "where the *real* work of the Agency gets done."

Within the DO, there are two main positions, he explained— reports officers, who take raw intelligence and prepare it for the DI analysts (primarily by making sure the source of the information is obscured), and case officers, the ones who gather the intelligence in the first place. "The case officers are the actual spies," he said.

There was no doubt in my mind when I left the meeting that day: If I was going to work for the CIA, I was going to be a case officer. The DI seemed like a confederacy of dweebs, and the reports officers sounded like glorified secretaries.

Like everyone else at the meeting, I left Washington with an application in hand—a fifteen-page document far more exhaustive than the Harvard application I had filled out four years before. I found a seat by myself on the train back to Boston, pulled my knees up to my chin, and began thumbing through it. In addition to essay questions and biographic queries about everyone in my family, it asked me to list all the places I had lived, and give a personal reference for each location. I thought about the room I'd rented in a Boston University frat house the summer after freshman year, and shuddered to think what anyone would say about me from those days.

It also asked about criminal activity and drug use. I knew a polygraph exam would be administered before I was hired, so I decided I would be honest about the fact that I'd used drugs. My father's words rang in my ears: "You've smoked pot. They'll never hire you."

Dad might have had a valid point, but I was no less determined to prove him wrong. As soon as I arrived home, I returned to my apartment, shared with two other postcollege friends, and hunkered down in the makeshift bedroom we'd created for me out of curtains and screens. Using a black ballpoint pen, I began to fill out the application. Eventually, one of my flatmates called through the curtain, "Are you okay? What are you up to in there?"

Recalling the bald guy's instructions not to tell anyone except immediate family members that I was applying to the CIA, I stashed the stack of papers under a pillow. "I'm fine!" I called back, sounding—I am sure—slightly panicked. "I have cramps. I'm just lying in bed."

About two hours later, I put the completed application in my desk drawer, intending to send it in the next day.

That night, I had a dream in which my family was reunited for a picnic in a grassy park, a place where Mom and Dad had taken us as children to hear Peter, Paul and Mary perform. In my dream, my deceased grandparents were there, sitting on a patchwork blanket spread out over the lawn. Even my mother and father, who in reality had been divorced for years, were laughing together as Mom assembled plates of fried chicken and potato salad. Everybody was got up in the kind of loose, hippie clothing we used to wear. My older brother was with some girl I didn't recognize, but who appeared to be his wife. I approached the group and went to give my grandmother a hug. She didn't acknowledge me, but rather turned away and sat stonily facing the opposite direction.

"Tell Memo it's me," I said to my father.

"Who are you?" he said.

"It's me!" I cried. "Lindsay!"

My mother laughed. "Lindsay?! We haven't seen her in years."

"You must have the wrong family." Boompah lit his pipe, then dismissively tossed the match over his shoulder.

When I woke, the dream, on the cusp of my decision to apply to the CIA, freaked me out. I couldn't help but interpret it as a sign that I was on a course I would later regret. Perhaps my family was right; maybe the CIA wasn't for me, at least not now. I was too young to embark on such a serious career—to embark on any career at all, for that matter. And so I never sent that application.

Instead, I moved to California, waitressed in a coffee bar, and worked as an assistant to a man who was writing a "Complete Guide to Cocktails." Later, I went to graduate school in New York. When New York had exhausted me, I took a job overseas—teaching English to exceptionally bright young students in Bulgaria, an unlikely and at that time dismal locale, but a country I would come to love and whose people would entrench themselves in my heart. After a year in Bulgaria, I came back to the States and—eventually—back to the CIA.

Why?

The Agency was like an itch that I had to scratch. In 1997, I was working as a writing teacher at a community college in San Francisco when that itch resurfaced. I had lived overseas and loved it. I missed Bulgaria terribly. Thinking of ways to return, the idea of the CIA resurfaced. *Why not spend my future living abroad?* I thought excitedly. *Why not make a career out of learning foreign languages, experiencing exotic cultures, having adventures in far-off lands? Why not go through with it this time?* Now I was older; now I felt ready.

The CIA also seemed to me a way to fulfill a sense of civic duty. The fact that my brother was serving our country in the U.S. Navy inspired me and provoked my own patriotic urges, but I knew I wasn't military material. Teaching—a profession of inarguably noble intent that I'd hoped would assuage my feelings of civic obligation—ultimately left me restless and bored. The CIA began to seem like the answer to me: a way to serve both the needs of my country and those of myself.

About the same time that I sent in an application to be a Fulbright Scholar back in Bulgaria, a decent if not surefire backup plan, I again sent my résumé to the CIA. I was twenty-six years old now, five years older than when I'd originally expressed interest. I wondered if the CIA had a record of me, and whether it would give me a second chance.

Again, the Agency responded quickly. Within a month, they had sent me another application, which I filled out *and* sent in. A few weeks later, someone called and, without introducing himself or saying whom he represented, informed me of an interview the following week at the Holiday Inn Fisherman's Wharf. He instructed me to make no inquiries at the reception desk and to take the stairs, "*not* the elevator," to Room 219 and knock twice. I briefly wondered if the caller might be one of the few people who knew I was applying to the CIA, my brother or my boyfriend, playing a prank.

But a few days later, I presented myself at the rather shabby-looking Holiday Inn, taking the stairs and knocking twice on the door of Room 219. I felt silly and was more than a little apprehensive that I would startle whatever tourists actually were staying in the room, the predictable punch line of this elaborate hoax.

But a man answered the door and, after darting his head out and looking up and down the hallway, quickly ushered me into Room 219. This man, who introduced himself as "Dave," seemed more auspicious than the previous CIA recruiters; at least he was young and fit. As Dave walked across the room to the small table by the closed blinds, I noticed he had a slight limp. I was pretty sure that he had been shot in the leg, performing some kind of supersleuth derring-do. Years later, Dave—who would end up being one of my instructors—confessed to me that he had sustained the injury in a softball game against some guys from the FBI.

As we began our conversation, Dave turned on the television—"sound masking," he explained—to an episode of *Teletubbies*. The singing, dancing, and hugging multicolored creatures were incongruous, not to mention distracting. I strained to focus as Dave spoke.

Dave said that he was a case officer and described some of the places he had served, all of which sounded exotic and exciting. He spoke several languages, had lived all over the world, and seemed slightly annoyed at spending a year Stateside, conducting interviews for new recruits.

Still, the interview went well, and at the end of it Dave said he thought I was a strong candidate to be a case officer. At his recommendation, I probably would be called to Washington for a week's worth of screening and further interviews.

I left the meeting giddy with excitement, even though my family and boyfriend were all dead set against my joining the Agency. My father remained convinced I would never be hired, owing to my liberal, lawless ways. My brother, on the basis of his military experience, felt this male-dominated profession would be hard on any woman and would especially curtail my free spirit. My mother was just plain worried: She was sure I'd go to some godforsaken place and immediately get myself killed. My boyfriend merely thought I was insane.

"What if you ever want to quit?" he said. "Will they, like, *terminate* you?"

Looking back, I think they were all a little bit afraid they'd lose me—if not literally, then figuratively. Or at least they would lose the person that I was then: open and friendly, always telling stories—even if those stories were often a bit exaggerated—and ever ready to share a laugh.

"What's the point of having adventures," my boyfriend asked, "if you can't ever tell anyone about it?"

My mother concurred. "My friend Rhoda's next-door neighbor works for the CIA," she said. "Rhoda said he's the most boring guy she ever met."

"I hope you're prepared to give up marijuana," my father warned me ominously, as if I seldom made it a day without smoking a bowl.

My brother sent me an article about a group of female employees who had sued the CIA. "None of them could get anywhere in their careers," he cautioned later on the phone. "Are you sure this is what you want?"

"I haven't even been hired yet," I countered their valid concerns. "Anyway, I probably won't make it through." I fell back on this retort for lack of any other adequate response. But a part of me thought I *would* make it through, and—buoyed by this inexplicable confidence—when invited, I readily traveled back to Washington, D.C., for the week's worth of screening.

The CIA put me up at the Hilton in McLean, Virginia. I had received a letter warning me that I was not to share with anyone the nature of my business and that I should report to Building X, not far from my hotel, at eight on Monday morning.

The first order of business was a complete physical and the drug test. I had smoked pot once between the time of my initial application—in which I'd reported drug use as "a few times in college"—and the current test.

Seated in a barren conference room, eight other candidates and I were handed slips of paper and told that, before undergoing our drug test and the polygraph, we should write down any "criminal activity or incidences of drug use" that we had not previously reported. I was the only person sheepishly to pick up a pen.

After the physical exam, we took a series of multiple-choice tests. One particularly asinine test contained in excess of two thousand questions. There were bizarre true/false statements like "I would rather be a florist than a firefighter," and confusingly worded ones such as "I rarely like to torture small animals."

Still, I thought I was doing okay until the following day when I met with one of the Agency psychiatrists. A shriveled old man, the psychiatrist wore a white lab coat and 1950s-style spectacles perched on his hawkish nose. Judging by his appearance, I was pretty sure the guy had worked for the Agency back when it was the OSS, and that this building had been erected around him and his sterile little desk. I got a bad feeling, but I was also aware that he must be some kind of ancient gatekeeper of sorts. I was eager to please, or at least to prove to him that I was as sane as they come.

The doctor began by telling me that I had scored the highest among all the candidates on the verbal and the mathematical aptitude exams. I felt myself beaming with hope and pride. Then he turned to the "psychiatric" portion of my evaluation.

"There were some disturbing results on your psychological exam," he started out.

I was taken aback. A classic overachiever, I was used to acing every test.

"Some very disturbing results." He clicked his tongue disapprovingly.

My heart sank. Clearly, I was out of the running.

"For instance," he went on, "you designated *false* in response to the statement *I have never wished that I were a member of the opposite sex.*"

"Well, sometimes, occasionally, I have thought it would be nice, I mean, you know, *easier* to be a boy."

The old man continued to stare at me impassively.

"*I'd* like to earn a dollar to a woman's sixty cents!" I joked, failing to elicit so much as a smile. The old man jotted down something in my file.

"Another statement which you indicated as *false*," he said. "*I have never engaged in unusual sexual practices.*"

I could feel my face reddening. "Well, I . . . I guess that depends on what you consider *unusual*," I stammered.

"I would be curious to know what *you* were considering to be unusual," the old man leaned forward, "when you marked this statement as false."

"Well, perhaps I am wrong," I was already angry at myself for letting the old man get the better of me. "But I assumed the question referred to anything other than, say, missionary-position sex."

This was followed by an agonizing silence. The old man's eyes bore into me even more intently.

"I mean, if other positions and, you know, experimentation are considered unusual, then I guess I'd have to say I've engaged in unusual sex. . . . But I . . ."

"What sort of experimentation?" he shot out.

Should I just get up and bolt? But I had come so far; I wasn't about to let some second-rate shrink intimidate me.

"I mean anything, ahem, *oral* . . . or otherwise," I said.

The old man now was scribbling furiously in my file. "Yes," he said at last, looking up. "I would classify that as unusual . . . even deviant. You clearly have some sexual deviancy, of which I have made note in my evaluation of you."

I was stunned, and surely visibly upset. I couldn't tell if he really believed me to be a sexual deviant, or if he was just trying to throw me off. I left, shaken, and went back to my hotel. I plopped down on the bed, called my mother, and told her, with a lot of embarrassed hedging, what had occurred. My mother was outraged.

"That's not deviant," she hollered into the phone. "I could give him something deviant, for chrissake!" Once we both had calmed down, my mother and I agreed that the guy was probably a pervert who was just getting his rocks off. "Are you sure you want to work for these people?" my mother said before she hung up the phone.

Oddly, I was surer than ever; now I had not only my father to disprove but also that dirty old psychiatrist. Furious but all the more determined, I decided that I would not let the polygrapher—by whom I was to be interrogated the following and final day—coerce me into making any kind of confessions, the way the shrink had.

Early the next morning, I showered, dressed, and headed out for another generic redbrick building in Northern Virginia, where the polygraph would be administered.

One thing I would come to realize for the first time that

morning, and on several occasions later in my career: The prospect of taking a lie-detector test is a surefire cure for constipation. I spent the half hour prior to my poly running back and forth from the waiting room to the restroom, nervous energy acting as a virulent laxative on my already queasy system.

One by one, the examiners opened a door at the far end of the waiting room and called us in by our first names. By now, those of us still in the running had formed a loose camaraderie, notwithstanding the fact that we were all competitors. We winked at one another and mouthed the words "good luck." I was heartened not to be chosen by one startlingly handsome polygrapher around my age—I wasn't wholly convinced I could make it through the next few hours without crapping my pants.

My polygrapher turned out to be a sturdy, attractive African American woman who introduced herself as "Kathy." Much later, I would realize that everyone with whom we came into contact used a fake name.

Like the other polygraphers, Kathy seemed incapable of managing so much as a smile. Wordlessly, she led me to a small windowless room and seated me in a BarcaLounger, stationed in front of a desk. Behind the desk was a swivel chair, and a computer whose screen I couldn't see.

Kathy matter-of-factly explained that the test would measure my physiological reactions to each question she asked, and that when I was lying, it would show up on her computer screen as well as on a printout.

She handed me a waiver stating that if, during my polygraph, I revealed having committed any serious crimes (such as murder, rape, or any federal offenses), the CIA was required by law to turn that information over to the Department of Justice or the FBI. I was pretty sure that my short-lived career as a petty shoplifter at the age of seven would not land me in a federal penitentiary, so I signed.

At dinner the night before, one of the other candidates had regaled us with polygraph lore: a story about a man who, with shockingly little probing, had admitted to killing his wife, dissecting her body, and then storing parts of her dismembered corpse in mason jars in his cellar.

Surely, whatever offenses I'd committed would pale in comparison. By the time Kathy had strapped coils around my chest and waist, a blood-pressure gauge around my arm, and nodes around two fingers on each hand, I was less nervous than I was curious, and even a little excited.

Kathy ran through a series of what I considered physiologically unchallenging questions: Was I a member of any terrorist organization? Had I ever willfully damaged any government property? Did I intend to answer all the questions truthfully? Was I working for a foreign intelligence service? Other than the instances I'd already reported, had I used any illegal drugs? Had I committed any crimes? Was I keeping from the CIA any relationships with foreign nationals?

The last question bothered me, mostly because of the Bulgarian rock climbers. I already had provided the CIA a complete list of my foreign friends, most of whom I'd made when I took up mountaineering while living in their country. I'd felt awful providing their names in the first place and wondered how they'd feel knowing I had reported them to the CIA. It was one thing to subject *myself* to the U.S. government's scrutiny; it was quite another to hand over the names of others. I justified it with the assumption that the Agency would just check them against a database of foreign spies. And, on the very remote chance that one among my friends *was* some kind of bad guy, shouldn't I know about it?

After several rounds of the same questions, Kathy said that we were going to take a break. Relieved, I assumed that I was doing okay. But then she plunked herself—almost angrily, it seemed—in front of me with a clipboard in her hand and a nasty look on her face.

"You're not doing well," she said.

Once again, I was taken aback. Ever since I'd begun pursuing an intelligence career, my tendency to excel had faltered increasingly.

"You're holding something back," Kathy said. "I think you should tell me what and why."

"I'm really not," I said. "I'm telling the truth."

"If you were telling the truth, we wouldn't be having this conversation," Kathy said. At that moment, I noticed that Kathy's blouse button had come undone and her black brassiere and ample bosom were showing. I wondered if I should tell her. I even wondered if it was part of the exam! I said nothing and averted my eyes. My unwillingness to make eye contact must have aroused Kathy's suspicions further.

"You're having issues with one particular question," she said. "I want you to tell me which one it is."

"I have no idea," I said. "I mean, I was honest about using drugs. . . . Maybe I did 'underestimate' by a few occasions the number of times I smoked pot, but—"

"It's not drugs!" Kathy said firmly.

"Well, then, I really don't know. I reported all my foreign contacts."

"It's crime," Kathy said. "You're having a reaction to the question about crime."

"You've got to be kidding?!" The crime question was worded something like: *Since the age of eighteen, have you ever committed murder, rape, or theft of items worth over 200 U.S. dollars?*

"I'm telling the truth," I said defiantly.

"Have you ever stolen anything?"

"I stole candy bars when I was seven," I said. "But not two hundred dollars' worth!"

"What about when you were a teacher?" Kathy continued. "Ever steal paper from the Xerox machine?"

"Certainly not." I was starting to get angry. "Once in a while, I may have reproduced a *Far Side* cartoon with the school copier, if that's what you're after. But it was usually for the benefit of the entire faculty. I mean, I would put it on the fridge in the teachers' lounge!"

Standing abruptly, Kathy said she was going to leave for a while to consult with her "superiors." During that time, I was to ponder what other crimes I'd committed that I was not revealing and, if need be, compile a list. I decided Kathy must be a complete nutter.

While she was gone, I stared at the wall and wondered how I had gotten myself into this mess. What if they didn't believe me and then turned me over to the Feds?! I thought about spending the rest of my life behind bars for some unknown crime that I didn't commit. Meanwhile, I glanced around the room, wondering where the hidden camera must be; we had heard that all of the rooms were equipped with a discreet video-surveillance apparatus so that the testers could observe your behavior while they were out of the room.

I tried to look cool and unaffected.

Finally, Kathy came back, her blouse rebuttoned. Not surprisingly, she informed me that her superiors were also convinced that I was lying about something.

I was incensed. "I've told the truth," I said. "I don't have anything else to say."

"I am going to give you one more opportunity to get everything off your chest," Kathy sat in front of me again, her legal pad crooked in one arm, pen in hand.

"I'm not lying," I said. "And I have nothing to get off my chest."

Kathy sighed. "Well, we can give you the test again . . . or you can come back tomorrow."

I had a flight back to San Francisco the following day. I already had been sitting in the chair for over two hours. I was starting to feel that this was a lost cause. "I don't care," I said.

Kathy hooked me up to the machine again and we ran through the same questions, but this time she asked the "crime" one between every other query. That alone made me so nervous that I was sure my physiological reactions were off the charts. Finally, Kathy told me I could relax (*Yeah, right!*) while she consulted a long scrolling printout of my results.

"I'll be back," she said snappishly as she again left the room.

When Kathy returned, she looked even more serious and unfriendly than before.

"You passed the exam today." She began uncoiling the wires from around my chest and waist. "Thank you for your time." With that, Kathy led me silently down an interminable hallway back to the waiting area.

Oddly, as I left the building, I did not feel gratified in the least. To the contrary, I felt humiliated and foolish for submitting to this degrading process.

I flew back to San Francisco convinced that my miserable performance on the polygraph and psych exams would prevent me from being hired anyway. I went back to teaching and tried to put thoughts of my aborted career in espionage behind me. One day I found in my mailbox notification that I had been awarded a Fulbright Scholarship to Bulgaria, and I excitedly began making plans to return to Eastern Europe.

Three weeks later, I received another letter, this one offering me a job—as a case officer with the CIA.

TWO

"Do you know Lindsay Moran?" The man on the front steps flashes a black leather wallet containing some sort of official-looking badge.

"I am Lindsay Moran."

"Aha!" The man introduces himself as Frank, a background investigator from the Department of Defense.

"You mind if I ask you a few questions?" Frank pulls a yellow legal pad and government-issued ballpoint pen from his tattered briefcase.

I lead Frank into the foyer of the San Francisco house in which I've been renting a room for the summer. I recall that during the past few days, Tina, one of my roommates, has noticed a strange guy lurking about the neighborhood. Often parked in a blue van, he's been observing our comings and goings from across the street. Obviously, this was Frank.

The day before, Tina reported to me, Frank had arrived on the front porch of the elderly and inevitably inebriated Mrs. O'Sullivan, who wasted no time in slamming the door on Frank's face and immediately calling the police. According to Tina, Frank also unwittingly approached the halfway house for criminals located across the street, causing half the guys to flee out the back.

Now Frank and I sit in the living room, still strewn with pizza boxes and beer bottles from the previous night. Frank asks me a lot of questions about my financial situation and drinking habits. His eyes scan the debris on the floor. I downplay the details of my huge college debt and our relaxed—slightly hedonistic—living situation enough to make myself seem generally, if not totally, upstanding. I am pretty sure that Frank has encountered more degenerate cases than the likes of me.

In the middle of the conversation, a guy I've never seen before emerges from the basement. He is naked except for a towel wrapped precariously around his waist.

I am not nearly as stunned as Frank. Truth be told, on any given night, I do not know who might be sleeping in the house. Tina, a displaced Ohio farm girl with the most open of hearts, extends her goodwill to anyone who happens to show up. Many a wayward and weary traveler—a friend of a friend of a friend—has found refuge at our house on Second Avenue by Golden Gate Park.

The towel-wrapped guy thrusts out his hand, first to me and then to Frank. "Hi! I'm Guy."

"Guy?" Frank writes the name on his pad, just below some scribblings about how many glasses of wine I consume per week. "Perhaps when we're done here, Guy," Franks says without looking up. "I could talk to you for a few minutes about Lindsay."

"Who's Lindsay?" says Guy.

Frank is visibly confused; it is left to me to explain that Guy and I have only just met. Then I tell Guy that I am Tina's roommate and am applying for "a government job." "Frank is my background investigator from the Department of Defense," I add casually.

This information is enough to send Guy hightailing it back to the basement. I am sure "background investigator" and "Department of Defense" evoke nothing but negative and foreboding connotations for the kind of freewheeling rambler Guy appears to be.

Frank seems as relieved as I am when he finally finishes the interview. As he folds the sheaf of notes on me in half, he sighs heavily and confesses that "this is all very new" to him. Turns out Frank is a recently retired shoe salesman.

"This is the first background investigation I've ever done," Frank says, almost apologetically. "I don't want to, you know, screw the pooch."

I tell Frank I understand and that, truly, there is nothing in my past I am trying to hide.

As soon as Frank is out the door, I yell to Guy that it's safe to come up from the basement, but just then the doorbell rings again. It's Frank.

"I'm sorry to bother you," Frank says, his eyes cast toward the pavement as if in abject shame. "But there's one more thing." Frank looks both ways to make sure nobody is watching from the neighboring houses before he steps halfway through the open doorway. "You don't do any more of this, do you?" Wide-eyed, lips pursed like a fish, Frank mimics taking hits off an imaginary joint. It's clear he's never smoked pot before.

In fact, I have not partaken of marijuana for over a year, ever since I left for Bulgaria on the Fulbright. "No drugs for me anymore," I say to Frank. I can sense Guy has arrived from the basement and is looming behind me.

"Okay, just making sure." Frank makes another note on a fresh sheet of legal paper and then salutes me and Guy before he retreats down the front stairs.

"Wow, that was one creepy dude," Guy says as soon as I've closed and locked the door. From the window, we can see Frank get in his blue van and drive slowly down the street. This time, it seems he's truly on his way.

Two weeks later, I am truly on my way as well: back to the East Coast to start my new job at the CIA.

One year earlier, faced with the decision—Fulbright or CIA—I hadn't known what to do. On the one hand, I was anxious to start my career as a spy. On the other hand, a year in Bulgaria on scholarship seemed an attractive proposition. I would be doing my own research, no one looking over me. I knew that once I started with the Agency, all facets of my life might be under constant scrutiny. The Fulbright seemed to offer me a final year of freedom, one last hurrah.

I called the Agency and asked if I could put off my start date for a year to take the Fulbright.

"We're beginning to question your commitment," the Human Resources representative said. "And whether you really want to come at all." This was in reference to the fact that I also had refused to start at the CIA two weeks after being hired, as the recruitment office had requested of me. Notwithstanding the Fulbright offer, I was in the middle of a teaching semester at the time and felt a commitment to finish out the school year. It surprised me that an organization that relied so heavily on the absolute loyalty of its employees, such as the CIA, would be so thoroughly *un*impressed by my sense of obligation to my students.

The recruitment office ultimately agreed both to letting me finish out the school year *and* to taking the Fulbright, contingent upon my undergoing another polygraph and background investigation when I returned from Bulgaria. I was told not to contact the CIA under any circumstances while I was abroad.

As if. I wanted to relish what I presumed would be my last year of freedom, and I did. I spent the year interspersing my reading and research with trips to the Black Sea and forays into the mountains. I became an even more avid, if not accomplished, rock climber. I returned a year later with a new boyfriend—a Bulgarian rock climber, of course—whom I reported as a "close and continuing foreign contact" when I showed up for my polygraph.

The polygraph was just as harrowing as the previous occasion, this time with the examiner throwing in a math problem (of all curveballs!) and me getting hung up—or so he told me—on the question *Have you ever willfully destroyed government property or computer systems?*

After I'd explained for the umpteenth time that I had no idea why I might "indicate deception" on such a question, the polygrapher—a bony, middle-aged man with a wilting combover—looked at me and said, "I want you to think long and hard, Lindsay, as this question could cover a lot of offenses . . . such as . . ." He leaned forward conspiratorially. "Taking a sledgehammer to a fax machine!"

"Oh, *that*!" I felt like saying. "Yeah, you got me: Sledgehammering fax machines—the one habit I just can't seem to break."

After several hours of interrogation, the man told me that I had not passed and I would not be hired after all. A part of me actually was relieved; I had jumped through so many hoops, I felt that I was losing sight of why I wanted to join in the first place. I also was nervous about what my new job would mean for me and Sasho, my—at this point serious—Bulgarian boyfriend. More than anything, I found the prospect of taking the polygraph on even one more occasion unimaginable, let alone the countless times during the course of my future career that would be required during periodic security reinvestigations.

My emotions vacillated between profound relief and abject disappointment as the polygrapher began removing all the coils and straps. He excused himself, saying he would return in a few minutes to show me out.

In the polygrapher's absence, I rose from the chair, smoothed out my skirt, and stood by the door, purse in hand. By the time he returned, I was resolute, ready to leave.

"Welcome to the CIA, Lindsay!" The polygrapher was grinning almost maniacally. "And I hope you'll forgive me for, ahem, yanking your chain."

"I passed?"

"You sure did." He reached out to shake my hand. "I was just making that up about the 'deception indicated.'"

"To try to get me to admit to something?"

"Sure. We do it all the time."

I had never—and to this day, *have* never—heard of another occasion on which an Agency polygrapher showed his cards in such a way.

I walked away from that monolithic building both stunned and gratified. The relief that I'd felt only moments before—on being turned away—gave way to satisfaction, pride, and rapidly mounting excitement.

Polygraph out of the way, I was told I would have to wait at least three months for completion of my background reinvestigation. I decided to return for the summer to San Francisco, primarily because of my boyfriend Sasho, who was riding out the tail end of a tourist visa. He worked odd jobs in between climbing rocks.

Sasho and I spent the summer camping in Yosemite National Park, heading back to the city when Sasho ran out of money and had to paint a garage or clean out a gutter.

Once, as I was dropping off Sasho on the street corner where he and the other day laborers, all of whom were Mexican, waited for work, I thought about what a marked turn the course of my life was about to take. We had spent the previous three nights sleeping beneath the open sky and its endless display of stars. What would become of me and my foreign boyfriend once I worked for the CIA?

I felt tremendously conflicted. On the one hand, I was anxious for the investigation to be done and for my career to be on its way. On the other hand, I was troubled about what I might be leaving behind. I loved rock climbing, and I also loved Sasho. Both represented to me a connection to the elements and also a kind of inexorable freedom, privileges I suspected I might have to relinquish (although I had no idea to what extent) in my new life.

Rather than make a choice between Sasho and the CIA, I put the dilemma out of my mind, convincing myself that I could have my cake and eat it too. Sasho, who knew only that I was about to take a job "with the government," had agreed to join me once I found an apartment and had settled in somewhere near Washington, D.C.

When we said good-bye on the street in front of the Second Avenue house, he stood on the curb, his face framed by the driver's-side window of the rental truck in which I would spend the next few weeks conveying my stuff across the country. My hands were already on the steering wheel. Looking me intently in the eye, Sasho said, "Are you sure you want me to come?"

"Of course I do," I said, although my voice was more testy than it was reassuring.

The truth was: I did not know. Scared to leave Sasho altogether, I'd convinced myself that it was not *such* a big deal to have a foreign boyfriend—on the verge of becoming an illegal alien, no less—living with me while I worked at the CIA. But as I drove, I was having a harder and harder time envisioning how he'd fit into my new life. I was going to be a spy, for chrissake! What would Sasho think about his girlfriend working for the CIA? An even more daunting uncertainty was: What would the CIA think about Sasho?

After every long day of driving, I would sit by myself in a roadside diner, picking at another greasy burger or slice of day-old pie. Staring at the night-darkened window into my increas-

ingly anxious reflection, I would relive moments from my past
with Sasho, and imagine scenes from my future without him.

The day that I actually entered on duty—"EODed" in
Agency-speak—was, at nine A.M., an already sweltering Au-
gust morning. I'd donned one of my new little blue suits and
drove my incongruously battered, air-conditioning-less pickup
truck to the main headquarters of the CIA, a colossal structure
that is bafflingly and alarmingly well-marked by large signs
reading "CIA."

I did not yet have a badge to gain access to the building, so
I pulled up to a camera and microphone box stationed several
meters from the main gate.

"Hello, um, I am here for my first day," I said, feeling somewhat moronic, into the microphone box.

"Okay!" a voice boomed out at me. "You know this is the
Federal Highway Administration, right?"

"Oh no!" I felt even more like an idiot. Then I heard cack-
ling from within the box and the voice boomed out again,
"Sorry—just kidding. Drive on down." I was relieved to find
that at least someone here had a sense of humor.

I was given a temporary badge and told where to park. As I
walked into Headquarters for the first time, I stood upon the
great seal embossed on the floor and stared momentarily at the
wall of gold stars, each one of which—I knew from books I
had read—symbolized a CIA officer who had died in the
course of service. The untimely ends of these men and women
seemed to me as glorious as they were tragic.

I felt a surge of pride. I had made it; I was actually inside the CIA. No one had stopped me.

My swelling ego was punctured when I saw a goofy-looking sign featuring the cartoon character Alf holding a bunch of balloons and exclaiming "Welcome to CIA 101!" Beneath Alf were instructions for new employees to proceed to a room on the first floor of Old Headquarters Building. It would take me weeks to figure out the labyrinth of hallways connecting Old Headquarters Building and New Headquarters Building; sometimes I would get so turned around in the basement corridors, I would retreat into a ladies' room just to take stock and get my bearings.

The first two weeks, CIA 101 comprised a kind of general overview, during which we sat in a large room, viewed some interesting presentations (for example, a demonstration by the bomb-detecting canine force), and listened to some not-so-interesting lectures (for example, the designations of different security classifications and the implications and punishments if you failed to apply them accurately). The most relevant, and disturbing, presentation for me was made by representatives from the Office of Security, about all the regulations that applied to dating foreigners. Two robotic-looking men and one Stepford Wife–ish woman peppered their seminar with many woeful tales about lonely CIA women who had fallen prey to the romantic overtures of duplicitous foreign men, *spies!*, and who had sold out our country for what they'd thought was love. Needless to say, the careers of these women ended in disgrace, and some of them were even doing time in federal penitentiaries.

Early on, I recognized a vast double standard in the Agency's attitude toward male and female employees. It was okay for the men, so long as they accounted for their foreign girlfriends, to do whatever they wanted. "Prostitutes do not have to be reported," one of the robotrons announced munificently, "as long as you don't see the same prostitute more than once." Ostensibly, a male case officer could routinely frequent the same whorehouse, as long as he alternated his whores.

But it was a much different story for women. "We're not going to monitor your partners so long as they're American citizens," the Stepford Wife addressed the women in the room. "But you will want to be mindful of your 'reputation' and how it can impact your career."

The Agency's message was clear: Women were more susceptible to flattery, deception, and the wiles of foreign men, all of whom were shady. Women presented a greater security risk. Women were weak. The obvious sexism bothered me, and during these security briefings, my mind always turned to Sasho.

I knew Sasho was not a spy, but I also knew he'd be considered suspect regardless. Among my supervisors and peers, I rarely—if ever—had spoken of my Bulgarian boyfriend. My strategy of compartmentalizing my life in this way, however, would not last long.

While CIA 101 was required for employees from all four directorates—the DS&T, DA, DI, and DO—those of us destined for the DO quickly found the others. We formed an immediate clique, regaling each other with stories of where we

came from and how we had ended up here. We endlessly com-
pared our nightmare experiences with the polygraph. We were
the last wave of new hires who would join Clandestine Service
Trainee (CST) Class C.

The rest of Class C, we learned, already had been working
at Headquarters, waiting for us to arrive so that the group
would be complete and we could start training. We could see
the other CSTs in the hallways and the Agency cafeteria, easily discernible by their relative youth and confident swaggers.
Unlike most of the government drones in the building, the
CSTs did not appear to have been beaten down by the system.
Notably, they all still took pains with their personal appearance. The CSTs, for example, were the only employees to frequent the Agency gym. CST men had yet to develop the
archetypal bureaucrat's goiter: sallow skin billowing out of a
yellowing white collar. And CST women were among the few
female employees who'd not yet resorted to wearing elasticized
waist slacks, or white Reeboks, reserved beneath the desk in
order to make the long trek from parking lot to cubicle.

The other members of Class C resented us, "the final wave,"
because we'd have only nine months to work at Headquarters
before we commenced training down at "The Farm," whereas
they'd been languishing at desk jobs for more than a year.
At first, they'd glare at our small group, huddled together at
a circular table in the far corner of the vast cafeteria. But
soon emissaries were sent, friendships formed, and, ultimately,
Class C became a cohesive and bonded group.

Following CIA 101, we commenced a two-week orientation into the DO. During this introduction to the Clandes-

tine Service, I experienced my first misgivings about the career path I had chosen.

I started to realize that all the spy novels I'd read prior to joining the CIA had provided a warped—either glamorized or glorified—view of the job. Somehow, I still had imagined that being a spy meant me personally stealing other countries' secrets: breaking into safes; scaling the exteriors of buildings; escaping through uncharted labyrinths of underground passages. I'd even wondered when exactly my rock-climbing and rope skills would come in handy. Most important, I thought the only person I'd be endangering would be myself.

The reality, of course, was a far different story.

On the first day of our DO orientation, the job of a case officer was explicitly laid out for us. Our life's mission was to spot, assess, develop, and recruit foreign spies. These foreign spies—"agents" or "assets" in CIA lingo—would sell us, their case officers, *secrets*. Secrets, we learned, were classified information to which the foreign agent should have unique access. If things went sour—like if either a case officer or his agent was caught—the case officer would be sent home, representing a minor glitch in his career, whereas the agent would probably be thrown into prison for the rest of his life or, worse, executed.

There was little, if any, discussion about the moral and ethical implications of persuading another person to commit espionage. In effect, the DO motto was *Lie, cheat, and steal; just don't get caught.* We were educated on how to spot and befriend anyone who might have access to valuable information, keeping a vigilant lookout for potential vulnerabilities—such as alcoholism, a faltering marriage, a stagnating career, or a dying family member—that might make them more susceptible to our overtures.

Contrary to popular jargon, a CIA *agent* is not the actual employee of the CIA but rather the hapless schlub who has been recruited by a CIA case officer to spy on behalf of the United States, usually in exchange for money. The whole process of spotting, assessing, developing, and enlisting foreign agents is called "The Recruitment Cycle."

Once we had spotted someone with potential access and determined his (most agents are men) vulnerabilities, we were supposed to play upon those weaknesses and introduce ways in which "our organization" might help. If the target, as a potential agent is commonly called, wanted to send his son to school in the United States, we could offer to arrange it and pay for it. If there was a daughter dying of some rare disease, we would offer to provide treatment. This, of course, did not sound like such a bad thing: I imagined myself some sort of covert do-gooder. But if the target refused a recruitment pitch, then the offer was withdrawn. And if the target accepted, but then later decided that treason was too dangerous an occupation—or if he failed to produce adequate intelligence—we would terminate all contact and cut off whatever assistance we'd been providing.

In cases where the potential asset exhibited no obvious vulnerabilities, we were encouraged to wine and dine him, ply him with alcohol and glimpses of the good life. If all went well, ultimately we could weaken his resolve.

"Everybody has some Achilles' heel," our instructors frequently assured us. "It's your job to figure out *what*!"

Our careers, we were told, depended on the number of recruitments we secured. While some recruitments were looked upon more favorably than others—for example, the "hard targets," such as Russians, North Koreans, and Chinese—quality seemed to be far less important than quantity. Legendary recruiters were the heroes of Agency lore.

I started to have momentous second thoughts. I did not like the idea of preying upon people, especially people who already might be experiencing a run of bad luck. I did not like the idea of pretending to be someone's friend, all the while intending to use him for my own career progression. I particularly did not like the idea of putting someone in danger by asking him to do something—betray his country—that I myself would never do.

The veteran case officers provided myriad justifications. *We're doing these people a favor. They want to work for us. They need the money. It makes their lives better. A lot of them exist under oppressive regimes; their betrayal of those regimes is something positive and brave.*

Intellectually, I could see that the experienced Agency officers had a point. It was easy to understand why we needed to recruit foreigners to have an adequate intelligence service. And I should not have expected spying to be anything but an inherently dirty business. But I was unsettled nonetheless. Already I could see that my usually crystalline sense of my own moral parameters was becoming blurred.

By the time we completed DO orientation and had been assigned to offices for our first "interim," I found myself becoming a bit withdrawn. This was unusual for me, because I'd always been an open, social person. But none of my friends "on the outside" knew where I worked and my conversations with them had become increasingly stilted and strange. "On the inside," there was nobody I felt I could trust, especially given how fiercely competitive the trainees tended to be. Ambition, independence, and singularity of purpose—combined with an ability to trust in and rely on nobody other than yourself—were all characteristics essential to one's success as a spy. It would have been foolhardy to confide in anyone at work.

Occasionally, I tried to raise questions among my classmates about the morality of harrying down-on-their-luck foreigners into spying for the United States. I generally received either blank or suspicious stares. "If you feel that way," one classmate said to me, "you shouldn't be here."

Looking back, perhaps he was right. At the time, I still felt as if I could do something good for my country by working for the CIA. But I began to let go of my idealism and to accept the fact that becoming a successful spy might mean confronting issues that were not always clear-cut, or doing things with which I was not always entirely comfortable.

In short, having no one with whom I could discuss my doubts, I pushed those doubts aside. As a result, I began to lose my sense of myself. I began to change.

Meanwhile, I was in a quandary as to what to do about Sasho, who would be arriving in a few weeks. During one of our seemingly endless security briefings, we'd been told that, in addition to the countless other regulations related to dating a foreigner, we were required to obtain special permission if that foreigner was going to stay with us for more than eight consecutive days, and particularly if he would have "unfettered access" to the home. On the one hand, I could see the need for the Agency's concern. On the other hand, I was incensed by the rule. If I was following standard procedure and "living my cover," there should be nothing in my home even to link me to the CIA. Needless to say, it wasn't one of those careers where you could take work home with you, at least not physically. (Every Agency officer, I would come to realize, carries home his job in the form of unparalleled stress and near-constant anxiety.)

Still, I drafted a memo to the Office of Security, asking permission for "my Bulgarian boyfriend, Sasho Todorov, to come visit for two or three weeks." In fact, I had no idea how long he'd be staying. We'd talked about getting married to prevent him from being deported, but I was hesitant for a number of reasons, not least of which was fear that Sasho would place my new career in certain jeopardy.

If a CIA officer marries a foreigner—with the Agency's prior permission only, of course—that foreigner is required to become an American citizen, meaning the couple must remain in the United States for at least five years. For a case officer, half a decade Stateside, especially early on, constitutes a career killer in and of itself. Prior to marriage, the intended foreign spouse also is required to take a polygraph exam and undergo a thorough background investigation. Meanwhile, it's a security violation for the Agency officer to reveal his true employers before the day of the polygraph. One can only imagine what it would feel like to learn, after getting engaged to someone, that you've been lied to throughout the entire relationship, and that to add insult to injury, you—the one who's been systematically deceived—will be required to take a lie-detector test!

Not surprisingly, this particular "nondisclosure" rule is routinely ignored. Every case officer and trainee I knew who was dating a foreigner had let that person in on his Agency employment early on. A lot of Agency guys even used what they euphemistically referred to as their "true affiliation" to pick up easily impressed foreign women in the first place.

Although I sent the memo requesting permission for Sasho to visit weeks in advance, a few days before his arrival I had not yet received approval. I was told repeatedly that the memo still had to "circulate" among several different offices. "It could be months before you hear anything," one particularly unsympathetic security officer said to me. "That is, if you hear anything at all."

"Meanwhile, it's a security violation if I have him stay with me without your permission?" I said.

"It is indeed," the security officer said. "In fact, that would be considered a serious breach."

I was exasperated. Making what I considered a valiant attempt to follow the rules, this conspiracy of petty bureaucrats seemed to take almost perverse delight in deliberately creating obstacles.

The day before Sasho's arrival, a security officer finally called and asked me to come to his office. He was concerned, it turned out, because he "just now" had noticed, on the first page of my memo, that I had reported Sasho's father as residing in Libya.

"What's he doing in Libya?" the security officer, in imitation of some kind of hard-boiled criminal investigator, asked me.

"His father is a surgeon," I explained. "But he can't make enough money in Bulgaria, so he moved to Libya to practice."

"Why Libya?"

"I guess there is a large Bulgarian community there," I said.

"Well, it doesn't look good."

"He's not Libyan himself."

"It still doesn't look good."

The officer left me in a panic that my request would be denied; I went home wondering what I should do. Should I quit my job? Should I tell Sasho not to come? He'd already spent the entirety of his day laborer savings on a ticket. I couldn't sleep that night, anguishing over the right course of action, and all the while sensing that this problem was only the tip of the iceberg.

I decided to ignore the situation, and in the end, permission was granted, although not until several months *after* Sasho had come and gone. What's more, the Office of Security misspelled Sasho's last name and, having run traces on the wrong person, granted permission for some nonexistent foreigner, Sasho Podorov (instead of Todorov), to stay with me for "a period of time not to exceed ten consecutive days."

When the albeit moot memo finally arrived, it read: "We have conducted traces on employee's reported close and continuing contact and have surfaced no derogatory info on the foreign national." A ringing endorsement of my alien boyfriend.

Sasho's visit was bittersweet. He stayed with me for about a month, during which time we spent weekends climbing in West Virginia. I found temporary solace in the enduring hardness of the rocks, and the sun-sparkling waters of the New River, into which we recklessly hurled ourselves from unimaginable heights. Sasho was a brief herald to me of who I was; he reminded me of peaceable Bulgaria and carefree summer days. He tried to comfort me when I grew angry and brittle—*I can't talk about it!*—all the while not having any idea what was wrong.

But the lying was wearing me down. Sasho, who thought I worked at "one of the government agencies" in Washington, D.C., would often try to walk me to work. I was evasive and, I am sure, transparent as every day I came up with some excuse as to why that was not possible. *I have to drive to Virginia first to pick up panty hose. It's my turn to get donuts for the office from the Krispy Kreme in McLean. The gas is cheaper at this station near Langley, Virginia.*

Sasho must have thought Washington, D.C., was a dreadfully inconvenient capital city, with no place to purchase stockings, snacks, or reasonably priced gas.

In the end, our relationship proved untenable. The constant lying made me irritable, and my erratic behavior was tearing Sasho apart. I felt guilty all the time, and my guilt manifested itself in anger and bouts of crying. Sasho, I think, just felt sad.

When one day I finally said, "I think you should go back to San Francisco," it wasn't hard to convince Sasho that this was for the best. I will never forget his searching eyes, welling over with tears, when we finally said good-bye at the airport.

"Good luck with the job," he said with a sad but ironic grin.

In his heart, he knew that my career had consumed me. He must have found it both insulting and absurd.

For days, I anguished over whether I'd done the right thing. Certainly, nobody in the Agency understood me, made me smile, or touched my soul in the way that Sasho did. And for sure no one there cared about me that much—or even *at all*, for that matter. Why had I turned Sasho away?

And why, with all my mounting misgivings, did I not just cut my losses and quit? I would have had every opportunity available to me. I was young and accomplished. I had Harvard on my résumé, and a Fulbright under my belt. I could have gone back to teaching, which I had loved, or to Berkeley Law School, where I'd deferred admission for two years running until I finally turned it down for the Agency.

Quite simply, I wanted to see the Agency through. That itch had not yet been scratched.

I wanted to finish the training. I wanted to live overseas. I still even wanted to be a spy. I wanted to be able to look back and say, even if only to myself, *I did that!* Moreover, I thought the Agency needed people like me, people who were bright and motivated and people who might shake the dust that seemed to have settled on the cubicles within this behemoth organization, people who actually might get something done. I believed that all the things that bothered me about the Agency could eventually change if only smart, reasonable people were in charge. Maybe someday I could be one of those people.

So I would keep going, I decided, even if that meant swimming upstream. I would make my own rules and maintain my own sense of morality, and I would not let my spirit be squelched.

I said these things to myself nearly every morning as I shimmied into stockings, and put on pert little pumps, and pulled back my unruly hair into a tight bun. I said them to myself as I drove to work each day, trying not to veer outside my lane while I searched in my purse for that tiny, yet inflexible, blue badge.

THREE

I am at a party somewhere in Manhattan with my two best friends. For the moment, I don't know where Emma and Emily have gone. I am standing in the corner, arms crossed over my chest. I feel like an imposing, unsightly monolith. Everyone else is rolling on "E" and falling in love. I am the weird and menacing friend, from phenomenally uncool Washington, D.C., with the spooky-sounding government job.

After another long and monotonous week at Headquarters, I took the six-o'clock train from Washington last night, arriving in Penn Station at ten P.M., just enough time to make it to the girls' apartment, change from my little blue suit into some outfit borrowed from Emily's closet, and head out on the town before midnight.

We spent Saturday afternoon nursing our hangovers with greasy food and getting foot massages in Chinatown. Now it's near midnight and we're out and at it again, this time at the penthouse apartment of some lithe, bedroom-eyed trustfundafariun who—from what I gather—routinely holds the preparty before any given allnight rave. His real name is Tucker, but people call him Thrash.

Thrash, whom I also assume to be the primary supplier of illegal substances, eyes me suspiciously, as if I were an undercover cop. I wish I knew where the girls were. I think they must have headed to the rooftop with some of the others.

Neither Emma nor Emily knows the nature of my job, but they both know that, ever since I started working in Washington, I am adamant about saying no to drugs. My abstinence doesn't bother the girls—it's good to have at least one responsible person in the party. But probably, like Thrash, they half wonder if I am some kind of informant for the DEA.

I met Emma and Emily through what we call "the Bulgarian connection." Emma, an American girl of Bulgarian descent, arrived in Sofia around the same time I did in the early nineties. Her artist parents—having escaped Bulgaria's oppressive regime two decades earlier—returned with their now grown daughter shortly after the fall of communism, to reclaim a villa outside Sofia and give Emma an inkling of her Balkan roots.

Emily showed up in Sofia later with her then husband, who had been awarded a small stipend to help post-Communist Bulgarian businesses segue into capitalism. Emily had used her idle days in Eastern Europe to write a novel and figure out her life. Eventually, she and her husband separated and Emma, Emily, and I became our own goofy version of the Three Musketeers: meeting for borscht nearly every day at Sofia's Cold War relic of a restaurant The Russian Club, pounding whiskeys and Cokes with fried-egg-topped pizza dinners; running around to Bulgarian discos at all hours of the night.

Around the same time I started with the Agency, the girls moved back from Bulgaria to New York City. Emma is working in film. Emily has a job at a publishing house. They work hard all week and put just as much concerted effort into partying on the weekends.

I know that my training schedule will soon be too heavy to go anywhere, so for now I try to make it up to New York as many weekends as I can. In addition to being clueless about where I work, the girls probably don't know how important they are to me. As I recede further into the strange and insular world of the CIA, they're my link to the outside.

They remind me of a time when I did not have to report anything and everything I did, when I did not have to ask permission to travel or to talk to a foreigner, and when I could make my own decisions about what risks to take in my life. The girls remind me of a time when I did not feel so desperately lonely.

Now I wish I knew where they were. The din of the party seems abnormally loud, like a roar, and the techno music booming out of the speakers makes me uneasy. I retreat from the living room, thronging with people, to the brightly lit kitchen, where I find Thrash, arranging lines of coke on a cheese-cutting board.

"Excuse me," I say.

Thrash leans over his project as if protecting a final exam from the roving eyes of the cheater seated next to him.

"S'up?" He points his chin at me in a single defensive thrust.

"I'm just looking for my girlfriends," I say, already stepping backward out the door.

Much later, I do find Emma and Emily—huddled together by the bathroom door. They are obviously high and laughing hysterically over something.

"What's going on?" I ask.

"Nothing!" Emily shouts between convulsions of hilarity. She moves to put her arm around my shoulder, and Emma hugs me on the other side.

"It's just Thrash," Emily gasps. "He's totally paranoid. He thinks you're going to flash some kind of badge and arrest everyone here."

I cannot help but laugh too. The girls, although half out of their minds, flank and protect me from the awful anonymity of this party. I chuckle to myself, wondering what the folks from the Office of Security back in Langley might think. It's moments like this when I realize my life's becoming really odd.

There was more than one reason that I did not just up and leave the CIA when my doubts began to surface. From the beginning, the Agency made us feel as if we could *not* leave, at least not by choice. We all had signed secrecy agreements pledging to let the Agency prescreen anything and everything we might ever write, say, or do. If we broke our secrecy agreements, the Office of Security cheerily informed us, "we'll go after you."

"We've done it in the past and we'll do it again," said a sturdy woman, sausaged into her blue rent-a-cop uniform, standing behind a podium and pounding its wooden surface with her meaty fist. "In my mind, anyone who tries to disparage the Agency is the worst kind of mole there is!"

"And don't even *think* about putting CIA on your résumé," she hounded us from her pulpit. "This organization is *not* in the business of building up *your* credentials. We have and we will deny any knowledge of you when and if potential employers call."

I imagined myself sitting in a job interview sometime in the future, saying, "Yes, I *could* explain the two-year gap in my résumé, sir, but I'd have to kill you first."

Little by little, I began to feel as if the options for me outside of the CIA had already dwindled and that perhaps the best thing to do was just stay the course.

Aside from instilling fear in our hearts, the Agency also dangled bunches of carrots in our faces. We were all promised overseas postings within a year, with sly assurances that case officers live in fabulous houses, far better than those afforded State Department officers. No matter, I should add, that the CIA's luxury accommodations abroad, relative to that of State Department counterparts, represent an obvious inconsistency that undermines the Agency officer's cover, making it easy for the locals to "spot the spook."

We were told the Agency provided all-terrain SUVs for us to drive and flew us Business Class everywhere we went— again, unlike our State colleagues. In a number of so-called undesirable places, we would receive danger and hardship pay. I was shocked to discover that Sofia, Bulgaria—which I knew to be cosmopolitan and comfortable—was considered a hardship post, and that Agency officers assigned there received the maximum pay differential.

In fact, most of the supposedly objectionable locales were places where I *wanted* to serve. I didn't join the Agency to live in London or Paris. I was intrigued by rife-with-conflict Balkan hellholes and the mysterious outposts of the "Icky-stans," as the southern provinces of the former Soviet Union were commonly called in the halls of Headquarters. I calculated that if I served a couple of tours in one of these purportedly miserable territories, I could pay back my college loans in less than five years.

Another among the Agency's enticements was the training itself. Following our interims—three-month stints in at least three different Headquarters offices—we would head off for paramilitary training. At the end of PM training, we would learn how to "jump"—that is, skydive out of an airplane. Someone was going to *pay me* to partake of extreme-sporting adventure!

And so I pushed my misgivings aside as I looked forward to better days ahead. My first interim was in the Central Eurasian Division, where I'd occupy the Kazakhstan cubicle, dutifully performing the most mundane tasks. A week into it, I discovered that for several months no Kazakhstan desk officer had existed at all. As a result, much of the correspondence from our officers in and around the Kazakh capital, Almaty, had been ignored completely.

The CIA chief in Almaty took advantage of my fleeting tenure at Headquarters to propose a trip for our counterparts in the Kazakh intelligence service. For their visit, I was told to make hotel reservations and research entertainment possibilities—specifically, area tittie bars.

To maintain my cover, I would not meet any of the Kazakhs face-to-face. For this, I was thankful. Judging by their photographs, they were a bunch of fearsome thugs. Meanwhile, I was given ten dollars per Kazakh to buy them gifts at the Agency store. I bought a dozen shot glasses bearing the CIA logo and similarly adorned ballpoint pens.

Planning the visit was a lot of work, and none of it particularly glamorous: making countless hotel and dinner reservations, chartering busses, checking store hours, ensuring there would be diversionary—although far tamer—activities for the Kazakh wives during the nocturnal tittie-bar runs. I was a cross between a glorified girl Friday and a pimp.

Afterward, the chief in Almaty e-mailed my boss at Headquarters in praise of my efforts. He reported that the Kazakhs got drunk and ate big steaks and enjoyed countless taxpayer-funded lap dances while their oblivious wives indulged themselves in the hotel hot tub and relished mountains of clothes they purchased each day from The Gap.

"The trip was a raging success," the chief wrote. "Due in no small part to the efforts of your diligent and able new trainee. It goes without saying that she has a promising future in our organization."

My second interim was a modicum more substantive. This time, I worked as a reports officer on the Balkans. At that

time, the Balkans were a foreign-policy priority and the dy-
namic office attracted energetic young employees with an ap-
preciation of the absurd and a sense of adventure.

I was responsible for the little-known Former Yugoslav Republic of Macedonia (FYROM), a tiny country bordering my
beloved Bulgaria. I had never visited Macedonia during the two
years I lived in Bulgaria, but the place had always intrigued me.
It was home to mystical Lake Ohrid, the largest and deepest in
the Balkans, whose alluring black water separated up-and-
coming Eastern Europe from the lawless territory of Albania.

Macedonia, at that time, was the sole former Yugoslav republic not to have disintegrated into civil war and rampant
ethnic cleansing, even though a substantial percentage of its
population was Albanian Muslim and the majority was Slavic
Orthodox. It seemed to me an astounding anomaly in this
otherwise tragically disharmonious part of the world.

As a reports officer, my job was to sanitize information—
that is, remove any source-revealing material—sent from our
officers in and around Skopje, the capital. Once I had transformed an intelligence report so that it was no longer "Top
Secret," I sent it down to the DI analysts, who would incorporate this information into their own reports, some of which
ultimately would be used to brief members of Congress and,
on occasion, I was told, the president. The work was not
thrilling, but it was better than scoping out tittie bars.

The members of my class frequently met for coffee in the
Agency cafeteria. We were not as eclectic a group as one might

imagine: some former cops, a lot of ex–military people, hardly any academics. The Agency certainly no longer was the natural extension of the Ivy League, as it had been in its earlier era. There was only one guy from Yale—a campus whose student body at one time had constituted the CIA's most fertile feeding ground—and another Harvard grad.

Warren had been a year ahead of me, and our paths had never crossed. He had gone on to law school at Harvard as well, and was notorious for claiming to have left a six-figure salary with a London law firm to join the Agency. He was also, as a trainee, flagrantly incompetent. It wasn't that he was not smart; to the contrary, he likely was brilliant. He spoke half a dozen foreign languages fluently. It was just that Warren had no common sense whatsoever. This was not, unfortunately, an expendable trait in a CIA case officer.

Aside from his tendency to overreact and/or panic in the face of simple tasks and basic simulated exercises, Warren routinely showed up late for class, missed appointments altogether, fell asleep in the middle of nearly every given lecture, and, most egregiously, blew people's covers in public venues.

One time, Warren hosted a party to which he invited, in addition to our training class, a dazzling array of voluptuous foreign women, most of whom, it emerged, he had met in airport lounges. The members of our group stood in mortified silence while Warren boisterously conducted introductions, mangling most of our names by mixing the real names with our Agency-assigned aliases. Upon realizing his error, he would smack his hand to his forehead and emit a Homer Simpson–style *"Doh!"*

For whatever reason, I liked Warren, as I liked the few other characters who added a bit of color to our class. Aaron, the Yalie, was a Renaissance man with countless stories about his former life in the African bush, doing research for his doctorate and leading groups of high school students on bike trips. A tall white guy who looked every bit the academic, he would sometimes break into one of those tongue-clucking languages and none would have known if he was faking it. Rob, a former Louisiana cop, loved to point out the irony of him and "Little Miss Harvard"—as he called me—being classmates. Gung-ho Ike, a marine who was forever ending our conversations with "Semper Fi!," had a sick sense of humor that kept me laughing when the absurdity of our environment warranted antidepressants.

For the most part, however, the group formed a collective posture of nearly obscene arrogance. This was no wonder. Case officers were treated as the cream of the crop within the already exclusive Agency. We were reminded on a near-daily basis that we were the "best and the brightest." I found this concept laughable, having attended school among geniuses and prodigies at Harvard, where I'd grown acutely aware of my own intellectual limitations and relatively meager talents. "The best and the brightest" the CIA trainee cadre was, quite simply, *not*.

As CSTs, we were catered to and coddled, much like spoiled children. Even when performing grunt work, we were made to feel that we were contributing invaluably to the larger mission. A good thing, as this illusory concept was in large part what kept me going.

. . .

During training, we were all paranoid about "cover." Having been assigned the first of many Agency-provided aliases, none of us knew one another's real last names. And we almost never divulged details about our out-of-Agency lives.

In counterintelligence briefings, we learned about the nefarious traitors Jim Nicholson and Aldrich Ames, CIA case officers who turned out to have been working for the Russians and who effectively devastated Agency operations. Over the course of several years, Ames had sold out countless Soviet agents spying on our behalf, most of whom the KGB consequently executed. Nicholson, who at the time of his perfidy had been an instructor at The Farm, provided the KGB a list of CIA officers-in-training, CSTs. The names of young men and women slated to go to Moscow, we heard, had commanded a particularly high price. Instructors now, consequently, were not given the true last names of any of their students.

The Nicholson and Ames fiascos had caused Agency morale to plummet during the late 1980s and early 1990s. Security measures grew even more rigid, and all information became highly "compartmentalized." Even a DO case officer with a top secret security clearance received information only on a need-to-know basis.

Unfortunately, this mandate, while conceptually valid, was rarely enforced. Office and hallway banter—as well as just plain failures of the computer system—meant that most employees (myself included) knew significantly more than they needed to know.

Most comically, we were told that employees wearing gray badges, such as cafeteria workers and custodians, had the least need to know and were—as a matter of policy—"uninformed as to the identity of their true employers." Yes, I thought, these people who drive into the Headquarters parking lot each day like the rest of us are surely unaware that they're working for the CIA.

While most Agency employees—analysts, scientists, and administrative workers—could tell their families and friends where they worked, as future case officers, we could not. As a result, we were neurotic about maintaining our covers. I was thrilled when the Harvard alumni magazine—which my college roommate had informed of my plans to join the foreign service—mistakenly reported my plans to "join the forest service." The farther from the truth the better, and I embraced my new identity as some kind of lady park ranger.

Most people in Washington, D.C., aren't idiots, though. If, at a party, I answered a question about my job by saying that I worked "for the government," the immediate and invariable response was "Oh! You mean you work for the CIA."

As one's career progresses, we were told, one's cover naturally erodes.

"You can always identify an Agency officer," one of my first bosses said. "He's the one out working a cocktail party while the State Department weenies cower in a corner."

Although we knew our cover was flimsy, in the beginning we fiercely defended it. The CST class did everything together, and it was a tacit courtesy to check beforehand if you planned to invite an "unwitting" guest along, since the nature of the conversation would have to shift so drastically. Discussing something other than the Agency was a skill we'd all evidently lost.

One guy in our class was pretty much excommunicated from the group when it was discovered that he had revealed to his girlfriend, whom we all knew, that he actually worked for the CIA. "He compromised all of us!" one of the more fanatical cover guardians cried, rallying the others to communal outrage. "We don't know who this girl really *is*!" another zealot shouted.

For me, protecting my cover meant becoming more and more insular and guarded. At Thanksgiving dinner with my cousins, who I imagined already were suspicious about what the hell I was up to, I was hard-pressed to explain things as simple as how I commuted to work each morning and whether or not I had a view from my office. Only once in my life had I been inside the government agency in downtown Washington where I was supposed to be working and, frankly, I wouldn't have recognized the building were I plopped directly in front of it. I reverted to nebulous claims such as "I get a ride with a colleague" and "I work in the blue hallway," vaguely recalling the color-coded corridors of my cover organization headquarters. But usually people, such as my cousins, pressed for more-detailed information. Finally, I ended up telling them that I worked in a government "annex" in Virginia, which I am sure they accurately interpreted as "the CIA."

In fact, each trainee had a D.C. office phone number for cover, one we could give to unwitting family and friends. The name of my ersatz office was "Regional Issues"—a dead give-away, in my opinion.

One day I told my mother to call the number and ask for me by name, just to test it out. Mom said that the phone rang at least fifteen times before someone finally answered with a kind of exasperated "Hullo?" When she asked for me, the person hesitated for a long while before requiring Mom to provide my Social Security number. Then Mom was left dangling for several minutes, during which time she could overhear what sounded like banter in some cavernous space, as if she'd reached the pay phone in a state penitentiary.

After what seemed like an interminable search, the person finally returned to report that although Lindsay Moran did work in Regional Issues, she was not in the office. Mom's message could be passed on, but only if it was urgent. That was the last time I gave out the number for Regional Issues.

My mother, even more so than I, was at a loss as to what to tell her friends. "If you want to know what Lindsay is doing, ask her!" she would snap irritably whenever anybody asked. One of her neighbors even speculated that, given my mysterious comings and goings and evasive answers, I must be a high-end call girl. Mom just shrugged and said, "How would I know? I'm only her mother."

A few of my friends outside the Agency would grill me relentlessly about what I did, and—little by little—I added enough details to my cover that I had a decent rap. By the following Thanksgiving, when I held court for several minutes regarding the duties of my nonexistent job, my performance was so convincing that my mother later said she'd actually started to believe that I worked somewhere else after all.

Still, I never grew comfortable lying—funny, considering how adept I had been at it as a kid. The difference is that it was no longer deliciously subversive but *required*—and it pervaded every interaction. "Be careful," one veteran female case officer said to me. "You start to lie about your job, and soon the line is blurred. Eventually, you're lying about everything." This woman also had been through three intra-Agency marriages, and her other words of caution were: "Mark my words, you'll end up marrying one of these assholes."

That said, my own prospects for ever tying the knot, I felt, were diminishing daily. None of the men I worked with seemed even remotely interesting. Contrary to the image perpetuated by movies like *Spy Game* and *The Recruit*, in which the neophyte CIA officer is played by some breathtaking hottie like Brad Pitt or Colin Farrell—a protagonist who's as introspective as he is hunky and who ultimately recognizes and confronts the moral dilemma presented by his job—most Agency men are self-consciously slick and preternaturally shallow. The male trainees spent hours on coffee breaks debating how best to achieve their next promotions.

I was lonely, terribly lonely, in fact—but I figured my love life was just on hold. And I actually missed Sasho less than I missed my girlfriends. I spent the majority of my final interim in a remote, altogether dormant office of the "counterintelligence" bureau. Sequestered in a tiny cubicle, I'd fritter away the hours exchanging banal e-mail messages with my fellow trainees, all the while listening to Mrs. Yee and Mrs. Rosen-feld, two longtime Headquarters employees who occupied adjacent cubicles. These women never spoke. They simply released an ongoing litany of sporadic, and seemingly competitive, gaseous emissions. The ladies would fart their way through an entire afternoon, as I grew ever more dispirited about my own fate within this bizarre organization.

FOUR

Sheer terror of being left alone in the woods—to be eaten alive by wolves, the remains of my corpse decomposing in the summer heat—is what compels me to focus.

The first day of paramilitary training has been devoted to Land Navigation. Following what I consider some alarmingly basic classroom instruction, we each are provided a compass and two fluorescent light sticks. Some hours later, a dump truck transports us to the edge of an eerie fairy-tale forest. The instructors assign every trainee a set of arbitrarily designated coordinates that lie at least one wooded mile away. We're supposed to make our ways, individually of course, to our particular points located on the other side of the woods. By the time we get started, it's the middle of the night.

I curse out loud again and again as I find myself inextricably tangled in thickets of dense bramble and thorny brush. I stop, take a deep breath, and squint at my compass. Everywhere around me, I hear leaves and branches breaking under the cautious footsteps of what I presume to be nighttime predators tracking me from all sides. I would not be surprised in the least to come face-to-snout with a wild boar, or have a snake coil its way around my legs. My mind transforms a barberry bush into a snarling African panther.

This nighttime slog through the woods for which the instructor cadre has allotted sixty minutes has now gone on for hours. I begin to give up hope of ever reaching the other side. Panicky, I look around for some small clearing in which to sit and weep. But then I imagine the extent to which I will be mocked and maligned if I don't make it to the other side. I draw upon my reserve energy, pick myself up, and move on.

Bramble by bush, I finally make my way into a clearing and find stationed there an instructor. Seated on a collapsible movie director's chair, he's smoking a pipe and humming softly to himself. The instructor pauses his melody long enough to exhale a white streak of smoke, which lingers in the air as he addresses me: "What took you so long, little lady? I was 'bout ready to drop off to sleep."

"Am I the last one across?" The euphoria of seeing another human already has transformed into mortification.

Just then, his handheld radio crackles to life. From some other spot in the woods, another instructor indicates that his student, Ike, has also just made it across. I can hear Ike in the background on the other end of the radio: "Semper Fi!"

"No, darling, you're not the last one across," the instructor turns to me. "In fact, you're one of the first. Now get on back to the bar-

racks and give yourself a thorough checking for ticks. I bet you're covered in 'em."

I turn and head toward a spotlight beaming from the far edge of this clearing. Every twenty-five yards or so, I am greeted by another instructor waiting for his student to emerge.

Finally, I arrive at an idling pickup truck, in the back of which sits Ike and one other student, a former Green Beret named Derek. Ed, the only instructor whose name I've committed to memory so far—in part because his reputation as a "mean bastard" has preceded him—stands between me and the truck. Legs apart, arms crossed over his chest, Ed looks like a small-town sheriff in the throes of a serious power trip.

"Good job, kiddo," he says, breaking his belligerent stance long enough to slap me on the back. I crawl up on the truck bed with Ike and Derek. Ed nods at us as he slams shut the back. "I'll give y'all ladies a ride home."

As the pickup barrels over the bumpy, unpaved ground, Ike and I shout to each other, reliving our navigational sagas. Derek is silent. I get the feeling he's both stunned and annoyed that a woman finished so close behind him. As he glowers into the darkness, I feel a surge of pride and inspiration. I look up at the countless stars that, back home, are obscured by the lights of Washington.

It's hot and sticky, and I can feel my body bruising with each bump and pothole. Still, I relish this ride. I've just excelled at something I thought would be the end of me. I've already overcome at least one fear. I lean back and let the darkness envelop me. It's the middle of the night and I'm in the middle of nowhere, and it's been a long time since I felt this alive.

. . .

In the spring, I broke the lease on my apartment, put my belongings in storage, and, along with the rest of CST Class C, boarded a yellow school bus headed south, to a CIA-owned site near Williamsburg, Virginia, commonly known as "The Farm." We would spend the rest of that year at The Farm, rarely returning to Washington even for weekends.

To explain my mysterious absence during the next several months, I crafted a bogus but plausible story: "The government" had sent me to a military base in Norfolk, Virginia, where I was employed as some kind of minion for a military-diplomatic Balkan task force. I figured the time I spent in Bulgaria lent credence to the story, and the military aspect explained why I'd been wearing in a pair of combat boots for months beforehand. "It's a real hassle to call from the base," I would say, explaining why I was completely incommunicado, all the while anxious that my story might only provoke further inquisition. In fact, I'd never even been to Norfolk, and wouldn't have been able to explain how to get there from D.C., or even how long it would take.

The first few months would be devoted to paramilitary (PM) training, culminating in our airborne jump qualification and—we had heard—some sort of POW camp experience. The PM groundwork was probably my favorite, and just what I needed to reinvigorate my enthusiasm. We were divided into teams of nine trainees, with whom we'd eat, study, and train. My team's potentially strongest asset was Derek, the former Green Beret. Unfortunately, his irritation at taking part in rudimentary exercises with hapless beginners prevented him from being much help.

My teammate Mark, who'd also served in the Army, acted as a buffer between Derek and the rest of us—in particular a woman we called Tornado Sally, an unstoppable whirlwind of both energy and errors.

Derek was particularly frustrated with Sally's performance as the team's catastrophic caboose on the obstacle course, a series of hazards that included: tire formations through which to hop, enormous walls over which to hurl oneself, thick ropes with which to swing over deep ravines, metal tubing through which to belly-crawl, and a number of precariously high balance beams and monkey bars to traverse.

The most daunting obstruction was a series of meter-plus-high horizontal logs. Jumping them was all well and good for the likes of Mark, Derek, Rob, and Gung-ho Ike—all more than six feet tall. But the hurdles came up to my chest, and were placed in such close proximity that even if I managed to get a running start and fling myself—in some obscenely un-flattering manner—over the first log, there was another one right in front of me, and I still had five or six more to go. The guys from other teams would congregate around the log hurdles, enjoying the pageant of women trying to get over them. I finally formulated a technique whereby I'd embrace the timber with both arms, then straddle it awkwardly in the manner of a deranged cowgirl, before unceremoniously flopping down on the other side. Then I'd haul myself back up, face the next log, and start over again.

The team's time was not recorded until the slowest participant had completed all of the stations and sprinted the final obstacle-free quarter mile. As a team, we made a pact to jog together in formation over the finish line. But Sally, consummately uncoordinated, was inevitably bringing up the rear, tripping over her bootlaces and fighting back tears. Derek would roll his eyes as she collapsed in a red-faced heap just inches beyond the finish line. The nastier he was to her (grumbling "whiny bitch" under his breath), the angrier I grew at him (growling "arrogant ass" loud enough that all could hear). Our dysfunctional love/hate triangle did little to abet the cohesion of the team.

The first week of PM culminated with a particularly challenging exercise. We each had to navigate to a different initial point, somewhere on the vast multiacre base, using a contour map and compass. There, we'd find coordinates for the second point, and so on, until we'd located ten points in order, terminating at a common rallying spot, to be reached by dusk.

We started out as the sun was rising; by noon, I was exhausted. I'd managed to find all of my points so far, but not before getting turned around several times, having to retrace at least a mile of steps back to one point and start that segment of my route all over again. I bumbled about in all different directions, talking out loud to myself. Occasionally, a deer would take notice of me, but I saw no one else.

For hours, I'd been staving off the desire to consume my single-issue freeze-dried meal-ready-to-eat (MRE). The exercise was meant to be competitive, and I knew guys like Derek, Rob, and Gung-ho Ike wouldn't even think to waste time breaking for lunch. Ultimately, though, I conceded that if I took the time to eat, I'd be rejuvenated. As it turned out, the downright gourmet "pasta with primavera sauce," squeezed like toothpaste from its foil tube, would revisit me for the rest of the day. For the next several hours, I burped and farted my way through countless marshes and increasingly opaque patches of woodland.

I arrived at the rallying spot close to dusk, just behind Derek. Not surprisingly, he was visibly irritated by the proximity in our times. His unabashed chauvinism was in part what inspired me, and nothing provided me greater delight than watching his ever-confident face darken into an angry sulk whenever I succeeded. Every minor triumph represented some small retribution on behalf of Sally, whom Derek considered incompetent and absurd.

In fact, many trainees didn't come close to completing their all-day navigation routes. One of my friends, Ophelia, a petite and resolute glamour-puss, had given up early and decided to sit by the side of the road, scowling over her contour map, until an instructor came and hauled her back to camp. Poor Warren was stuck in the woods for hours before he stumbled back onto the roadway, where eventually he, too, was offered a ride. Sally was found close to dark, half naked in a swamp. Frustrated by her inability to find her destination, she'd inexplicably decided to bathe. Sally wore her calamitous nature as a badge of honor, really, and the two of us later laughed about her foray into exhibitionism.

Although CST Class C was becoming increasingly cohesive and supportive, the competition was intense. Perhaps the fiercest competitor in our class was a Korean American woman named Jin Suk. Even before our scheduled group Physical Training (PT), which occurred at seven each morning and consisted of anything from five-mile runs through the woods to an hour of swimming to the obstacle course, Jin Suk would be up at four A.M., jogging on her own or doing push-ups in the barrack bathroom. She was silently but visibly outraged on the day of the standard Army PT exam—a timed two-mile run, two minutes of sit-ups, and two minutes of push-ups—when, much to both her and my astonishment, I managed to do more push-ups and sit-ups than she had. From that point on, I became Jin Suk's unwilling nemesis, our polar personalities simultaneously drawing us together and pushing us apart.

A defensive-driving course, affectionately called "Crash and Burn," comprised the next two weeks of training. On the first day, we were timed on a driving route: several laps around a racetrack at full speed, a few back-and-forth shuttles weaving among orange cones, then maneuvering around the cones in reverse as well. I was no stellar driver to begin with, and my first time through, I effectively demolished the course, knocking down practically all of the cones and thereby adding several "penalty seconds" to my already preposterously slow time. Mine was the worst effort in the class, and earned me the nickname "Miss Daisy," which caused Jin Suk to fairly beam.

We spent the next five days, from morning till night, practicing various evasive driving techniques on the racetrack and among the cone formations. Part of my problem derived from the rental cars, which were designed with back ends so high that, as a short person, I had difficulty seeing when I drove in reverse. "No problem," the driving instructor said when I feebly brought up this point by way of explaining my miserable performance. "All reverse driving is to be done without turning around; you should just use the rearview mirror in the center of your windshield."

From then on, whenever I shifted into reverse, I was met with my own frowning reflection: the bulging blue vein down the center of my forehead, the eyes boring into the mirror. It dawned on me that perhaps I was just as competitive, in my way, as Jin Suk. The driving course caused me considerable private anguish, and yet I was determined to make it through: I would not allow myself to be paralyzed by fear.

Which is not to say I ever grew comfortable taking turns at a hundred miles per hour, or screeching to tire-burning *Dukes of Hazzard*–style halts. For two weeks, my queasy stomach had me ever on the verge of a mortifying public bout of puking.

During one exercise that caused me particular anxiety, dramatically enraged instructors would jump out of roadside hiding places and bang on the hoods of our cars with large sticks. In response, we were supposed to calmly reverse and zigzag backward through a formation of orange cones. In a near panic, I forgot to shift out of drive and thereby rear-ended an instructor's Saab that he'd unwisely parked in my path.

I was only mildly chastised and did not suffer near the degree of humiliation as Jin Suk, who, normally so self-possessed and focused, somehow managed to drive her car into a ditch, activating the air bag. The burn marks it left on her face for the next several weeks seemed to bother her less than the profound public failure. Tornado Sally, meanwhile, succeeded in wrecking two of the rental cars, but was mostly just amused by her spastic driving record.

On the final day of the first week of Crash and Burn, we retook the driving test. My palms sweated profusely on the steering wheel as I waited for my turn. The instructor who timed us later told me that he'd never seen such a look of determination as I burned rubber out of the start. I tore through the course at what I was sure was an unprecedented pace.

And although in the end my time was still among the slowest, I didn't knock down a single cone, and later was awarded the title "Most Improved."

The second week of Crash and Burn consisted of smashing old beater Cadillacs and Monte Carlos, probably seized from drug dealers, through barriers such as parked cars, wooden fences, and solid walls. The instructor would let fall a flag, like Natalie Wood in *Rebel Without a Cause*, and from a standstill the student was expected to floor the gas and drive unflinchingly into the barricade. The point was to demonstrate that, indeed, we could collide into a number of different obstructions and still live. When it was my turn to launch head-on into two parked cars, I actually shut my eyes at the moment of impact. I opened them a couple of seconds later, stunned to discover myself alive and well, beyond the wreckage of the barricade.

After four days of slamming into large stationary objects, we were told to prepare for a nighttime exercise. To me, any activity that took place after dark and didn't involve martinis was ominous and unpleasant. For one thing, the whole base had the aura of some southern backwater where small, slightly ethnic people like me might get lynched or bubba-raped after nightfall. I hardly looked forward to incorporating darkness into our already harrowing demolition exercises.

That night, we convened in a large classroom near one of the many firing ranges, ostensibly to take a test on our knowledge of explosives, the topic of a single day's seminar earlier that week.

While we were completing the multiple-choice explosives exam, a trio of instructors would arrive and select a single student to take outside. Those who returned, about twenty minutes later, would resume their tests and—as per instructions—not utter a word. I had a vague idea of what was in store when I caught a glimpse of Tornado Sally being blindfolded outside the door as it slowly swung shut.

When it was my turn to go, my heart was racing. Blindfolded, I was positioned in the front passenger's seat of one of the beat-up cars. The instructor reversed out, then drove fast for about two minutes. When the car stopped, I heard the doors open and I was told to slide over into the driver's seat, as the instructor took his place next to me in the passenger's seat.

"Okay, drive on," he said. Still blindfolded, I accelerated slowly, giving my anxiety ample time to mount, while the instructor told me when to turn right or left. Finally, commanding me to halt, he pulled my blindfold off. We had stopped at a makeshift "border crossing" where various instructors, dressed as border guards, wielded weapons and enormous flashlights. Jorge, an instructor who'd spent his career in Latin America, moved toward the car, shined his flashlight in my eyes, and demanded something of me in Spanish, a language I don't speak or understand. I assumed, given the border motif, that he wanted my passport and so provided my base badge, which weeks earlier we'd been told would serve as "identification in any simulated frontier or hostage situations." I surmised that this was a simulated frontier situation.

Meanwhile, I looked around frantically for some way to escape, something through which I might crash the car. Then I remembered that we'd been given a lot of instruction on just keeping our wits about us, talking our way through difficult situations, and avoiding any rash or unnecessary maneuvers. Just because we'd learned how to Evel Knievel our way through an impasse didn't mean we were supposed to do it in every situation.

This seemed to me one of those scenarios from which I could emerge without doing donuts or barreling through a brick wall. Jorge was haranguing me by this point about my "passaporto," something along the lines of it was "nono-authenticatico," and also saying something about "narcatico." Another instructor was meticulously examining the front bumper and hood of my car. Still, I did not think the solution was to run him over.

I soon gathered—drawing upon the fact that Jorge was dangling a zip-lock bag full of dirt and onion weeds in my face—that this was about to become a trumped-up drug charge. I had no bribe money with me and half thought such a gesture would only invite more trouble. I kept repeating, "Americano. Americano diplomato!" I felt like a deranged Starbucks customer, trying to make my order clear to the uncomprehending barista.

I was told to unlock the doors so Jorge and the others could search the car's interior, from which, no big surprise, they managed to unearth more zip-lock bags, these containing white powder. I calmly denied knowledge of the drugs.

I can only assume my defense was less than convincing. *It's just an exercise,* I told myself, while something nagged at the back of my mind. A disquieting seed had been planted, and further training would provide endless fertilizer: *Am I really going to be able to handle myself when faced with such a situation in real life?* Confronted with damning evidence—genuine or fabricated—by armed foreigners, would I indeed be able to keep my wits about me? Or would I crumble, blow my cover in panic, and desperately insist on calling the ambassador or, worse, the CIA chief, to rescue my sorry, apprehended ass.

Finally, Jorge either tired of my performance or decided I'd objected willfully enough to suggest that I was neither going to admit to smuggling nor go apoplectically commando through the frontier. He handed me back my passport and pulled aside the wooden pony barrier to let me drive on. Later, I found out that a few students—including Sally and Warren—had completely freaked as soon as their blindfolds were removed and careened through the barricade as Jorge and the other instructors leapt out of their path.

Once through the "frontier," I was blindfolded again and told to drive on. Several more minutes of sightless navigation ended with the instructor commanding me to stop and then pulling the blindfold off my face.

This time, I was parked (astoundingly) in a sort of cul-de-sac formed by a six-foot-tall brick wall. A gang of masked men began launching themselves over it, landing with echoing thumps on the hood of my car and banging on the windshield. You'd think I'd be used to the instructor-turned-banshee routine by now, but my stomach cinched tight.

Luckily, I'd remembered to lock the car doors after Jorge and gang had checked for "drugs." The masked men grabbed futilely at the door handles, continued to beat on the hood and scream unintelligibly, and pressed their wild-eyed, grimacing faces against the windshield. Observing that the car was surrounded on all sides except the rear, I quickly figured out the point of this exercise. I threw the car in reverse and, eyes fixed on the rearview mirror, flew backward until there was enough distance to make a three-point turn and blow dust in the air as I tore out of there.

No sooner had I caught my breath than the blindfold was back over my eyes. I prayed that we would be heading back to the classroom now, that I could finish my explosives exam and return to the barracks to collapse in my bunk. I was sore, tired, and stressed out from two weeks of sitting in a car all day, high-speed chasing, maneuvering on two wheels, screeching to halts, and craning my neck to weave among orange cones. On the one hand, I felt proud, acutely aware that my limits were being tested and that I was rising to each occasion. On the other hand, I wondered, *What the hell am I doing with my life?* At some point, didn't I just want to find a nice guy and settle down? Drag racer/demolition gal here would have to start cruising Monster Truck rallies for dates.

I relegated these thoughts to the back of my mind as I concentrated on the task at hand, driving blindfolded through the woods. I was told to stop the car again, and this time, as soon as the blindfold was off, a new gang of baton-brandishing thugs emerged from the darkness and commenced the now-hackneyed beating of the car and shrieking obscenities. One of them even had an AK-47, which he shot off merrily into the air. I was no longer scared so much as amused, though later I heard that one of the trainees wet his pants. The instructors, I figured, must be having the time of their lives. The Farm, it occurred to me, was all part of an elaborate game for men who'd never really grown up. And the world of espionage, I thought warily, might well be just a global playing field of this little boys' game.

This time, I discerned that I was surrounded on all sides except in front, where two parked sedans formed a barricade. One of the attackers had somehow managed to get the back door open, and was crawling in when I thrust my foot down on the accelerator. Just as I'd practiced all week, I headed straight for the weakest point in the barrier, the joint where the two cars in my path met, bumper to bumper. Sure enough, I broke through to the other side, turning briefly to see the vehicles through which I'd just smashed, now with their headlights facing forward and a large smoldering gap between them. I pushed down the gas pedal as far as it would go and barreled through the woods, the instructor whooping alongside of me, "You go, girl!" Exhilarated, I thought, *This may be a silly game, but I'm actually getting good at it.*

Afterward, I was told that I'd performed appropriately and admirably on each of the Crash and Burn exercises, but that I'd failed the test on explosives.

. . .

Explosives, a topic that enthralled the men in our class, did not interest me in the least. All afternoon, we occupied a stuffy, chemical-smelling, glass building where we learned how to assemble bombs out of C-4 and Clorox, which we then watched explode spectacularly in the open fields in front of us. The *boom*ing sound reverberating throughout the base always made me uneasy.

I could hardly imagine, moreover, that I was actually going to inspect my car each and every morning, which we were told was a necessary precaution when living overseas. Having heard countless rumors about case officers who had succumbed to paranoia and eventual insanity, I figured the mental deterioration must begin here, learning how to assemble and dismantle weapons of grave, if not mass, destruction. Even if I *were* to detect a bomb, I certainly had no intention of disabling it myself in the manner in which we were being taught. I determined well in advance that I would just get the hell out of there.

I spent the majority of our explosives seminars daydreaming, staring wistfully at the sultry Virginia swampland, and waiting for the instructor to blow up a car in the distance, which was mildly diversionary.

Soon we would travel several hours south for an entire week's worth of explosive training. This would have been purgatory to me except that I fell in love with the strange atmosphere of the new base; we got to sleep in quasi–motel rooms instead of barracks, and the cafeteria ladies served up plentiful vats of southern home cooking—crisp fried chicken and buttery biscuits and baked apples topped with cinnamon. The air was ungodly hot and buzzed with cicadas. At night, we would drink beers by the bay and I would swim out under the luminous moon, half wanting to keep going till I reached that spot where the dark of the sky met the black of the sea.

During explosives week, we were familiarized with all kinds of biological agents, only one of which was fit for training purposes. For a much-dreaded exercise, about which we'd been provided troublingly scant details in advance—I recall Ed mumbling something about "examining one's threshold for pain and discomfort"—we were to march, hands behind our backs, in a single-file line into a small chamber where gas-masked instructors gaily assailed us with cans of pepper spray.

The discomfort was intense; our eyes burned red and we moaned in protest and cursed. Water, we were told, would only aggravate the stinging, but several people could not help themselves and ran to the bathroom to douse their faces. I wandered around blindly with my knuckles burrowed into my eye sockets, willing the pain to go away. Jin Suk dealt with the situation stoically, of course, retreating under a tree, where she sat cross-legged with her eyes closed like some kind of meditating yogi.

Another explosives-week exercise was called "Secondary Interrogation While Traveling in Alias." We all had been issued alias identities and documents, the details of which, by this time, we were expected to have memorized.

"Real-life INS agents will be here by tomorrow," Ed told us.

"They will enact a simulated, but highly realistic, frontier crossing. These guys are professionals. They will grill the bejeezus outta you. Y'all had better have your stories straight."

I prepared by studying the details of my alias identity every night. I even knew the astrological signs of each member of my alias family.

Like most suburban high school kids, I'd used fake ID to buy beer and get into bars since the age of thirteen; "Secondary" was a breeze for me. Some other students had trouble with the exercise, particularly those who grew combative with the INS agents, whom, curiously, I found to be some of the nicest people I met during training.

INS brought to mind Sasho, whom I'd not seen nor spoken to since that autumn day when I drove him to Dulles Airport. I recalled how his eyes had welled with tears as he scanned the departures board for his flight back to San Francisco. I hadn't cried then, but I'd sobbed the entire drive home, all the while wondering for whom I was sorry, him or me.

Thinking about Sasho now was painful. Memories of him, no matter how vivid, seemed like recollections from somebody else's life: Sasho's face smiling up at me when I looked down from a climb; his rugged hands firmly gripping the rope from which my life suspended; his lips brushing my forehead when my feet finally touched the ground.

I pushed these images of Sasho to the recesses of my mind. As much as I missed him, I remained convinced that I had done the right thing. I thought of how much I'd learned since I started PM training; even the relatively mundane stuff back at Headquarters—traces, cables, classification systems—represented a pool of new knowledge for me. And I was doing well so far, making a good impression. I was on the road to becoming a successful spy.

I thought about how Sasho would have complicated my life, muddled my thoughts, and thwarted my progress. I couldn't have done this with him around. While I might have been able to deal with the dubious eye the Agency cast toward my foreign boyfriend, I could not have withstood Sasho himself, his innocent questions that made me second-guess the course of my life. Sasho had been so human, while I was learning to be a machine. Sasho was inherently honest, and I was starting to build a life on lies. And Sasho represented to me freedom, which I was well in the process of leaving behind. It was painful to think about, so I pressed on with my training and let the images of him gather dust, figuring they'd eventually fade away.

Following explosives, our reward was to return to The Farm for a week of "Maritime." This was Crash and Burn, but on sun-streaked open water.

There were skills to learn—nautical distances, navigational direction, recognition of tidal and storm patterns—as well as some degree of proficiency we were supposed to achieve in operating high-speed boats. I grasped the basics, then focused on the feel of the wind whipping through my hair as we lacerated waves and raced the setting sun.

At the end of each day, we scrubbed down the boats while listening to Motown tunes and spraying each other with hoses. The entire thing felt very fun and wholesome, like a Mountain

Dew commercial. I was glad that, no matter my initial reservations, I'd decided to see this thing through. More than anything, I was happy to be making new friends. My fellow teammates, at first glance an assortment of egomaniacs and freaks, now formed a close-knit circle of comrades.

I would eat meals with Tornado Sally and good-natured Mark and Green Beret Derek, and we would all rib one another, talk over and past each other, lean in to whisper about the hard-ass instructors, or strategize against other teams. We seemed more and more like a family.

While we spent days on the water, we spent nights in the air. After morning maritime activities, we occupied the afternoon setting up "drop sites." In clouds of mosquitoes and suffocating humidity, we arranged patterns of fluorescent panels in a wide pasture so that a plane, flying overhead, could release boxed materials on target.

One night, I was in charge of actually shoving an enormous wooden crate—which earlier we'd packed with cement blocks—out of the small propeller plane. As soon as I recognized our T-shaped configuration of fluorescent panels hundreds of feet below, I braced my back against one side of the small plane and—hoping mightily that no animal or person was occupying the field below—used both feet to give the crate a vigorous heave.

I accomplished the mission a second too late and our drop box missed the landing site altogether. It did, however, hit a power line during its descent, thereby eliminating electricity on the base for the next several hours. My ineptitude, which quickly gained notoriety, was surpassed some days later when Warren nearly shot off his own foot during firearms training.

For the following week, we spent every morning on the range, firing off Beretta revolvers, Browning pistols, AK-47s, sawed-off shotguns, hunting rifles, and weighty shoulder-contusion-causing submachine guns. Occasionally, an instructor would tack atop the silhouetted target's head a photo of Saddam Hussein or Usama bin Laden—who may not have been *public* enemy number one in 1999, but certainly was within the CIA.

Warren routinely ignored instructions and, swinging his loaded weapon every which way, presented a lethal hazard on the range. Alarmingly, our firearms evaluation hinged not on hands-on performance but on a written multiple-choice and true/false exam, administered at the end of the week. Warren received the highest score.

Weapons week was followed by five days of hand-to-hand combat, combined with medical training; we spent the afternoons tending to the bruises and wounds we'd inflicted by beating the crap out of each other earlier that day.

I proved hopeless at hand-to-hand combat. As the only two left-handed people, my friend Ethan and I were consistently matched as adversaries. Pitted against each other, Ethan and I couldn't bring ourselves to maul and kick. We danced in circles, occasionally ejecting one arm in a spastic, ineffectual jab.

The "hand-to-hand combat consultant," flown in from

Arkansas, lavishly extolled Jin Suk when she nearly fractured the leg of a fellow trainee by punting him in the shin while delivering a diversionary wallop to the underside of his jaw.

During PM training, I was surprised to discover that I hardly missed home at all. Increasingly, my life revolved around The Farm. The relationships I thought about were those with my teammates and our instructors. The days followed a comforting pattern: morning PT, bacon and eggs at the mess hall, three to four hours of practical training, a sandwich for lunch, afternoon activity (usually outside), fried chicken or macaroni casserole for dinner, evening exercise—and, if we were lucky, an occasional free night to drink beers and play darts at the base bar. Every night, just before collapsing exhausted into our bunks, we checked one another thoroughly for ticks, chiggers, and lice.

The near-constant activity saved me from worrying about anything relevant to my real life: my family's seeming doubt in my ability to succeed within the Agency; the failing health of my one surviving grandmother, whom I never had time to visit anymore; and the fact that I was approaching thirty without a boyfriend, sequestered in the equivalent of a maximum-security penal colony. I soothed myself by thinking of PM training as a kind of intense adult summer camp experience, and eventually I succeeded—so much so that I was loath to leave The Farm.

One weekend, we were bussed back to Washington for a few days of R&R. I was idle and restless at my mother's house, confined and nearly claustrophobic in the shopping mall, and inordinately annoyed by little things such as standard suburban traffic or the dizzying array of beverage choices at Starbucks. Most of my friends "on the outside" had given up on trying to get in touch with me, so even the forty-eight hours back in society seemed lonely and purposeless. I took the opportunity to launder my army fatigues and polish my boots in preparation for two weeks of "jump camp."

As trainees, we were not *required* to jump. Truth be told, virtually none of the PM training was relevant to the reality of our future careers. In actuality, we would have little reason to be traipsing through the woods with nothing other than a compass or doing donuts and wheelies in our diplomat-plated vehicles.

Jumping out of airplanes represented perhaps the most gratuitous exercise. It wasn't as if we were going to arrive for our first overseas posts via airdrop, like some kind of Flying Elvis Brigade. A few of the guys—Rob the ex-cop, Gung-ho Ike, and former Green Beret Derek—might end up in Special Operations, but the rest of us would be working desk jobs by day, trolling the diplomatic cocktail circuit by night. Jumping, we recognized, was primarily intended to build our confidence.

Derek was already Airborne Qualified, and thus indifferent, but the rest of us were mostly scared shitless, though we hid it with varying degrees of bravado. Before actually jumping, we would spend a week preparing, learning: how to land ("stop, drop, and roll"); how to run in a serpentine, immediately gathering up the parachute so as not to be dragged across the ground by the wind; and what to do in the event of a water, wire, or tree landing.

The latter consumed my psyche during the days preceding our first jump. We would spend mealtimes discussing which of these three represented the biggest misfortune. Most people thought that a water landing would not be so bad: All you had to do was shed your combat boots and pack, and fill part of the chute with air to use as a flotation device.

"As an alternative to reinflating the parachute," an instructor assured us, "you can craft a trouser floatie."

To do so, you would remove your pants, tie each leg at its hem, capture air by swinging the pants above your head, and then tie off the open waist—all the while remaining clearheaded and frantically treading cold, brackish water. During practical application of this skill, which took place in the base swimming pool, I did not see one person succeed in making an adequate trouser floatie. I decided that a water landing would be almost the worst of all possibilities, second only to a defective parachute that did not open at all.

To become Airborne Qualified, we each had to perform five jumps, including one "equipment jump." The equipment jump entailed attaching a seventy-pound military-style pack to the front of the jumper's legs that, during the descent, he was to uncouple from his body and let drop to the ground. If he couldn't manage to get the pack off, he'd land with it still attached, likely breaking both legs.

As the instructors read out the supposedly random order in which we would jump, a collective gasp rose from the crowd when Warren's name was called first. The PM instructors thought he was a total fool, and his Harvard pedigree had only increased their collective ire. During jump week, Warren unnerved everyone with his unfettered fear—howling in terror each time he had to leap, albeit attached to Peter Pan–style cables, from the thirty-foot-high training tower. I was pretty sure it was no accident that he was our designated pioneer of the sky.

The plane could carry up to nine students at a time. During each flight, the pilot would make three passes over the landing zone and students would be pushed out in rounds of three. The rest of us assembled to watch from the ground. It was a clear and beautiful day, with only a few white clouds streaking the baby-blue sky. My heart surged with pride when, all of a sudden, we saw a small khaki-colored blob tumble out of the plane, a chute pop open, and Warren sail gracefully to the ground. The rest of us, even those who probably held him in private disdain, erupted in cheers.

From my team of nine, I was the second to be shoved out, right after Derek, who earlier had cautioned me not to "steal his air" on the way down.

Perched in the open doorway of the Twin Otter aircraft, hands braced and ready to go, all I could think about was how unprepared I was to die. I experienced a random and pathetic regret: that there would be no bereaved boyfriend to mourn me upon my death. I briefly wondered if the funeral attendees would find my spinster status an added element of the overall tragedy. I also conjectured as to how the CIA, and for that matter my parents, would explain my demise—the result of jumping out of an airplane over an undisclosed location—when everyone thought I was doing administrative work at some government annex.

The land looked as land does from above: inauthentic,

patchwork, limitless—a gentle hint at one's own insignifi-
cance. In the distance I could see the bay, a vast span of blue,
in which I hoped I wouldn't land. I didn't have much time to
worry about it, however, as the jumpmaster shouted "GO!"
and then shoved me out of the plane.

Much to my relief, my chute opened. As soon as I saw the
canopy spread out above me like an enormous umbrella, I
calmly grasped the toggles and began maneuvering my descent. Enveloped by the still and silent air, I felt overcome with
freedom. Suddenly, I knew I would be okay.

Being one of the lighter jumpers, I descended at a slower
pace than the others. As we neared the landing site, Wolf, a
Vietnam veteran and former paratrooper who bore an uncanny
resemblance to Willie Nelson, roared through a megaphone
from below, "More to the right, you big dummy!" "Knees bent,
you big dummy!" "Steer, you big dummy!"

My first four jumps, though exhilarating, were uneventful.
When it came time for the equipment jump, my initial terror
resurfaced. I think I would have preferred to die rather than
break my legs. I had a vague premonition that there would be
trouble releasing the pack. Sure enough, midway through my
fall, as I yanked on the tail of twine that was supposed to dis-
engage the pack, the knot merely tightened. The seventy-pound
pack remained dangling from my left leg like an anchor.

"Oh, Lord, don't let me break my leg," I said out loud, and
felt guilty about my sudden religious conviction, especially
given that—all things considered—a fractured limb wouldn't
be such a big deal. I suppose that, more than anything, I feared
an injury that would get in the way of the rest of my training.

I knew that I would need to be at least ambulatory for the tradecraft course; the idea of being sent back to Headquarters to heal, while my friends and peers moved on, was more than I could bear.

I yanked harder, merely causing the knot to cinch tighter; at this point, the ground loomed toward me like an opaque wave. Then a rush of adrenaline must have endowed me with some kind of superhuman strength. Momentarily releasing the toggles, I used both hands to snap the twine. The pack plummeted to the ground, landing with an impressive thud and a small cloud of dust. I immediately focused on maneuvering my way toward Wolf, who by this time was hoarse from shouting over and over, "C'mon, you big dummy!"

The final two weeks involved an exercise that was supposed to incorporate everything we had learned during PM. Our primary mission was to conduct an "exfiltration" of a group of American hostages from hostile territory. We were told we would have a number of auxiliary missions en route.

"A helicopter will drop each group at a different undisclosed location," Ed, standing at the front of a classroom, briefed us. "Y'all've got five days to reach the exfil point, rescue the hostages, and make it back to this room, which will serve as your headquarters. During that time, you'll be sleeping in the woods and constructing shelters with what materials you have on your person."

Warren looked panic-stricken; Jin Suk was eagerly taking notes.

"You should expect at least one water-based element of your journey," Ed went on. "Each student will be provided an AK-47 and several blank rounds, should you encounter hostile forces en route."

Ethan glanced at me from across the room and silently mouthed, "For faaaaack's sake . . ."

As a group, we also received two ancient handheld radios—to communicate with and receive intermittent orders from headquarters—as well as a couple of contour maps and a single global positioning system device. We packed crates of MREs, which would be delivered to us via plane in drop zones we would set up ourselves and whose location we would communicate, in code, to headquarters.

Ed delivered his final words of caution: "You are expected to traverse in some clandestine manner through the woods, never on one of the open roads. You are not to communicate with any other groups. And you are not to get caught!"

We commenced our operation one evening under a relentless, pounding rain. Our group of nine was taken up first in the helicopter, flown to the opposite end of the enormous base, and dumped in what as far as I could tell was quicksand. Once we'd managed to crawl out of the pond of goop, our battle-dress uniforms (camouflage pants and jackets) were soaked through, weighted down by mud.

We hiked until we reached an area that seemed as if it would serve as an adequate drop zone. There we placed fluorescent panels in formation. Later, we would convey the geo-coordinates of our site to headquarters and, sometime the following evening, a plane would fly overhead and deliver us the prepacked crate of MREs. In the meantime, nearly everyone had stashed at least an apple or a granola bar.

During our months together, certain alliances had formed. Derek and Sally were constantly at each other's throat, and Derek was vexed by my tendency to rush to Sally's defense. Mark could irritate people with his know-it-all demeanor and rambling sagas of fly-fishing, his "real life" hobby. But everyone got along for the most part, and, no matter our varying degree of skills, we had bonded.

Our camaraderie proved critical once the mission got under way. That night, we were intermittently terrorized by the appearance of huge camouflage-covered trucks, each one filled with machine-gun-wielding "rebels" who, if they spotted us, would shoot wildly into the air and sometimes chase us deep within the woods.

Our first food drop never arrived, an error that we later discovered was the result of Derek—much to our surprise and his consternation—miscalculating the coordinates of the drop zone. Disappointed that food was not forthcoming, we erected makeshift shelters with our ponchos and took turns sleeping while at least two sentries stayed awake, on alert for the enemy. All night we could hear random shooting and explosions reverberating throughout the base.

In the morning, we were to check in with headquarters to receive a coded message. At first Sally had taken on this responsibility, but when she garbled the first message—constantly consulting the slip of paper that contained the code key, and recontacting headquarters six times—Derek finally wrested the radio from her and handed it to me.

I determined from the message that we were to press on toward a location on the opposite side of base, from which we would be given further directions. After several hours of hoofing it through the woods and another few run-ins with the gun-toting rebels, we came to a small clearing in which had been stationed two deflated, overturned Zodiac boats. A note affixed to the underside of one of these thick rubber boats instructed us to row to a spot several miles down the swampy estuary, where we would find the group of American hostages to be rescued.

The inflation of the boats was left to Sally and me, under the assumption that we couldn't possibly screw it up. Sally held out the floppy rubber like a blanket to be folded, while I operated a handheld pump that Derek had had the foresight to include in his pack. As much as I outwardly reviled him, I had to admit there was no other trainee I'd rather have on my team. Indeed, he seemed always to know what to do, and to think of precautions and consequences that never would've occurred to the rest of us.

We split into two groups and each took a Zodiac and four paddles. Upon first attempts to row forward, our boat spun in circles like the teacup ride at Disneyland. Derek suggested that one of us use a paddle as a rudder, while the others sculled. I took up the rudder position and, after much maddening experimentation, finally got us moving slowly in the right direction. It dawned on me that I should have paid more attention during Maritime.

We rowed and rowed along this flat marshland-surrounded tributary. Dragonflies buzzed and snapped above the water, and occasionally a heron would swoop down from overhead. I felt like a guerrilla.

Hours later, just as we were nearing our destination, I noticed two men hiding in the brush atop a riverside crag. Their faces were painted a motley camouflage of green and black, as were all of ours. One of the men regarded us through a set of binoculars.

"Don't look now," I whispered to Mark, paddling next to me, "but we're being watched."

We stopped rowing and waited for the second Zodiac to catch up. Sally, meanwhile, was shouting out remarks about every form of wildlife she observed—*Oh, look at the birdies! Did you see that fish?! Ewww, a snake!*—like some overzealous river guide. I shushed her, and as the other boat drew up beside ours, I mouthed to Derek that there were enemies lying in wait on the riverbank. I was sure we were headed for an ambush, and wanted to continue down the river instead of disembarking at the predesignated spot. Derek insisted we must go on with the mission as planned.

"If they ambush us, open fire," he said.

Sure enough, just after we'd finished hauling the Zodiacs out of the muck and onto the shore, someone let out a hideous battle cry. The hair on my arms jumped to attention, and the nine of us scrambled to ready our weapons. I felt that same sick sense of nervousness that I did as a kid playing cowboys and Indians. Because my mother wouldn't let us have toy guns, I'd always been one of the insufficiently armed Indians, lamely awaiting capture or some other unfortunate fate.

Within seconds, we were all shooting randomly through the brush. I was amazed by the immediate and collective suspension of disbelief. Focused on nothing other than emptying each successive round, I was fighting for my life. Had it been a real battle, I am pretty sure at least half, if not all, of us would have perished in friendly fire.

The shoot-out was followed by an eerie calm. I figured the instructors and base staff posing as our enemies had three other groups to terrorize and hadn't wanted to waste all their energy and ammunition on us. I sat on the ground to catch my breath.

"I think they're gone," I said to Derek, who, I suddenly noticed, was lying on his belly about a foot away from me.

"I think you're right," he said—in spite of himself, I was sure. He rolled over onto his back and leapt in one swift, impressively acrobatic movement off the ground.

Tornado Sally emerged from behind a small plot of reeds, looking as if she'd just survived a plane crash; face smudged with dirt and hair askew, she began wandering around in a semidisoriented state, looking for her ammo belt, which she'd dropped at the onset of the melee. Derek suggested we regroup and move on to a safe location where I could contact headquarters.

Our next instruction was to traverse by night over many more miles of hostile territory, to find a shelter serving as base for a suspected terrorist cell. Once there, we were to infiltrate the premises and collect as much detailed information, "intelligence," as we could.

We were exhausted, but we knew there was no choice but to press on. That day we managed, somewhat miraculously, to make the entire leg of the trip undetected by the bad guys, although we could hear them patrolling the roads with their noisy Mack trucks, engaging the other groups in firefights.

After several more hours of hiking, we came upon a shack in the woods with a light on inside. Our reconnaissance of this shack, clearly the terrorists' base, was comical at best—the nine of us huddled behind a wall to whose other side we all quickly scuttled when someone thought he saw movement in the wood. We must have looked like the Keystone Kops, and I don't think Derek appreciated it when I asked whether such tactics brought him back to his days with the Special Forces.

Finally, the "terrorists" shouted out in forced foreign accents, "We go now!" before evacuating their base. Once they were out of sight, we skulked forward, stumbling into one another in the darkness and cursing in stage whispers. The shack appeared for the most part empty, until Sally shrieked delightedly that she had found a trapdoor leading to a basement. Sure enough, the basement was chock-full of terrorist wares: Arabic magazines and newspapers; some materials that by now we knew could be used to make bombs; playing cards and Western nudie mags. The jackpot!

We all set about feverishly jotting down our findings. My task—given that none of us knew how to operate the

high-tech digital camera with which we'd been furnished—
was to hand-draw the terrorists' "compound." I sketched a
simple wood cabin that reminded me of young George Washington's house, and added a long arrow pointing to the floor,
labeling it "trapdoor." As the others bustled around the basement, the situation suddenly seemed ripe for an ambush, and—
sure enough—within seconds, I saw the lights of a convoy
truck creeping across the grass.

I readied my weapon and positioned myself behind the
uneven curtain, like the maniacal grandma from *The Beverly
Hillbillies.*

A man I'd never seen before, cradling what appeared to be a
broken arm in a muslin sling, emerged from the truck and approached the cabin. *Should I shoot him?* I was at once ashamed
of myself for the barbaric impulse.

"I'm hurt; there are people hurt!" the man called.

I yelled down to the others, and once they'd all scurried up
from the basement, I opened the front door, my weapon
poised.

"We're American missionaries," the man cried from the
lawn. "Our plane crashed in the field. Several people are
injured."

I immediately smelled the point of the next exercise: im-
plementation of the medical training we had received. Sure
enough, the wounded man transported us, via his conveniently acquired truck, to an open field in which lay the gut-
ted remains of a large passenger plane and, next to the plane,
clusters of wounded persons with varying degrees of injury. I
was impressed with both the props and the actors.

I radioed into headquarters and was told that a helicopter would be arriving shortly.

"The potpie can only feed five," the voice on the other end added cryptically, abandoning our agreed-upon code. I interpreted this comment to mean that the helicopter could transport no more than five of the wounded.

Derek agreed with me: "The rest will have to remain in the field."

"*Gee*, I wonder what the point of this exercise is?!" Mark said, his voice thick with sarcasm and fatigue.

"Yeah. If they wanted to teach us about prioritizing people by their relative value," Derek grumbled, glancing at Sally, "they should have cut half the idiots from this program the first week."

After a quick divvying up of duties, I set about interviewing the wounded to determine who should get a spot on the helicopter. I recognized some of the base personnel who obviously had been shanghaied into festering in this mosquito-plagued and tick-infested field for hours on end, moaning about imagined injuries and being manhandled by frantic—and by this time, foul-smelling—groups of trainees. I arbitrarily decided that the cafeteria lady, who always let me have both sausage *and* bacon with my eggs in the morning, certainly ought to be saved. The others overruled me when it was discovered that one among the wounded was an "American ambassador."

"We've got to save the ambo," Tornado Sally said. "Or we'll be in hot water for sure."

"Any victims whose injuries are life-threateningly severe

should be left to die," Derek added. "We don't have the time or supplies to tend to all of the wounded."

When the helicopter arrived, we began to transport the five persons deemed salvageable. It was a calamity of tragicomic proportions, as we exacerbated the victims' pain and suffering with our bumbling efforts to lift and carry them to the chopper. The "American ambassador," in fact one of the base custodians, acted out his exalted role with flourish and passion, moaning with every move we made and grumbling about "when the secretary of state hears about this!"

Once the chopper had lifted off the ground, leaving us all with windswept hair and muddied faces, the remaining victims broke character long enough to shoo us out of the area. The next group of students was on its way.

The cafeteria lady was removing her bandages and repositioning herself by the "smoldering" fuselage of the downed plane. I discreetly waved to her, and she waved back, just before we crossed into the woods.

As we continued to trudge through the forest, the sun began to peek through the trees and our minds moved toward sleep. Before setting up camp, I radioed into headquarters again. I could almost hear the perverse glee in the instructor's voice on the other end: "We've got one more mission for you." In code, he gave me the coordinates of an "enemy pharmaceutical plant, rumored to contain materials for weapons of mass destruction."

We were to locate the camp and conduct nighttime reconnaissance, perhaps even infiltration, and return with sketches, descriptions, and photos. In addition to the high-tech digital camera, each group had been equipped with two pairs of night-vision goggles, which, for some reason, our group had yet to employ.

By this time, we were all rank and tired, not to mention running short on food. We'd experienced only one successful MRE airdrop and we had eaten all of them, except for a few safeguarded peanut butter packs, industrial-strength saltines, and Tootsie Rolls. Aside from being famished, we were uniformly cranky. I was pretty sure that Derek and Sally would either kill each other or end up sleeping together, their animosity had reached such a fervent and passionate pitch.

It was decided that Mark and I would conduct the first recon mission in the middle of the night. I had a few hours to acquire some degree of proficiency with the digital camera, and so spent the evening taking pictures of my own feet and of Sally, blissfully sleeping under a poncho suspended from a branch.

Later, Mark and I tromped not so stealthily through the woods—he smoking one of his contraband cigarettes and me lumbering awkwardly under the jumbled load of equipment. Our faces painted for battle, we sported the night-vision goggles, whose effect was more disorienting than enabling, causing us to plunge into small ditches and run head-on into large trees.

When we heard the roar of an approaching truck, Mark and I dove into a roadside ravine. I nearly impaled myself on a storm-truncated tree, while he landed with a thump on the muddy ground alongside me. As the truck passed, someone shot a few rounds into the air.

For the last several meters before our destination, we slithered on our stomachs, side by side, until we reached the barbed-wire perimeter of the industrial plant. The compound contained three buildings, one downed chopper, and a huge truck in which sat two brutish-looking guards.

I managed to draw most of the buildings and take several photos with the digital camera, while Mark surveyed the perimeter to determine if there was an opening in the fence or any other means of breaking in.

"Nada!" Mark said when he returned from his crawl-about and collapsed on the ground next to me. As we lay there, wondering what should be our next move, his handheld radio suddenly sputtered with static and then angry shouting from the other end. "Oh, shit!" He rolled over to muffle the noise; obviously, he'd forgotten to lower the volume or change the frequency on his radio. The guards perked up at once. They were dismounting from the truck as Mark and I clambered to our feet and hightailed it back through the woods. This time we didn't bother with the night-vision goggles, whose strap garroted me around the neck as I raced after Mark.

When we arrived back at the campsite, I could feel my heart pounding. I was afraid, exhilarated, and exhausted—all at once. It did not take great powers of observation for Mark and me to realize that the others were gone. The makeshift tents were still standing, and some remnants of occupancy—for example, Sally's purple jog bra, drying on a branch—remained around the campsite. But there was not a person in sight.

That was soon to change.

Six armed, masked men came crashing from the wood and surrounded us. Mark and I jumped back, slamming into and ricocheting off of each other like colliding billiards.

"Drop your weapons!" one of the men shouted, a demand with which neither of us wasted any time in complying. Two of the other men threw pillowcases over our heads. Sightless, I felt panicky at once, and struggled to remind myself that this was all part of the game. We were marched several meters before being hurled into some kind of cavern, amid what I recognized—by the pungent body odor and subdued grumbling—as the rest of our team. The cavern, it turns out, was the back of a truck.

We'd all anticipated our eventual "capture"—PM training was scripted to culminate with a simulated POW experience—but I was frightened nonetheless. As the truck's engine rumbled into operation, I had an arbitrary, yet intense, desire to see my friends. Emma and Emily, I imagined, would be slurping margaritas at Tortilla Flats in the East Village right about now, or perhaps they'd headed out to Brighton Beach as we all had before, drinking vodka and eating small salty fish at a Russian restaurant by the sea. *Why am I not with them?* I thought. *What in the hell am I doing here?*

We careened blindly over potholes, my backside sliding to and fro across the gritty metal truck bed. I fumbled to remove the disk from the digital camera and to tear my sketches into tiny bits. I stashed the disk in my boot and the scraps of paper in my pocket. Finally, the truck skidded to a halt, its back doors flung open, and we were deposited, still blind, onto some muddy turf. Tinny Balkan music blared over a loudspeaker.

Good Lord, I thought. *Where are we?*

For the next hour or so, we were made to march single-file

up and down hills and in circles, with both hands on the pillowcase of the person in front of us. All the while, unfamiliar
male voices bellowed at us to tighten the pillowcase around
the neck of whomever we followed. If anyone slowed down, or
tripped, he was quickly kicked or rifle-butted. At one point, I
heard Sally choking and gasping for air, inviting immediate
abuse, and I thought grimly that though I'd known this POW
simulation was coming, I was unprepared for how realistic it
would be. I struggled to loosen the pillowcase, thus singling
myself out for a few swift kicks to the backs of my legs, coupled with some colorful verbal invective: "Move it, you goddamn sloth!"

Finally, we were led to a dark but roomy chamber where our
pillowcases were removed, and where we found the three other
teams sitting subdued and silent on the concrete floor. It was
unsettling that none of our captors was recognizable as an instructor or member of the base staff. Looking around for the
sunny face of the cafeteria lady, I briefly considered the possibility that perhaps this was not an exercise at all. Was it possible that enemy forces had taken over The Farm and killed the
entire cadre of instructors and staff?

We were told to sit up straight while our arms were tied behind our backs. One guard commanded us to keep silent just
before he and the rest of the guards filed out, leaving us behind
on the dank concrete.

As soon as the "bad guys" were gone, we looked around and
smirked bravely at one another. We'd been warned that no
matter what happened, we were to stick by our cover stories,

not reveal that we were "CIA." I'm sure we were convincing as war-painted, camouflage-clad, gun-toting "tourists," carrying night-vision goggles and digital cameras, who just happened to be vacationing near a top secret nuclear arms facility.

Mark and I were among the first called out for interrogation. So was poor Ethan, whom I'd not seen in days, since he wasn't on my team. He looked ashen and panic-stricken as the guards dragged him and Ophelia up off their feet. Unlike Ethan, Ophelia appeared merely tired and pissed off. Scowling at the guard yanking on her comically large battle-dress uniform top, she defiantly took a moment to straighten her hair.

The guards redistributed pillowcases over our heads before pushing the four of us out the barely cracked door. After more awkward and aimless marching around, I was led into a trailer, my pillowcase was removed, and I was shoved before a man whom I assumed to be the interrogator. An anemic-looking guy with the face of a ferret, he was flanked by two other armed guards.

"Name?"

I answered.

The interrogator grinned upon hearing my alias. "Okay, Miss Mosby." He leaned forward and twirled one end of his mustache. "What are *you* doing here?"

While the interrogator grilled me, asking the same questions again and again, I stuck by the preposterous "tourist" story. At long last, the interrogator produced some notes—in barely legible scrawl that was unmistakably the work of Mark—about the pharmaceutical plant–cum–nuclear facility.

"We found these in the pocket of that big fellow you were caught with." The interrogator arranged the notes in front of me meticulously, as if he were putting together a jigsaw puzzle.

"I don't know anything about that," I said. "We just thought it was an interesting site, like a museum or something."

We both knew it was a feeble explanation. The interrogator's eyes narrowed, and he said, "Your friend Mark is telling us something very different."

I knew Mark wouldn't have ratted us out, so I just chuckled. This, it emerged, was a momentous offense. One of the guards lunged forward and knocked me off my chair. Struggling to right myself, I was not so much hurt as shocked, and more than a little bit humiliated.

Mercifully, I was then returned to the concrete grotto where the rest of my classmates were now marching in a circle, shouting out over the thunderous Serbian folk music, "I am a coward! I am a coward!" Three guards provided aggressive encouragement to the parade in the form of theatrical screeching and frequent rifle-butt jabs. The pageant halted almost immediately upon my arrival, and I was told to stand in the middle of the room.

"You see this woman?!" a guard shouted. "She just betrayed all of you! She told us the real story—that you're working for the CIA."

I felt my face flush and resisted the impulse to cry out in my own defense. Surely the others would know I wasn't a traitor. I certainly would not have capitulated after a single interrogation! Just then, Ophelia, Ethan, and Mark were returned. Each was publicly accused of treachery, exactly as I had been, and then the four of us were made to stand in the center of the room and eat cookies, while the others were commanded to "heckle the traitors." I wondered if I was supposed to defiantly refuse the cookies, but I was famished and they tasted very good.

When the captors had wearied of this game, we were allowed to return to our spots on the floor. There we sat in silence for more hours, wordlessly tolerating the horrid folk music and intermittent sieges when one or another student was called out for interrogation and the rest of us were yelled at, or made to stand on one foot for several minutes, or do push-ups, or parade around in circles, loudly attesting to our own idiocy or cowardice.

I was called out for at least half a dozen interrogations, as were Ethan, Mark, and Ophelia. I could scarcely believe the lengths to which the Agency had gone in order to re-create the harsh reality of a prison camp; it seemed a whole new staff had been employed. And this staff showed no indication of the friendly sort of contrived antagonism maintained by our instructors; these guys were downright mean. I perceived that it might be dangerous to look one of them in the eye, but occasionally I made a quick study of a face for some sign of empathy, or even reservation. More than anything, I was looking for any indication that this was still just a game. Little by little, my confidence began to waver.

At one point, as we were circling around with our arms in the air, shouting, "I am a loser," a generally reserved and obedient classmate named Ted tried to enact a revolt.

"There's only a few of them," Ted shouted suddenly. "There's more of us. Let's charge them. Let's go!"

The rest of us stood there mutely as Ted was set upon by the guards and hauled out, screaming, "Come on, guys! Help me!" as he tried to resist.

Ted's failure to rally the troops was disheartening, to say the least. I was embarrassed for the whole lot of us. It was painfully clear, as proved by our collective inertia, that nobody was prepared to rebel just yet. No matter that the line between reality and make-believe was becoming increasingly blurred, we still figured the exercise would end soon enough and that we'd be let out. I had calculated that it was probably Monday when we were captured, and we had to be released by Friday, because the PM course was scheduled to end and some students had families waiting for them at home.

Several hours into our captivity, the guards returned with the pillowcases. "Put these on, you pussies!" They separated the women from the men, and we were herded outside.

Minutes later, thirteen girls jostled for space in a concrete cell the size of a broom closet. "Stay standing!" one guard shouted right before he wrenched shut an iron door whose devastating sound, as he turned the lock from the outside, made my heart freeze.

As soon as the guard disappeared, we pulled up our pillowcases so we at least could make out the shapes of the other women in the darkness. We groped around to find spots on the ground to sit or squat. When we heard the guard returning—heavy thumps across the gravel outside—we all scrambled to our feet and quickly repositioned our pillowcases. I was struck by what little time it took for the conditions of captivity to victimize our normally strong wills.

The next wave of interrogations commenced. Each woman was called out at least once, and some of us several times. Every once in while, a few of us would be summoned to take part in some kind of humiliating exercise, performed for an audience of smugly spellbound male guards. They made us maintain a squatting position until we collapsed on the floor, crawl through the mud while being sprayed with an industrial-strength hose, and run around the camp blindly while machine guns were fired in the air.

The punishment that the guards clearly supposed would be most effective was one I actually grew to like. "Going to the fence" meant you were handcuffed to a chain-link barrier, which I assumed encompassed the circumference of the prison camp. There, you were pretty much ignored, unless a captor stopped by to spit on you or dangle a cookie in front of your nose. I found myself "fenced" quite frequently during our captivity—"due to failure to cooperate," I was told.

Meanwhile, I derived a certain amount of both pleasure and inner determination from knowing what my captors did not— that the fence represented a respite to me. No matter the awkwardness and immobility, and not to mention the swarms of mosquitoes (that, on account of handcuffs, were impossible to swat), at least I was outside—a warm, late-summer drizzle washing over me, along with an occasional tranquil breeze. These circumstances were far preferable to languishing among a dozen other type A women, each in the throes of panic, irritation, and/or PMS, in some claustrophobic and stinky little cell.

A few of the women, in fact, were quietly weeping by this point. Jin Suk, on the other hand, was emotionless and utterly silent, both with the captors and with us. For the entirety of our incarceration, she sat with her arms crossed in front of her, staring straight ahead. For some reason, Jin Suk's imperviousness to both the cruelty of our adversaries and the distress of our friends irritated me greatly. I sat next to her, longing for the relative serenity of the fence.

Occasionally during interrogation sessions, we were given an apple, cookie, or small package of crackers—some insultingly minuscule treat, but one that each girl would bring back to share with the others. Jin Suk, of course, refused any offer of nourishment—on the one hand, a show of enormous will; on the other, an example of her priggishness and self-assumed superiority.

At one point, a girl named Brenda was returned to the cell convulsing in tears. Several of us reached to comfort her once the guard had slammed the metal door shut. "They hit me," Brenda sobbed, pulling up her sleeve to show us marks that would eventually darken into bruises. Seconds later, the guard returned. A steely-eyed guy with Aryan features, he hollered, "Shut up, you cow!"

A few girls rallied in front of Brenda like a human shield, but this only encouraged the guard toward further cruelty. "You're a fat piece of shit," he yelled, prodding us away from Brenda, who was still seized with tears.

For some reason, nothing that we'd endured so far upset me as much as this man's abuse of Brenda, which seemed mean and unnecessary, and caused a revolution in my psyche.

"We've got to plan an escape," I whispered not long after

the guard had disappeared, leaving Brenda a soggy and dispirited lump on the floor.

"This is bullshit," I said. "Ted was right . . . we outnumber them. Let's get the hell out of here."

I thought I saw Jin Suk flinch, though she remained silent. The other girls thought a revolt was too risky.

"The weakest among the guards can overpower even the strongest one of us," Sally argued.

"And they have guns," Ophelia pointed out, her voice shrill more with irritation than fear.

"If they're doing this to us, can you imagine what the guys are going through?" Sally shook her head in genuine pity for our male classmates. No matter her own travails, she always worried more about other people than herself.

"Look, I can't stay in here another *goddamn* night," I said, even though I knew I could, and probably would. I suppose that, more than anything, I longed for some sort of diversion.

A few of the other girls felt emboldened enough to attempt an escape, but just as we started to devise a plan, the door swung open and the same despotic brute who'd been berating Brenda now commanded both her and me to come out.

Through the thin material of the pillowcase, I could perceive light outside. On my arms, I felt the warmth of the sun. The air smelled like early morning.

"Get on the ground!" the evil guard shouted. For the next several minutes, Brenda and I crawled through thick, gloppy mud, being careful not to raise our heads from the mire lest the guard wallop us. All the while, he hurled insults, some of which I found absurd and even amusing, such as "You two smell like shit!" But any humor was quickly squelched whenever I heard Brenda choke or cry out in pain. I wanted to comfort her in some way, but I figured that would only invite more punishment for the both of us.

Finally, Brenda was evidently hauled away and I was escorted to another trailer, where my pillowcase was removed and in which I found—in addition to a lineup of the by now familiar interrogators and guards—Rob and Warren, both handcuffed to metal chairs.

"Do you know these men?" one of the interrogators said, turning to me.

"No." Obviously, we were *not* supposed to let on that we recognized anyone outside the team members with whom we'd been caught.

"I thought you told me you knew this woman," the interrogator said to Warren while pointing at me.

"I do!" Warren pronounced almost gaily. No matter that I looked like Swamp Thing, Warren clearly was just happy to see me. "We went to Harvard together," he said. "That's Lindsay—she dated my roommate!" I groaned audibly, and Rob rolled his eyes.

"You must be mistaken," I said, my eyes boring into Warren. In fact, I hadn't even ever met him in college, let alone dated his roommate. I had no idea of his roommate's name, a claim that I spent the next several minutes defending to our interrogators, who were obviously delighted to have in their custody what appeared to be two Ivy League idiots. The evil guard, standing on the sidelines with a gun in his hand, looked particularly smug.

Aside from making asinine false assertions to jeopardize the both of us, Warren dramatized the effect of his internment by sobbing demonstratively and howling about how he was a "lawyer."

"I'm going to sue the whole lot of you!" he cried.

Ignoring Warren, the evil guard turned to Rob. "Since you say *you* don't know her, there should be no bonds of attachment."

"If I shoot this woman"—he gestured with his gun at me—"you'll be freed immediately."

Rob was shaking his head no, but Warren, in the throes of his own private melodrama, seemed oblivious to my fate.

"One of you is *going* to admit that you're CIA," the guard shouted, lunging forward and pressing the aperture of his revolver against my head. "Or I will kill her!"

This guy's out of his mind, I thought. Willing myself not to vomit or faint, I looked frantically toward the door. I didn't care if we were in the world of make-believe anymore or not: I wanted *out*.

It did not take long for Rob's normally stoic resolve to crumble. He struggled to lift his body, still handcuffed to a chair, off the floor. "Enough." Rob lurched forward so that he was between the evil guard and me. "Enough." The chair dangled awkwardly from his wrists. "Okay, we're CIA," he said.

I felt my face awash with tears. Though angry at myself for crying, I felt wrought with relief as the hot, salty liquid dribbled into my trembling mouth.

Suddenly, there was the by now familiar hum of convoy trucks approaching outside. Our captors, simulating panic, dropped their weapons, fumbled to release Rob and Warren, and then fled from the trailer. I tried to embrace Rob, but he was scrambling to retrieve the array of discarded guns before Warren could get to them. Warren, meanwhile, failing to comprehend that freedom was imminent, continued to snivel and moan.

Outside, we saw for the first time the "camp." It was a large muddy area surrounded on all sides by a barbed-wire fence. The Serbian folk music had ceased. In the distance, I recognized one of my favorite instructors, jauntily kicking open the door of a small concrete hut and thus liberating the other women.

"Whooey!" Sally shouted as she stumbled out into the light. Ophelia, looking pissed off as usual, shuffled out after Sally, followed by Brenda, her face and clothes covered with mud. I looked down at my own body, just as sodden and dirty. Again my emotions got the best of me and I struggled to contain my tears. It could not have been more than a few days, I thought, but I felt as if we'd been incarcerated for weeks. Watching my cohorts file out one after another—disoriented, shocked, and blinking into the sunlight—made me realize how close to most of them I had become.

That night, we were allowed showers and, at long last, civilian clothes. Notwithstanding the Office of Security's deluded and paranoiac attitude toward alcohol, we continued the Agency

tradition of getting plowed. We spent hours swapping rau-
cous, inflated stories from our incarceration. Jin Suk was heralded by the instructors as an incomparable stalwart for her
refusal to exhibit any signs of distress at all.

At one point, the austere instructor Ed approached me.
Shielding his mouth with a can of Coors, as if sharing some
top-secret information, Ed said, "I heard you planning that escape, missy."

"I thought you guys had abandoned us," I said.

"That's what we *wanted* you to think." Ed cracked an uncharacteristic smile. "I had no choice but to turn you in,
which is why you got singled out toward the end." Ed winked
at me before he turned and walked away.

Nearly everyone in the group reveled in our release from
captivity. Even Warren was emboldened by his unexpected
survival. As we celebrated, however, Brenda brooded over the
injustices that had been wreaked upon her. She kept a careful
record of her bruises and, weeks later, would threaten to sue
the Agency, thereby eliminating the POW exercise for future
trainees.

As much as I'd hated it, I did find the experience useful. I
was surprised both by our strengths—sharing food, standing
up for and comforting one another—and even more so by
our weaknesses. I recollected the intensity of my shame and
frustration when our captors publicly accused me of treachery,
or when I was made to eat those damn cookies. I marveled
at the onslaught of my tears—a mixture of terror, guilt, self-
preservation, and sadness—when, staring down the barrel of a
gun, I'd confronted the notion of my own end.

I left that day, with the others, the same way we'd arrived weeks before—on a large, yellow school bus, reminiscent to me of both the trauma and tranquillity of early childhood. As I rested my forehead against the window and watched the dense forest give way to the comforting scenery of green high-way signs and fast-food restaurants, I was content. I had been afforded a long, scrutinizing look in the mirror, and I had confronted my reflection free of ego or expectation.

There was a long way in our training to go, I reminded myself. This end was only the beginning, but it wasn't such a bad beginning after all.

FIVE

Ethan and I are riding bikes in the darkness. It's nearly midnight; we're back at The Farm. The air is thick and smoggy with the dying days of summer. Clusters of deer peer out at us from the trees, and the frogs churn out a symphony of cacophonous croaking. I live for these bike rides; I think Ethan does, too.

The instructors and other students are curious, as rumor has spread that Ethan and I take off on bicycles late every night. But there's nothing but friendship between Ethan and me. On these rides, we shout stridently about our creepy instructors and the crap nature of this course. The outdoors is one of the few places we can be sure we're not audiotaped or video-surveilled.

"The only bugs out here are the crickets and ticks," Ethan says. Every night he asks me, "Where should we go?"

"*I dunno,*" I respond. "*Maybe our usual route.*" After PM training, we know nearly every nook and cranny of The Farm.

Ethan likes to go by the driving range that, only weeks earlier, had been converted into the POW camp. "*The death camp,*" he calls it. Ethan was perceptibly altered by that time in captivity. "*It was goddamn fucking ass-licking awful.*" For one thing, he's developed a penchant for uniquely invective language. "*But, you know, I wouldn't have missed it for the world.*"

Now we have been back at The Farm for two weeks; already, the months ahead seem grim. We've been told that, while we are permitted to drive home for the weekends, we're unlikely to have time to do so.

"*You'll find the work during the week just piles up,*" the tradecraft course supervisor, Adam—whom we quickly nicknamed "*Saddam*"—gleefully informed us on the first day. "*Don't plan to go to any weddings; don't plan to see your families . . . we own you now. This is your life.*"

Adam went on to tell us a story of a former trainee who had driven back to Washington for the weekend, attempting to defy the effects of weeks' worth of sleep deprivation. Somewhere along the way, the guy had fallen asleep at the wheel, run off the road, and died.

"*If something like that happens to one of you,*" Adam said, "*what can I say? It's your own damn fault.*"

"*What a douche bag that guy is,*" Ethan says, pedaling his bike furiously across the pavement; steam rises from the swamps surrounding us as if we're in a colossal cauldron.

"*It's like we're in the depths of hell,*" I say.

"We are, we are." Ethan laughs loudly, and together we sub-merge into a lightless tunnel of trees.

As luck would have it, Ethan and I were assigned to the same Small Training Group (STG), six people with whom we would share the next several months of our lives. I couldn't have asked for a better STG. Aside from Ethan and me, there were: Ophelia, Mark, Tornado Sally, and a self-defined ne'er-do-well named Alec. An uncommon wit, Alec would deadpan jokes, his eyes all the while riveted to his computer, and have the rest of us doubled over in stomach-aching laughter many a late night.

Each STG was assigned a workroom equipped with six computers and a large centered table, at which we would sit with the STG instructor to review the daily round of missions and assignments. Our STG instructor was an elfin man named Paul, who drove a red Mercedes convertible that stuck out ab-surdly among the squad of Fiats and Corollas belonging to the other instructors. He'd enjoyed a long and illustrious, by *his* description, career with postings all over the world. Why then, we wondered, did Paul find himself an instructor at The Farm?

We'd been assured that things had improved since the years when The Farm's reputation within the Agency was that of a glorified rehabilitation center where dysfunctional case offi-cers were sent to dry out. Still, we suspected that each instruc-tor here must have committed some offense, or had his career hit a sizable wall, in order to end up in this dismal swampland.

Paul's weakness, we would soon discover, was women. After

weeks of watching him try unsuccessfully to avert his eyes from Ophelia's V-necked blouses, we pretty much figured that Paul was on the lam from some sort of sexual harassment charge. Still, except for Ethan, who thought Paul was out to get him, we pretty much liked our STG instructor. He stood as an advocate between us and "Saddam," and his mild perversions caused more amusement than concern.

We surmised that each STG room was equipped with a hidden camera. The suspicion was confirmed when word spread about two former students who'd been expelled for having sex after hours on the rectangular worktable. The six of us derived infinite pleasure from talking in jest for the benefit of the hidden camera, which we deduced must be positioned at the high-ceiling corner of the otherwise sterile room.

An occasional late night, we would turn up the CD player (radios were not permitted in classified areas) and dance. Ophelia was in fact a recreational belly dancer, and we could hardly imagine Paul's delight at watching her undulate around the room and on the tabletop.

We also amused ourselves by using the workroom phone to crank-call other STGs, whose members always seemed terribly earnest and self-serious.

"This is Miss Abbott from base maintenance and security," I would claim. "We're having problems with the power system. We're going to have to ask you to turn off your computers and lights for about thirty minutes and remain exactly where you are. We'll call to inform you when you can turn everything back on."

Then our group of six would creep around the hallway, stifling our laughter as we peeked into each room where the other students sat, mutely wringing their hands and waiting for the go-ahead to turn the lights back on. Jin Suk, meanwhile, would continue her composition by hand, with the aid of a miniature flashlight.

All told, however, there was little time for fooling around. The six-month tradecraft course, we knew in advance, was intended to apply maximum pressure to the students, as we were saddled with more and more, not to mention increasingly daunting, tasks.

In addition to being habitually deprived of sleep, we had no real contact with the outside world. The Farm was set up under an elaborate make-believe scenario, in which we were supposed to be Agency officers assigned to the CIA Station within a fairy-tale land called Vaingloria, like some mythical Marx Brothers country.

Our job was to spot, assess, and recruit Vainglorians, role-played by our instructors, and thereby to acquire foreign intelligence, which we would report back to "headquarters" through endless bureaucratic correspondences that were due each morning. Hence the sleepless nights.

With my background in writing and teaching, I didn't find the work as overwhelming as someone like Tornado Sally, who couldn't cobble together a grammatically correct sentence to save her life. Ethan and I ended up editing much of her work for her, just so the poor girl could get a few hours' sleep.

Meanwhile, each student was subject to near-constant criticism from the instructors. And we all faced the very real possibility that, at any given time, the "Murder Board" would deem us unfit. The Murder Board was the name given to a bi-weekly event when the instructor cadre reviewed every student, with particular attention to those who were failing to perform. The instructors would vote, and if a simple majority advocated elimination, the student would be escorted off the base within twenty-four hours, suddenly jobless and homeless.

To make the process "fair," we each were pitted against a number of different instructors for a variety of exercises. The first exercise—exaltedly dubbed "The Ball"—required us to attend the Vainglorian National Day Reception. There, we were supposed to spot our first target, make contact with him or her, and secure a follow-up meeting for lunch or dinner. The entire simulated scenario assured the instructors at least one free meal a day.

We were not told the exact names of our targets, but we each were given some identifying piece of information. They might be a "college professor in nuclear engineering" or "first secretary at the Embassy of Arrogancia." In addition to the United States, there were countries diplomatically represented in Vaingloria, and their embassy officers were viable targets as well. If we successfully worked the cocktail party, making the rounds and initiating conversations with as many instructors as possible, we should be able to identify our respective targets.

Equipped with a small supply of fake business cards and wearing my stupid blue suit, I arrived at "The Ball" in search of a "prominent Vainglorian journalist." I scanned the crowded room, not knowing how or where to begin. I was reminded of a childhood "getting to know you" game that involved wandering around making a particular barn animal noise—like a pig, goat, or chicken—until you found the only other person making the same animal noise, at which point you could both switch to regular humanlike conversation. I was now half tempted to "oink" as I circulated the room. Instead, I headed toward the bar.

A critical trainee skill was attending a cocktail party without getting completely soused. While not forbidden from drinking, we assumed that our habits were being closely observed, and that it would be unwise to linger by the bar ordering successive scotches—as might have been my inclination under other circumstances. Aside from the smattering of Mormons— a community from which, incidentally, the Agency recruits many case officers, owing in large part to their squeaky-clean pasts and notwithstanding their general lack of social skills— most of us ordered at least one drink to fortify ourselves.

Stirring my vodka tonic with its tiny plastic straw, I surveyed the room. Finally, I strolled toward Ophelia, who stood glowering behind the table of second-rate hors d'oeuvres. Ophelia, I'd discovered during an after-hours rap session outside the STG, shared my aversion to the recruitment process.

"This is revolting," she said, obviously *not* referring to her cracker smeared with sunset-colored cheese. "This whole thing is foul. I don't want to meet any of these people. I don't even want to talk to a single one of them."

I had to agree with Ophelia, although I was more disheartened by the bleak appetizer spread than anything else: Triscuits and cheese; bitter celery stalks; cold chicken nuggets in a puddle of coagulated grease. Ophelia and I commiserated for a few minutes until Ethan, looking unhinged as his eyes darted wildly about the room in search of his target, joined us.

"I can't find the goddamn ambassador of Malevolencia," Ethan cried. "Have you seen or talked to him?" Ethan, unlike Ophelia or I, was neurotically eager to please the instructors, and consumed with worry over his standing at The Farm. We were evaluated for each exercise and would receive any number of "lesters"—that is, less than satisfactory ratings—depending on our performance. Ethan maintained an obsessive tally of how many "lesters" each student had.

"I haven't talked to anyone yet," Ophelia retorted. "And, quite frankly, I don't want to."

"I think I'll get another drink," I said. "Anyone want to go to the bar?"

Our ambivalence only added to Ethan's anxiety, and he tromped off, but not before fixing an altogether fake smile across his face and discreetly flipping us the bird.

Close to an hour later, I had engaged in trivial conversation with nearly every instructor in the room when I finally deduced that my target—as misfortune would dictate—had been cornered by Jin Suk, who was talking at him rapidly and enthusiastically.

Prominent journalist indeed, he was an enormously large man who bore a close resemblance to Santa Claus. Bracing myself, I sidled alongside Jin Suk, who didn't pause to take notice of me but continued chattering away. Our STG members had agreed to help one another find and meet our respective targets, but I could see Jin Suk wouldn't be doing me any favors. She even shifted her position so as to shield Santa Claus from me. I was left pathetically lurking the fringes of their conversation.

Finally, I shoved my arm between Jin Suk and the probable target and introduced myself with my new training alias, "Hello: I'm Liddy Morton."

Jin Suk looked censoriously at my extended hand, as if she'd never seen a more dismal debut in her life.

When Santa Claus responded to me, "And I am Barry Bennington," Jin Suk turned on her heel and stalked off.

Some initial pleasantries enabled me to determine that Barry Bennington was indeed a prominent journalist, native to Vaingloria. The cocktail party was winding down, and the other students leaving, when I finally managed to secure a lunch date with Barry for the following day. By no small coincidence, Barry suggested the exact time to which I'd been assigned: twelve o'clock.

Mission accomplished, I headed back to the STG room, where we were expected to spend the rest of the night writing up cables about our experience at "The Ball." We were evaluated not just on our performance in each exercise, but also on our ability to accurately report the details of it later.

I was careful not to embellish upon any rapport I'd established with Barry, since I knew he would be the one reading and grading my report. Each instructor had a reputation for being easy or tough, and I'd heard that Barry was tough.

Developmental meetings with our targets generally took place off base, somewhere in the surrounding area of Williamsburg. The fairly large radius within which to operate, no matter its scope, in the coming weeks would seem increasingly claustro-phobic.

Prior to any operational exercise, each student was required to drive a one- to two-hour "surveillance detection route" in order to determine that he was not being followed. If he *was* being followed, he was supposed to "abort"—that is, not go to his meeting.

Some rudimentary surveillance-detection training back in Washington—four weeks of driving around Maryland and Northern Virginia while intermittently being followed by clusters of "shadows"—had prepared us for the more intensive training that we would undergo in the near future. Habitual failure to detect surveillance was a surefire way to get oneself evicted from The Farm. Obviously, if you couldn't perceive that you were being followed, you were not going to make a very effective spy.

I'd always viewed driving as a chance to zone out and sing along with the radio, pretty much oblivious to my surround-ings. In fact, I was one of those people who considered herself insulated and anonymous within a car. Using the cab of my truck as a makeshift powder room, I would apply lipstick and mascara, pluck my eyebrows, and, without a second thought, excavate my nose.

Such indulgences were no longer possible at The Farm, where we all lived in constant fear of being watched and fol-lowed. Now as I drove, I always kept a pen and small pad by my hand so that I could take notes on suspicious cars and li-cense plates.

My first developmental luncheon with Barry was to take

place at the T.G.I. Friday's in nearby Newport News. At this meeting, I should garner enough information from Barry that I could begin to determine his potential access to state secrets. I also should present myself as someone engaging enough that Barry might agree to another meeting with me. In reality, I would later learn, a foreign man/potential source rarely, if ever, turns down the opportunity to have lunch, dinner, or drinks with a young female American "diplomat." But this wouldn't become clear to me until long after my first date with Barry.

Having conducted the requisite hour-plus driving route in and around Williamsburg and Newport News, and thereby determined that I was *not* under surveillance, I walked into the T.G.I. Friday's, where I was at once assaulted by the *über*-friendly wait staff, who seemed nearly ecstatic to encounter the first customer of the day. (It was, after all, eleven-thirty in the morning.) The group descended on me, proffering menus and solicitous greetings.

I asked to be seated in a booth in the most remote corner of the cavernous restaurant, where I spent the next twenty minutes reviewing in my mind the details of the political, economic, and military infrastructure of Vaingloria, with which each of us was expected to be thoroughly familiar.

The point of immersing ourselves in the "scenario" was twofold. To begin with, many among the instructor cadre were quasi-retirees who'd been banished to The Farm years earlier. They knew this fake and incredibly elaborate scenario better than they knew any real current events. Often I wondered if some of them actually had started to believe it, perhaps even spent sleepless nights fretting about the nuclear

capabilities of the hostile nation-state Malevolencia. These instructors derived perverse pleasure from trying to trip us up by
demanding the name of some obscure official at the Embassy
of the Republic of Infirmia, or the details of a treaty signed between Arrogancia and Vaingloria years before.

In addition to this information memorized from a stack of
bursting three-ring binders, we would receive daily video news
briefs informing us of recent developments in the Republic of
Vaingloria, commonly referred to as the R.O.V. Such broad-
casts elucidated the second point of the scenario: Armed with
knowledge from the binders, and updates on what had been
reported via "open sources," we would be able to ask our potential targets pointed questions, and thereby determine their
access to state secrets and/or their willingness to share genuinely classified information. If a target merely reiterated what
had already been reported on the news, he obviously wasn't di-
vulging any secrets. If, on the other hand, he informed you of
something that, the following day, could be corroborated by
the news, you could use that to prove to headquarters that you
had a truly valuable potential asset.

Liddy Morton was supposed to be an American official
with the nebulous title of "Special Assistant for Vainglorian
Affairs." Semiconfident that I could hold court, or at least my
own, on all things Vainglorian, I spent the next few minutes
perusing the menu, settling on pea soup, which wouldn't require chewing or talking with my mouth full of food.

By the time Barry ambled in, there were exactly three other
T.G.I. Friday's patrons: a stay-at-home mom and her two children, one of whom was wailing loudly while the other threw a

tantrum over the unavailability of peanut butter and jelly. As
the exceptionally eager hostess led Barry to the corner booth,
it was the first—but certainly not the last—occasion during
which I felt acutely aware of the seedy implications of a young
woman in a quasi-clandestine meeting with an obviously
much older man.

To our mutual mortification, Barry proved too big to fit between the booth seat and the table.

"Oh, I'll just slide this toward me," I said as I grasped the
tabletop with both hands and executed a hearty pull. Unfortunately, the table was bolted to the floor.

"It's okay, it's okay." Barry was even more chagrined than I.
"I'll just sit like this." He turned sideways so that his rear end
was perched on the edge of the booth, his legs extended well
into the aisle.

For the next two hours, we talked primarily about Barry's
past as a prominent Vainglorian journalist, pausing only when
lunch was served or the ambitious young busboy came to refill
our water. During the first meeting, Barry dropped a few
nuggets: personal disillusionment with "the regime," brigadier
general brother-in-law, young daughter with a grave illness.

That night, back at the STG, I would write up my reports
to headquarters, expounding upon Barry's access (to the Vainglorian military structure, via his brother-in-law) as well as his
main glaring vulnerability: the young diseased daughter.

For the next several weeks, Barry and I met at least twice a
week for lunches and dinners. Often we would lean in toward
each other over the table, talk in whispers, or furtively glance
around to make sure no one was listening to our conversation.

This might have added to the impression that I was some kind of young home wrecker, but the only other option, I realized, was to talk audibly, and I already felt like an ass, discussing with passion and sincerity this make-believe country.

As Barry revealed more about his relationship with his brother-in-law, who, as per the scenario, "tells me everything," and also about his frustration at not being able to cure his beloved daughter ("if only we had the money"), I was supposed to reciprocate by subtly suggesting ways in which the United States government could help. I should also be moving our meetings to more clandestine venues. The whole developmental process was supposed to culminate with Barry agreeing to provide me state secrets in exchange for money.

This would require me to lure Barry back to my room on the base, the only suitably secure venue in which I could recruit him. The whole process of recruitment was not unlike a courtship: I was the suitor, and Barry the coy and reluctant object of my affections.

In spite of the fact that the whole thing was a sham, I began to dread my meetings with Barry. I felt distraught and guilty every time I wrote back to headquarters: "Subject is motivated by the desire to help his ailing daughter. If recruited, we can effectively control Subject by leveraging medical aid for the girl."

Ophelia and I would get together for dinner and commiserate about how disgusting we found the process. Ethan, on the other hand, was into it, as were the majority of our fellow trainees. On our bike rides, Ethan would reassure me that Vainglorians were an oppressed and troubled people, in need of the CIA's help, and also that I ought not to feel sorry for any of the Malevolencians, whom we knew—from the material contained in the binders—to be a bellicose and deceitful lot.

Driving back to The Farm one evening, after dinner with Barry at the Ruby Tuesday, I suddenly was seized by an intense feeling of loneliness. Upon reflection, it occurred to me that my only forays into freedom involved rendezvous with this corpulent man twice my age. Huddled together in a booth at depressing chain restaurants, Barry and I spent countless hours talking about people and situations that didn't even exist. I felt less like I was in a training program than caught in some endless, unsettling dream. As my car was delivered from one streetlamp beam to the next on the otherwise empty country road, I concluded that my life had become not only weird but also sort of pathetic.

I knew that I could head back to the STG, where Ethan and the others would be busily completing their write-ups, but the thought of it only compounded my angst. I thought about calling Emma or Emily, but the girls likely were preparing to go out on the town, which would depress me even more. Finally, I decided I would call Sasho, even if only to hear his voice.

I figured that Sasho would remind me that someone once had cared for me in a very human way—a way that seemed altogether foreign to me now. It would provide a semblance of hope: that something similar could happen again, that I was not irrecoverably lost to real life or to real love.

I pulled into a strip mall parking lot and headed toward the pay phone located just outside the Dairy Queen. Convinced that our room phones, and perhaps even the rooms themselves, were bugged, I rarely made personal calls, and only off base.

I had not spoken to Sasho in months, and it took me a while and several wrong numbers to track him down.

"It's me," I said when Sasho finally answered a phone number provided by some other foreign-sounding guy.

"*Who* is it?" Sasho sounded sleepy and disoriented.

"Me. Lindsay. Hi."

"Hi. Where are you?"

"I dunno. I mean, Virginia. I'm still in Virginia."

"Oh."

During the long silence that followed, I looked around the area surrounding the phone booth—a desolate strip mall; the darkened Michael's Craft Shop; a tiny pawnshop—a fluorescent glow from the Video Outlet providing the only discernible light.

I thought of all those nights Sasho and I had spent sleeping on the rocks, and the sense of enveloping awe I felt each time I got up to pee: the blue-black darkness, the crisp night air, the feel of the wind against the bare skin of my body. I thought of standing above the spectacular cascade of Yosemite Falls, when Sasho—whose face I could barely picture now—looked at me, and told me that he wanted to marry me someday. We would move to New Zealand, Sasho thought, where he could obtain a visa and "learn some things." I would teach school, or write. At Christmas and in the summer, we would go back to Bulgaria: hike the seven lakes in the Rila Mountains, visit his grandmother's village in the central plains, climb the rocks on the shores of the Black Sea.

Now I clung almost desperately to the phone, feeling abysmally lonely and depressed.

"I just thought I'd call," I said.

"You are working your job?"

"What do you mean? Yeah, I'm working."

"Is very important job, eh?" Sasho's smirk was nearly audible.

"It's not so important," I said. "What are you up to?"

"Nothing. Work. Climbing. School."

"School?" Sasho had never finished his education at the Technical University in Sofia, having immersed himself in rock climbing instead.

"I am studying computer science at the university in Berkeley," Sasho said. "I like it, but I have not so much time to climb anymore."

"Sasho, that's great," I stammered. "I'm so proud of you."

We spoke for a few more minutes, during which time Sasho told me: as a student, he had acquired legal status in the United States; he'd met a girl, from Korea, in his English course at night; they were living together now in San Francisco—"I guess you could say she is my family, here." I could see him, if I wanted, in a picture taken by a German photographer that would appear in the next issue of *Rock and Ice*.

When I hung up the phone, I was relieved—*Sasho's doing well, there's no need for guilt*—and, at the same time, panicked— *Sasho's doing better than I am, actually!*

And why had it been so hard to answer the simple question "Where are you?" What did I have to say? What had I done, or accomplished, in the past several months that I could ever even begin to explain?

Overcome! by sadness, I cast my eyes around the parking lot, as if looking for somewhere to go, some small harbor of comfort. In the far corner of the lot, I recognized one of the shadow vehicles, its driver and passenger looking directly at me.

Goddamnit, I thought. I noted the make and model, and calmly returning to my own car and exiting the lot, I jotted down the license plate number. My mind had already dismissed Sasho as I thought about what details to include on my "surveillance report."

The next day, I was commended for detecting that I was being followed, but also questioned and chastised for drawing attention to myself by stopping to make a call from a strip mall phone booth.

"You should have spotted the surveillance before you made the call," Paul told me.

"You shouldn't have been making any calls at all," Adam said.

I left the meeting angry and confused. Who was Adam to tell me I couldn't call my ex-boyfriend? Already, they'd made me feel as if dating a foreigner were some kind of unprecedented treachery. I thought ruefully of the countless adolescent tales, told by my male instructors and colleagues alike, about the Eastern European strip clubs they'd frequented or Thai prostitutes they'd solicited—only to discover, in the latter case, just prior to consummation of the deal, that the "beautiful young Oriental gal was actually a beautiful young Oriental guy!" So much for a case officer's common sense, foresight, and perceptiveness, I thought each time I had had to endure another one of these stories. Absurdly, such imprudent dalliances on the part of male case officers and male trainees were never looked upon as anything but that. The Agency's double standard remained flagrant and unapologetic.

I could not sleep that night, and found myself petulantly jealous of Sasho and his freewheeling lifestyle. When I sent him back to San Francisco, Sasho was heartbroken, penniless, and on the verge of deportation. I, on the other hand, had a straight path upon which I was about to embark. That straight path, it seemed to me now, had led me into a long, dark tunnel, with a light at the end that I felt increasingly ambivalent about.

My recruitment meeting with Barry, back in my room, was not going well.

"What do you mean you want me to work for the United States government?!" Barry roared. Jumping off the bed—on which I'd directed him to sit since there was only room for one chair—he disrupted the small tray of cheese, crackers, and cookies I'd set up in advance. Generally, within the first few minutes of any given meeting, Barry had consumed all of the "amenities"—the official term for the snicky-snacks we were supposed to provide at each developmental meeting. Today, however, Barry said he was too nervous too eat.

"You wouldn't just be working for *us*," I said.

"Who do you think I am?!" Barry's face reddened, and he wiped his brow. "This is an insult! An outrage! Are you CIA?!"

"I *do* serve in an intelligence capacity," I said. "But that is precisely why I am the person in whom you can confide things, such as what you have already shared with me . . . ahem, about your brother-in-law's intentions to stage a coup. I am the person who can securely convey this information back to Washington without anyone knowing where it came from. By providing me this secret information, you can help Washington policymakers plan for the new regime in Vaingloria, in which your brother-in-law obviously will play an important role. Like you, Washington actually has the best interests of Vaingloria at heart."

"I asked you a question!" Barry snarled. "Are you or are you not CIA?"

"As I explained, I am authorized by the U.S. government to deal with matters of intelligence. I am trained to handle and transmit sensitive information, top secret information . . . such as that which you have *already* provided." I was trying to impress upon Barry, as we'd been instructed to do, that he had already committed espionage. He had already betrayed his country. To now make the leap from informant to *paid* informant was pretty much a no-brainer.

My powers of persuasion did not appear to be working.

"This is an outrage!" Barry shouted, grabbing his jacket and readying himself to storm out the door.

Just then, we heard a violent pounding from the hallway, followed by Adam's booming voice, interspersed with some giggly pleading from Tornado Sally: "I don't know what you're talking about, Officer. It's just me in here."

"Quick, get in the bathroom." I pushed Barry's bulk toward

the bathroom door. "The Security Services are conducting a raid."

I dumped the cheese-and-cracker platter into a drawer, yanked down the bedspread, and tossed the pillows on the floor. Worst-case scenario, the "secret police" would find Barry fuming in my bathroom, and I would explain his presence by claiming we were having an affair—standard cover story for a female case officer and a male asset, I already knew.

But it was not my day to be raided, evidently; minutes later I heard Adam and the others tromping back down the hallway.

It was hard not to laugh when I pulled back the shower curtain on Barry standing there in the tub. Luckily, the time-out had given Barry's anger a chance to subside, or rather to evolve into fear.

"I guess you're right," he said, lifting one of his giant legs out of the tub. "I'm already in too deep."

"Don't think of it that way, sir," I said, assisting him out of the tub. "Think of this as helping your country . . . and your daughter." I could hardly believe my own sleaziness. But soon Barry had been recruited—that is, he agreed to provide me classified information in exchange for four-hundred Vainglorian munars a month, signed a secrecy agreement, and devised a communication plan such that we would never have to rely on the telephone. We shook hands, and I popped a bottle of champagne to toast our new relationship.

I thus successfully completed "The Ball." Later, during the feedback session with Barry, he told me I'd performed admirably every step of the way—an assessment that surprised me, since I had considered the final recruitment meeting a debacle.

But Barry said that I was a natural recruiter. Then Barry posed a question that I'd never heard, nor have I since, any other Agency officer voice: he asked me how it made me feel.

"Were you happy when you recruited me?" Barry looked at me quizzically. It was our first encounter outside of the roles we had played, the journalist and the diplomat-cum-spy. "Did you feel a sense of accomplishment?"

"No, actually," I said. "In fact, I felt awful. I felt really bad about manipulating you. And I was miserable over your sick daughter."

Barry laughed. "Don't worry, I don't even have a daughter."

"Oh, thank God!" Relief passed over me like a breeze, and my normally hunched-up shoulders began to relax.

Then Barry confided in me that he had started out as a case officer but found the job overwhelming, and far less gratifying than he'd hoped.

"I never had time for my wife," Barry said. "So I decided to switch to reports."

"Really?" I'd never heard of a case officer switching to reports. Undeniably, reports officers were considered second-class citizens within the DO.

"It just seemed the right thing to do, for me," Barry said. "Maybe it's not as glamorous or intriguing, but I was still doing my part. And I'm one of the few among us who are still married, and I mean still married to my *first* wife."

"Anyway," Barry pulled out the little blue book containing my evaluation, "I gave you exceptionally high marks. I don't think you have to worry about the Murder Board this go-around."

He shook my hand as I walked out his office door. "You have a bright future ahead of you, young lady," he said. "No matter what you do."

Barry's revelation got me thinking. Truth be told, I had found even the simulated process of recruiting a foreigner altogether unpleasant. But in order to be a successful case officer, I would have to recruit. In fact, recruiting would be the whole point of my existence. Faced with this fundamentally distasteful prospect, I began to consider another option. Becoming a reports officer was an inarguably *saner* path.

Not surprisingly, women in the DO were often drawn or relegated to reports. The job didn't require you to be out on the streets at all hours of the night, but it was also considered the less ambitious career track. As a reports officer, I might forgo some excitement, but I also might have some semblance of a normal life, and I'd still be serving my country.

The next day, I requested a private meeting with Paul and told him I was considering switching to reports. He was appalled; he rolled his eyes as if I'd announced I was off to join the circus.

"You don't want to do reports," Paul said. "You'll be bored. Your career won't go anywhere. Reports is for the people who can't do ops."

"I'm not comfortable with this whole recruitment thing," I said.

"What do you mean?" He looked at me warily.

"The idea of preying upon someone's vulnerabilities," I said, "manipulating them into doing something that I would never do. It's just not me."

Paul launched into the routine litany of justifications: "Everybody who gets recruited *wants* to be recruited. We're doing these people a favor, giving them a chance to influence the fate of their countries. Not all people enjoy the liberties we have here in the States, you know?"

"Look, Paul," I said, "I can see *why* we do it. It's just not for me."

He rolled his eyes again and gave me an *Oh please!* look.

"What did you *think* you'd be doing when you came to work for the CIA?" he said. Good question! I thought back to all my romantic preconceptions.

"I guess I pictured myself breaking into vaults and scaling walls in some kind of black unisuit," I said, knowing how naive I sounded and how naive I'd in fact been. "I thought *I* was the one who would be stealing secrets . . . not some foreigner down on his luck, who could get arrested or killed if I fuck up!"

"You *are* the one stealing secrets," Paul said. "You just need to find the right person to tell you those secrets. Believe me: Once you get out there, you'll see. Everything changes as soon as you get your first scalp."

I found this cliché, which instructors and trainees alike liberally tossed about, slightly revolting, and so it was hardly an effective enticement. Every case officer's success or failure, we were constantly reminded, hinged on the number of "scalps" he accrued.

We continued our circular line of conversation until each of us realized we were not making any progress in changing the other's mind.

The following day, I was called into Adam's office.

"I hear you want to switch to Reports," he said intensely.

"Yeah, I guess I do," I said. Adam always made me uncomfortable.

"Well, that would be a very bad decision," he said. "Very bad for us, and very bad for you."

Adam didn't even bother with the quasi-reasonable arguments that Paul had laid forth. He merely made clear that if I abandoned the case officer route, I might as well leave the Agency altogether. He had no sympathy for the cause of my misgivings. "Quite frankly," he said, "you should have thought of these things before."

I couldn't really argue with that. For the next week, Paul and Adam played good cop/bad cop with me: Paul trying to convince me that being a case officer was not as sleazy as I thought, and Adam reminding me that, *really*, I had no choice. In the end, I buckled. I agreed to continue the training as a case officer, with assurances from Paul that I could still back out at the last minute and go on my first tour as a reports officer.

My misgivings were assuaged somewhat during the next few weeks, when the focus shifted from "recruiting" to tradecraft, starting with an intense surveillance-detection course, to take place in a nearby city.

During the two-week course, we were to spend every day planning different routes—on foot, via public transportation, but mainly by car. Once we had planned a route, we were supposed to "conduct" the route, making various "cover stops" at local stores. If we determined we were under surveillance, we should garner as many details as possible about the vehicles or persons following us. All the while, we were to act normal and *not* try to lose our pursuers, but to appear as if we hadn't even noticed them and were going about our daily routines.

We were graded, foremost, on our ability to detect surveillance. If you were unable to do so, or if you reported that you were under surveillance when in fact you were *not* —what was called "seeing ghosts"—then you failed the course altogether, ostensibly lacking the most fundamental case officer skill. Adam made clear that if we did not pass surveillance detection, we'd be evicted from the training. It made sense: An asset who gets "wrapped up"—that is, discovered to be meeting in secret with a suspected CIA officer—surely will be arrested and, in most countries, executed.

For that reason alone, it was one area in which I would have been devastated to fail. The instructors bombarded us with stories about CIA officers who had grown lazy about their detection routes in seemingly benign countries. They'd been disgraced not because they were spies but because they were spies who got caught.

We learned to design an effective route that was wide-ranging and included both congested areas and isolated roadways. We also learned to accurately describe our shadows: the makes and models of cars, license plates, the physical appearances of drivers and passengers. Cars were not my strong suit, but I excelled in the physical appearance category, down to brand names, stores where the outfits could have been bought, and whether hats, purses, and shoes were this season's or last's.

Seemingly mundane, the course actually was incredibly stressful. We had no idea when or even if we would be followed, so we had to remain constantly alert. For most of the girls, who didn't particularly enjoy driving, the course was purgatory. I was especially anxious about driving after dark. My night vision had never been stellar, so I dreaded my after-hours routes. The city had some surprisingly seedy areas, in which I often found myself hopelessly lost. Maps spread out on my lap and mini-Maglite perched between my lips, I prayed I wouldn't be carjacked.

Equally as concerned about being caught with scribbled notes, I would instead write plate numbers and car descriptions on my upper thigh, easily obscured later by my skirt or shorts. Writing while driving was one of the hardest tasks, and I marveled that there were not more trainee-related accidents, although legend had it that one former CST from New York City, with no prior driving experience, had committed a hit-and-run while under surveillance.

In fact, one of the main goals was to appear as non-alerting as possible. You were not supposed to drive too fast, or too slow, run yellow lights, or commit illegal U-turns.

"The objective," one instructor said, "is to lull your shadows to sleep, bore them to death."

"This skill will come in handy once you're overseas," he elaborated. "In convincing whatever host nation security apparatus might be following you that you're an ordinary diplomat and not some CIA spy."

During one of my first runs, I was gratified when I could tell that indeed I was being followed. I quickly jotted down the license plate numbers of the two shadow cars. As I confidently turned into the crowded downtown area, already anticipating praise at my success, my cherry-red convertible rental suddenly malfunctioned such that the horn began to blare incessantly. For several minutes, I was stuck honking relentlessly in slow-moving traffic in the city's upscale shopping district, while a team of shadows trailed me from behind. It took me a while to live that one down, and I assumed I'd been set up by the instructors, who must have tinkered with my car.

One of my favorite pastimes during the course was luring pedestrian shadows into embarrassing cover stops: the lesbian bookstore; the sex shop; the porn section of the video outlet. Most of the shadows were retirees, likely former CIA or FBI employees, who could barely disguise their discomfort as I led them among displays of calendars featuring women in dog collars, or shelves of mechanical dildos. One female shadow complained about my "penchant for unsavory establishments," and I was threatened with a lester if I continued my antics.

The surveillance training was a lonely time. Aside from daily meetings with an instructor (assigned to each one of us particularly for the course), we were pretty much on our own. The instructor allocated to me, it was rumored, had had several of his assets "wrapped up," and some subsequently killed. Not surprisingly, my instructor was a deeply wounded and troubled man. He inevitably arrived at our meetings with a supersized Slurpee that I eventually realized had been spiked with vodka.

That was pretty much the extent of my human contact. We were staying in any number of hotels and motels in and around the city, but, since we were traveling in alias, we were not supposed to socialize. Eventually, loneliness and the desire to rebel prevailed, and a handful of us—Ophelia, Alec, Mark, and I—began to convene nightly in one or another's hotel hot tub. We developed the feeble cover story that we'd just randomly run into each other there. Better than nothing, but not much.

If there was one thing we had in common, it was this inclination, *need* almost, to act subversively. And the spirit of seditiousness was, in part, sanctioned from above.

One director of the DO had a reputation as a womanizer. This was not scandalous in and of itself, as intra-Agency infidelity was rampant. But he, purportedly, would carry on à la Bill Clinton, in quasi-official venues. Stories circulated like wildfire about his being caught atop the desk in his palatial office or in his reserved parking garage spot, where supposedly he'd been interrupted *in medias* blow job by several Security Police Officers. According to the story that was common knowledge around the Agency, the SPOs surrounded the steamed-up car, having witnessed on videotape what they thought was an important senior official having a seizure. No one begrudged him his alleged infidelities, or even that he undertook them during the workday—and on Agency property, no less. It was the fact that a head of the clandestine service had been caught—*and more than once!*—that was so appalling.

Personally, I could not have been less romantically intrigued by anyone even associated with work. But I, too, was drawn to subversion, in the form of Chris, a *tapas* bar chef whom I met during surveillance training.

I spotted Chris on the first of many dinners I would eat alone in this antebellum city. I was sitting at the bar, nursing some sangria and choosing among the dizzying array of dishes, when I noticed the chef—an incredibly handsome young man—bustling from brick oven to wooden chopping block to granite bar. As he sautéed shrimp, stirred salsa, and skewered steak, I found him, quite simply, *sizzling*.

To say that I "picked up" Chris would not be wholly accurate. I did, however, hang out at the *tapas* bar pretty much every night, writing home highly sanitized versions of what I was up to: "out of town for some boring seminars on military preparedness."

I found out later that Chris and the rest of the *tapas* bar crew had assumed I was a restaurant critic, a misperception that afforded me uncommonly good service, and likely secured my first date with Chris.

"What do you do?" Chris asked over breakfast at a Cuban diner one Sunday—the only day when instructors, shadows, and students were officially off duty.

"I work for the federal government," I said, despising the deadly dreary sound of it and wishing I could tell him the truth.

"Doing what?" he asked.

"It's . . . um." I picked at my frittata, distracted by Chris's earnest stare and his uncommon good looks. "Well, I'm training to be a diplomat, you know, overseas."

"Wow." Chris seemed genuinely impressed. He'd never traveled any farther than Jackson, where he went to college at Ole Miss. When I told him I'd gone to Harvard and lived for a while in Bulgaria, a place he'd never heard of (and evidently equated with the land where no children are allowed, from the old Dick Van Dyke movie-musical *Chitty Chitty Bang Bang*), he was bowled over.

"I've never met anyone like you," he said at the end of the day, which we spent walking idly around downtown, and later at an outdoor petting zoo. "When can I see you again?"

That night, I couldn't sleep as I anguished over that very question. Then I began to scheme and plot. We had been warned never to break the "no personal use of one's government-rented vehicle" mandate, but it made all of our lives miserable. If we wanted, for example, to head an hour south to Virginia Beach for a weekend respite, we would first have to drive three hours back to Washington, drop off the rental car, pick up a personal car, and drive four hours back, repeating this highway odyssey in reverse the following day. "Rental cars are to be used for casing and operational purposes only!" Adam had hammered into our heads.

At first, none of us took the rule seriously; we planned excursions to Busch Gardens amusement park and Virginia Beach. But, inevitably, someone had to be made an example. Some poor guy drove home for the weekend and, at the last minute, decided to stop at Tysons Corner shopping mall to purchase for his—no doubt neglected—girlfriend a small gift. Leaving Victoria's Secret, he had the misfortune of running into Etta, one of the battle-axes from Human Resources who served as a sort of den mother to the CSTs.

"What are you doing here?" Etta asked, eyeing the tissue-wrapped parcel.

"I came home for the weekend, and stopped to buy my

girlfriend a gift," he answered honestly. Two days later, Etta had processed the paperwork to have him removed from the program for violating regulations.

Etta was notoriously heartless. Back when I'd been fretting over Sasho, struggling to maintain my relationship with him while also abiding by the Agency rules, I had gone to Etta for guidance. "Why don't you just lose this worthless weight-lifter?" she said. I'd designated Sahso's occupation as "rock climber," and assumed she didn't make the distinction. "Eastern Europeans cannot be trusted," said Etta, herself a Cold War relic, escorting me to the door.

Once we learned the unfortunate fate of the well-meaning guy with the bra-and-panty set, we all took very seriously the personal car usage rule. "If you're hemorrhaging internally and coughing up blood," joked Ethan, "you'd better hail a cab to the hospital. Etta might be trolling the emergency ward parking lot."

Most personal errands—buying tampons, going to the dry cleaner's, using a pay phone to call home—could be accomplished legally, we were assured, during our surveillance-detection routes, or while we were "casing" an area. Suffice it to say that, after I met Chris, I spent nearly every weekend "casing" the nearby city where he lived.

At the time, I thought I was falling in love. I hadn't dated anyone since Sasho, and I was starved for male companionship. Many of the other trainees were married, with albeit increasingly forsaken wives, and in some cases children, at home. If the workload was not overwhelming, they'd drive back to their families late Friday afternoon.

Until Chris, I had nowhere else to go. My friends in Washington had written me off as flaky and unreliable. On the rare occasions when I did go back to D.C., I hung out primarily with my mother, but she'd become irritatingly concerned for my psychological well-being. "I don't like what this place is doing to you," she said more than once. "It's like you're shut off from the rest of the world."

Naturally, I preferred to drive to Chris's bohemian bachelor pad, where he would smoke pot (though I never did) and cook me delicious dinners. My only responsibility was sneaking into his neighbor's yard to steal rosemary from the herb garden. Chris and I would sit out on the balcony and have long, pretentious conversations about the beauty of random meetings such as the one that led to our acquaintance.

I came to rely on Chris, my only link to the outside world, in an unhealthy way. Needless to say, this put a strain on our relationship. Aside from that, Chris had many questions that I could never answer: Why did I always have to leave in the middle of the night? Where was I going? Why didn't I have a phone number he could call? How was it that I always showed up with a different car? (For "operational security," we frequently had to switch out our rentals.)

I always had some explanation for my bizarre behavior, but the lying was corrosive. I quickly lost track of what untruths I had told, and became increasingly uncommunicative and, in Chris's view, untrustworthy.

I had hoped that my fly-by-night inaccessibility would make me more attractive to Chris. Nobody could accuse me of being "too available." But over time, Chris found me and my situation less alluring than baffling.

"I've got to be honest with you," he said one night when I showed up unexpectedly, late. We were sitting on his couch, listening to Wilco and drinking wine. "You intrigue me, but I'm not sure this is going to work."

"What do you mean?!" I said. "Of course it's going to work." Somehow, I'd already decided that Chris was going to follow me around the world, preparing *tapas* for ambassadors and other dignitaries while I prowled about anonymously by night. "Chris, it *has* to work!"

"It doesn't have to," Chris said, smelling my desperation a mile away. "Lindsay, I've met somebody. She lives here. She works at the restaurant with me." He began gently rubbing my back. The thought of Chris's "somebody" crushed me; she was probably somebody who led a normal life, I thought. What was I? I was somebody who came and went, and who lied constantly and instinctively. I was somebody whose job was to *use* other people. Clearly, I was somebody not to be trusted. I wouldn't have wanted somebody like me, I realized, any more than Chris did.

"Okay," I said, straightening myself up. "It's okay." A few minutes later, I was back in my rental car, driving again toward Williamsburg, my vision blurred by tears.

Days later, I called Chris and asked to see him again. Hoping to salvage the relationship, at our next meeting I revealed to him that I actually worked for the CIA.

"That's why I come and go with no warning," I pleaded

over an untouched platter of sushi. "That's why I have ten different cars but no damn phone."

At first, Chris appeared relieved and even impressed. For the next few weeks, we resurrected our relationship: taking long walks on weekends; playing with his nippy little dog among the fallen October leaves; sharing a last beer on Sunday afternoon, before dusk, when I had to head back to The Farm.

But in the end I could only share so much with Chris. The weightiness of my job became a source of stress to him rather than anything genuinely intriguing or attractive. Chris wanted to hang out with friends who could talk about where they worked; who weren't petrified of inhaling secondhand pot smoke; whose eyes didn't dart around looking for "shadows." At some point, I think Chris took the whole CIA story to be a sham and started to worry that I was either dangerous or delusional, or both.

Eventually he retreated altogether, was suddenly "very busy" every time I called; this from a guy who made a second career out of concerted idleness. I started driving back to D.C. on the weekends, always feeling a pang of regret. I ached to hear Chris's smooth southern accent—his voice was like bourbon to me—as I headed north, toward the secondary comfort of Mom.

SIX

Alec and I are tromping around the pedestrian district of Colonial Williamsburg, licking our ice-cream cones and kicking up dirt. He is dressed in a Hawaiian shirt and white golfer's slacks, and has ice cream in his pencil-thin mustache. I am about eight months pregnant.

We're in disguise, masquerading in public as a tourist couple. In addition to this enormous pillow I've got strapped around my waist underneath a muumuu-style jumper, I'm wearing a frizzy red wig and large 1970s-style sunglasses. Glancing in a shop window, I realize that I look less like a pregnant woman than a fat, deranged clown.

Our outfits come courtesy of the Agency's official disguise division, who arrived at The Farm earlier today.

"This here could make anyone look like a moo-hodge-AH-

deen," *says a woman who's introduced herself as an "altered-identity engineer." She proudly displays what looks to me like a typical Halloween mask that you could buy for twenty bucks at Toys "R" Us.*

"These masks are handmade," the woman goes on. "Each one takes months to manufacture and costs thousands of dollars."

"The fleecing of America," Ophelia whispers audibly. Ophelia is an acquaintance of someone who works in the disguise shop. During the break, while our classmates stroke and ogle the other multi-thousand-dollar masks, Ophelia and I retreat outside, where she gives me the inside scoop.

"It's a bunch of would-be cosmeticians who can't find work at the local Hair Pair," Ophelia says. "The CIA is the ultimate boondoggle for them. My friend says all they do is fart around all day, giving each other pedicures and styling each other's hair."

When Ophelia and I return to the classroom, our fellow trainees have dispersed to the wardrobe, makeup, and accessories stations. We're supposed to spend the rest of the day growing accustomed to whatever disguise has been engineered particularly for us. I wonder what gave them the idea I should be pregnant.

"Ahh! This is great for you," the wigs woman says as she pulls a curly red mass of fake hair over my head.

Alec is now hamming it up: talking in a loud, midwestern accent and giving some halter-topped schoolgirls, obviously on a field trip to Colonial Williamsburg, the hairy eyeball. He could pass for a sleazy used-car salesman, or just a plain old-fashioned pervert. I put my arm through his and lead us into Ye Olde Tyme Museum, which is designed to look like a slave-quarter kitchen. Just beyond the butter churn, we spot Ophelia, with some outrageous

*hair extensions that make her look like Rick James, and Ethan,
sporting a full beard that hangs lopsided off his reddened, sweating face. With his black suit and wide-brimmed black hat, he
looks like an Amish man.*

*When Ethan's eyes meet mine, we both burst out laughing. I
can hardly believe I'm getting paid to have this much fun.*

Gradually, I settled into a routine at The Farm, willing
myself to ignore the disquieting sense that my world was becoming increasingly insular. For sure, there were moments of
serenity—long runs through the woods, early-morning swims
at the base pool, my nightly bike rides with Ethan—when I
would forget that, sooner or later, I'd actually have to *do* this
job. I basked, albeit prematurely, in a sense of nostalgia that
The Farm somehow evoked. I knew that here was where all
of the great case officers throughout CIA history had been
schooled in spying. I wondered if years later I would be remembered as one of them.

A few of our instructors I found likable and even inspiring.
The most impressive among them, a legendary recruiter named
Bill, was assigned to be my mentor. Bill differentiated himself
from the other instructors by refraining from making inappropriate cracks or sexist slurs. Much to my personal delight,
Bill sometimes even openly contradicted Adam. Since his
tenure at The Farm was merely a segue into early retirement,
Bill would tell it like it is, no matter whom he opposed or offended. Famous for having acquired a record number of scalps,
ironically, Bill was the only instructor who took seriously my

moral qualms about recruiting, and who had supported my short-lived bid to switch to Reports.

"I get a tremendous thrill each time I recruit someone," Bill said when I first confessed my misgivings. "But I can understand, intellectually, how you would not."

A bit old-fashioned, Bill thought women should not be case officers in any event.

"I would never want my daughter doing this," Bill told me more than once. "I can't count the number of times I've had to get dressed in the middle of the night and rush off to save a female case officer from some libidinous Arab agent.

"I had one young woman call me in hysterics at two in the morning," he said. "When I got there, she was being chased around the hotel room by a sheikh."

At first, I only alluded to my doubts with Bill, but in time, I spoke openly to him. He always listened empathetically, and provided thoughtful and reasoned advice. No matter his own love of the job, Bill was willing to consider that it might not be right for me. And no matter his own allegiance to the Agency, he saw its drawbacks.

"Don't lose yourself to this place, Lindsay," Bill once said to me. "It's not worth it. Even within the walls of Headquarters, the best among us will quickly be forgotten." He reminded me that the Agency's only famous spies were the failures and the traitors.

Bill's parting words, during one of our last one-on-one meetings, would echo in my mind for years to come: "At the end of your career, be careful on your way out that the revolving door doesn't hit you in the ass."

. . .

Ethan and I were barreling down Route 64 toward Virginia Beach, flagrantly breaking the "no use of rental cars for personal purposes" rule, since the beach lay far outside the confines of our operating area. At least had I been caught gamboling about with Chris, I might have claimed that I was "casing" the area, or—a more likely lie—that my car had broken down en route to D.C. But Virginia Beach was the opposite direction. If caught, we'd be in real trouble.

"I wonder what's compelling me to do this?" I had to ask Ethan, whom I'd somehow convinced to be my partner in crime. "Especially so late in the program."

"You want to test fate," Ethan said. "If you get kicked out, you don't have to decide for yourself to leave."

"Well, what about you?"

"I just want to test what we've learned," Ethan said. "I want to make sure we don't get caught."

After months of training, we were supposed to be spending this rare free weekend mentally gearing up for our "away trip." During the away trip, we would be operating in alias in an unknown city, implementing all of the tradecraft tactics we'd learned. The entire class had been split into two groups, one of which would travel to San Francisco, the other to Philadelphia. I was disappointed to draw Philly, which seemed to me the less alluring locale, a mere five hours north of Williamsburg by train. While most students chose to travel by air—in part to practice navigating airport security in alias, but also because the Agency would foot the bill for business-class tickets—I opted to take the train. It left from the city where we'd done surveillance training, and I thought I might want one last chance to see Chris.

With the weekend off, many students were home visiting their families. I'd decided that Ethan and I should go to the beach. We left the base and made off as if we were driving to D.C. Once we were sure we weren't being followed, Ethan made an abrupt U-turn and we started heading south.

"It *is* kind of like we're making use of our training," I suggested.

"Exactly!" With the convertible's top folded back, Ethan's hair whipped up in the wind. "Is that Adam's car behind us?"

I slunk down deep in my seat, and Ethan started laughing.

"Like that's gonna help!" he said. "If that asshole sees us, we're toast."

But Adam did not see us, nor did any of the other instructors. Ethan and I spent a glorious day at the beach—diving like dolphins among the waves and, later, strolling on the boardwalk, stuffing our faces with fried dough and ice cream as the sun set among the dunes.

I couldn't remember the last time I felt so happy or so free. It dawned on me how stressed-out I'd become. And I was probably one of the more chill members of the class. I'd yet to pull an all-nighter, as many of the others routinely did. My secret advantage was being able to write: I'd draft the entire slew of asinine fake correspondences, run them through spell-check, and hand them in without a second glance. Others, like Tornado Sally, would anguish over a single sentence for about an hour.

Most of the trainees looked as if they hadn't slept in days, because, in fact, they hadn't. And everyone, even Jin Suk, had gained weight since the time of our Army PT test. Recruitment and surveillance-detection training were to blame for the collective pork-out: days of doing nothing but driving from one Dunkin' Donuts to the next, eating out of paper bags one day and ingesting another alcohol-soused and fat-permeated developmental luncheon the next, then spending hours on end with one's butt bonded to a swivel chair. Ethan and I used to joke that soon our asses would be so large, they'd become permanently lodged in our work chairs and we'd have to walk doubled over, chairs protruding from our gargantuan backsides. This puffed-out, flabby group was the CIA's elite cadre of spy trainees.

At the end of Ethan's and my day at the beach, we both sported telltale sunburns and sand-swept hair. But we didn't care. Driving north, we bypassed The Farm and, later that night, Ethan dropped me off at a motel by the train station. The next day, I would take the train north to Philly.

All night long, I resisted the urge to call Chris. What would I say, anyway? *Hi, this is Alice . . . um, I mean Lindsay.* (I was traveling in alias, of course.) My sudden appearance at a sleazy motel in his hometown—under a false name, no less—would only confirm Chris's suspicions: that I was a nutcase, stalker, convict, or cop.

I thought about heading over to the *tapas* bar, where I was pretty sure Chris would be working dinner, but again, what would be the point? *I'm almost done with training*, I thought. *I'll be overseas within a year.* There was no point in trying to resurrect a relationship that already had died one slow, painful death.

I spent the night eating Domino's pizza, watching second-rate porn—slightly anxious that the charge on my alias credit card would designate "adult film," I insisted on paying for everything with cash—and feeling vaguely sorry for myself.

Obviously, I couldn't identify myself as "Lindsay" over an open telephone line, so there was really no way to call anyone. I supposed my mother would recognize my voice, but that would link Alice Applegate's room to my mother's home phone number, which would constitute poor tradecraft and, if detected, earn me a whopping slew of lesters. Traveling in alias turned out to be more boring and lonely than cool.

The next day, I bought a round-trip train ticket, again using cash, and headed north to Philly. I'd never approached Washington, D.C., a city around which I'd grown up, from the south, and I was stunned by how majestic and beautiful it was. Seeing the Capitol dome, the stark point of the Washington Monument, and the Lincoln Memorial in the distance, I swelled with momentary pride. *I am going to be serving my country*, I thought. *This country that I truly do believe is the best in the world. No one will know exactly what I'm up to, but I'll be behind the scenes, doing important things.*

In Philly, as elsewhere, we were to be constantly on alert for surveillance. This time, we were told, the shadows would not be retiree golfers, as in Williamsburg, but honest-to-goodness FBI agents, infinitely more honed and discreet in their surveillance techniques.

I dropped my baggage off at the hotel concierge and ran to my first appointment, dinner at a fancy restaurant with the Malevolencian ambassador to Vaingloria, whom I'd been developing for weeks now, and whom I had convinced to meet me in this "foreign" city. "To solidify and formalize the nature of our relationship," I had told him. We both knew I planned to pitch and recruit him to work for the CIA.

The ambassador was played by an elderly instructor, more suited to life as amateur thespian than the second-rate case officer he was reputed to have been. He took his role-playing seriously and relished our pompous discussions—sometimes conducted in French, no less—over cigarettes and port.

Dressed in a stylish black suit and nervously twisting a pearl necklace between my winter-chapped fingers, I approached the hostess's stand in this fancy seafood restaurant that I had researched in advance, and whose address I had provided the ambassador on a scrap of paper back at The Farm. When I gave my name, Alice Applegate, to the maître d', he said, "Oh, you are the one waiting for Ambassador Leroi?"

I was stunned. Was all of Philadelphia in on our hokey scenario? Or had I, too, totally lost sense of reality?

"I am," I said, unsure if I should be truthful, or if this was a test.

The maître d' reached into his jacket pocket and provided me a note: *Meet me at Le Bec-Fin in twenty minutes! M. Leroi*

Le Bec-Fin—located a twenty-minute cab ride away, on the opposite side of town—turned out to be an intimate French restaurant, something like where a man might take a woman on the night he intended to propose. When I arrived, I instantly spotted Leroi, sipping from a goblet of red wine at a far corner table.

Shit, I thought. *Surely I'll be docked for this.* For some stupid reason or another, Leroi must have objected to the seafood restaurant, which I'd selected after careful consideration and ample research. Perhaps he thought it was too central and crowded a venue in which to conduct an advanced developmental meeting? I would realize later that Leroi just wanted a more expensive meal, as well as the opportunity to order dinner in his cultivated French.

As usual, we shared a bottle of wine, then had an array of appetizers and a three-course meal, followed by brandy and dessert. If American taxpayers had any idea how much money goes toward fattening up CIA retirees, they'd surely protest. During the entirety of the dinner, Ambassador Leroi and I danced around the topic of Vaingloria, both more interested in discussing life, literature, and what to order next.

Ambassador Leroi, over the past several weeks, had grown worried that I'd not yet found a husband, a concern he expressed frequently and openly.

"I do wonder how will you meet someone of your . . . *calibre,*" he said at last. "Roving about the world aimlessly in your *decidement* seedy career."

Although I'd never formally "broken cover" with Leroi, the idea was that the target should know precisely what a case officer wants, leading up to the moments before an official recruitment. A potential agent shouldn't learn for the first time at the pitch meeting that he's been collaborating with the CIA. Somewhere along the line, the case officer ought to have dropped enough hints for the target to have figured that much out. A potential asset's willingness to continue to meet, even after he gradually accepts his complicity, represents his propensity to take risks.

"I guess finding a husband is not so important to me right now." My hand went for my necklace, as if the pearls were worry beads. "I figure I'll find someone eventually, or he'll find me."

"Tsk, tsk," Leroi put down his wine goblet and leaned in close to me. "You're not getting any younger, *mademoiselle*."

"Clearly," I said testily. I was anxious for our meal to end. Whereas initially I had found Leroi charming and gallant, especially in juxtaposition to some of the boorish other instructors, I'd grown weary of his proselytizing matrimony and motherhood when he was supposed to be teaching me how to become a spy.

"Right now I am thinking more of my career." I signaled the waiter to bring me the check. (We had learned never to let an instructor pay the bill, one surefire way to fail the entire exercise.)

"I'm also concerned for the good of my country," I said to Leroi. "As well as the future of your country, in its increasingly precarious position, Mr. Ambassador."

"You're a very clever girl." Leroi settled back in his seat. When the waiter arrived with the check, the ambassador ordered a cognac. "But your priorities at the moment are indubitably *en mélange*."

For the next half hour, I endured—as I had done on countless occasions—Leroi's unsolicited advice about my love life. At some point, it dawned on me: Not only was I not getting any closer to recruiting Leroi that night, Leroi was addressing himself to Lindsay Moran, not Alice Applegate.

Sometime around midnight, with both of us bleary-eyed and Leroi's Franglais growing less and less coherent, Leroi let me pick up the well over two-hundred-dollar check. With only fifty left in cash, I handed over my alias credit card, reminding myself not to unthinkingly sign my true name, a common case officer blunder.

A few minutes later, the waiter returned to the table and handed back my card, pinched distastefully between two fingers. "Your credit card is canceled," he sneered. "They said you have not paid your bill."

My face reddened; never in my life had I had a credit card rejected. The CIA's Office of Budget and Finance was supposed to take care of our alias credit-card bills, a fact that of course I could not share by way of explanation with this irate waiter.

"There must be some mistake." I fingered through my pitiful assortment of five- and ten-dollar bills. "Can you try it again?"

"We have tried it several times," the waiter said loudly.

Ambassador Leroi rolled his eyes and pulled out his wallet. My throat tightened: This would result in a smattering of lesters, at the very least.

The following morning, a note had been left for me with the hotel concierge: L'ambassador has taken the liberty of correcting your last night's faux pas. Leroi must have informed someone in the Office of Budget and Finance about my predicament. When I tried my alias credit card again, at a pet-shop cover stop—where I purchased a leather-studded collar for a dog I didn't have—I was relieved when the card was at once accepted.

In addition to the task of recruiting Leroi that week, I was also supposed to obtain from formerly recruited Barry, now code-named BTMYSTIFY, a computer diskette. I was to use an ancient and nearly defunct tradecraft technique called the "dead drop." This entailed me first making a "safety signal," a chalk mark on a predesignated telephone pole, indicating to Barry that he should make the drop within twenty-four hours. Barry then would deposit, in yet another predesignated location, the computer diskette, which he should have concealed in a fake rock that I'd crafted out of a chunk of Styrofoam. I had provided Barry the faux rock, painted and adorned with dirt and leaf fragments, along with all of the signal and drop "sites," during a "brief encounter" with Barry in an elevator, two days after arriving in Philadelphia.

Once Barry made the drop, he should give me a signal— this time, scattered orange Tic Tacs, at another prearranged site—indicating as much. I would retrieve the fake rock and immediately follow up with yet another signal—the curtains open and a red towel drying off my hotel room balcony— indicating to Barry that I had retrieved the drop and that all was well. Of course, none of these operational tasks could be performed if I was under surveillance, so for the next three days I conducted a kind of uninterrupted multimode surveillance-detection route in and around Philadelphia.

One day, as I was skulking about the waterfront area, I spot-

ted a woman whom I'd seen close to my hotel about an hour
earlier and on the other side of town. Now she was stationed
on a bench, pretending to read a newspaper.

Over the next hour, I was followed by a team of at least ten
"shadows," some on foot, some in a white Chevy van that I
spotted in the distance again and again. I already knew I
would not be servicing my signal site for that day, so I decided
I would attempt to "burn"—that is, identify and get as much
distinguishing info about—each and every one of my pursuers
by dragging them around town.

I knew we were not supposed to do anything alerting while
under surveillance, but I couldn't resist the urge to give the
team a run for its money. As I exited the waterfront area, the
bench lady lurking somewhere not far behind, I quickly
flagged down a taxi that had been whizzing by. Sliding across
the leather seat, I commanded the driver to take me, via the
most circuitous route possible, to the other side of Philly. In
the rearview mirror, meanwhile, I could see the bench lady
looking around desperately for another available taxi. A mustachioed man who had been stationed behind a phone booth
now was talking into the collar of his Members Only jacket,
where a microphone surely was hidden.

"Ha!" I said out loud as the taxi sped across town. I felt a certain exhilaration, even though I knew the point was not to lose
the surveillance team. Fifteen minutes later, as I stopped for
coffee in a deli, I was shocked to perceive at least two members
of the team casually walking down the street outside, both of
them got up in entirely different outfits from before. The formerly brunet bench lady now had a head of long golden tresses

cascading from beneath a white tennis visor. The mustachioed Members Only man was suddenly clean-shaven and sporting a plaid blazer. The trick, we'd learned weeks before, was to look at the shoes, which rarely would be switched out.

These guys are good, I thought. I paid for my coffee and continued on my route, this time hopping on a crosstown bus. These elaborate surveillance-detection routes were supposed to have been meticulously planned in advance, down to the very last pace and turn, but at this point I was pretty much winging it.

Sometime later that afternoon, I'd just rounded a corner into Philadelphia's historic district when three men in black suits and dark glasses surrounded me.

"Oh my!" gasped a rotund midwestern lady who'd just purchased a dozen miniature Liberty Bells that went spilling to the ground.

"You're under arrest," one of the Feds said. Another produced handcuffs and began reciting my Miranda rights.

"What for?!" I was peripherally aware of a cluster of Japanese tourists, elbowing one another out of the way to get a better snapshot of the scene. It seemed as if I could hear a thousand shutters going off.

"Drugs. Dealing," one of the Federal Agents—a big, beefy, Irish-looking guy—produced his badge, which coincidentally bore the last name Moran. "We have witnesses who saw you drop something in a dumpster the other day. We retrieved nearly three kilos of cocaine."

Intellectually, I knew this must be a ruse, but I was shaking nonetheless. I'd never been arrested before, let alone in such a public venue. I thought dejectedly about the dozen or so home slide shows in which I would later appear somewhere in Japan—the frowzy, handcuffed American lady.

"What's your name?" Moran said, obviously intending to trip me up.

"Alice Applegate." I handed over my wallet, containing my entire alias documentation.

"When's your birthday, Alice?" For the next several minutes, Moran fired off questions that would test my knowledge of my alias identity. What were my address, my telephone number, my parents' names and addresses and birthdays, the astrological signs of my family members?

The crowd of spectators, meanwhile, had grown significant. I think Moran started to fear that the onlookers might rally to my cause, since I was being exceptionally cooperative and not a shred of evidence had been produced. Probably in order to disperse the crowd, he led me to an unmarked car, idling across the street.

There, I sat in the backseat flanked by the two anonymous Feds, while Moran continued to question me from behind the steering wheel. Where was I staying, and what was my business in Philadelphia?

"I'm a consultant," I said, hoping that my jeans, sneakers, and backpack (mercifully now void of signal site and dead drop material) would not totally betray me. "I'm on a scouting trip to check out Philadelphia as a place to open up a new office."

"Yeah." Moran smirked. "Do you have any contact numbers we can call?"

Luckily, during the week, I had stopped by several temp agencies and office-supply stores, precisely in order to bolster my cover story. I'd even given out a few fake business cards. Now I readily provided Moran the addresses and telephone numbers of places I'd visited, information conveniently jotted down on a notebook in my backpack.

"Why don't you start calling some of these joints?" Moran said to the Federal Agent on my right.

While the first call was made, I felt anxious. What if no one remembered me? These guys seemed to be taking this whole thing very seriously. Could I be sure that this wasn't for real?

Luckily, at each establishment, the owner, manager, or at least a store clerk remembered a businesswoman who indeed had left her card sometime in the last forty-eight hours.

"Couldn't forget a stupid-sounding name like Alice Applegate," one of the store proprietors reportedly said.

The Fed also called my hotel, whose concierge—without much prompting, I was alarmed to discover—provided a slew of information about me, including the array of purchases I'd made from the minibar and the observation that when I returned at the end of each day, I often appeared frazzled and harried.

Finally, Moran started up the car. Nobody said a word as our unmarked vehicle wove among the crowded streets of downtown Philly. I felt my throat tightening. Would they really throw me in jail? And, if so, would they let me make a phone call? Who would I even call?

Moran pulled the car to a halt at the edge of the relatively deserted shipping dock area.

Shit, I thought. *Maybe they're not Federal Agents at all.*

Maybe they're just a trio of sex offenders, and I'm about to get gang-raped.

"Good job, kiddo," Moran said, as one of the other Feds stepped out, allowing me to exit the car. "I'll let your Agency know that you stood up to the test. No holes in your story." And with that, Moran closed the tinted windows and the un-marked car peeled away.

I walked for several meters along the windy waterfront, looking out over the endless expanse of opaque water with its flotsam and jetsam bobbing toward the horizon. I thought about how close I was to completing training and going back overseas. While my enthusiasm had ebbed and flowed over the past several months, I'd been rejuvenated by the away trip.

I can do all this stuff, I thought giddily. *It's all a big game, yeah, but it seems like I might be good at it. Maybe this is what I'm meant to do with my life. Maybe I can learn to overcome the loneliness. Maybe I'll be so satisfied with myself that I won't even care that I'm on my own.*

Farther down the quay, I bought a hot dog from a stand and an extra bun to break into pieces and feed to the pigeons. I found a bench upon which I must have sat for more than an hour, gazing out at the sea.

Sasho's forgotten. Chris doesn't matter anymore. I'm going away. I'm going to start a new life full of promise and excitement.

The last night of our away trip, those of us who'd spotted each other around town managed to spread the word and get together for an illicit rendezvous at a bar by the waterfront. Another flagrant violation of the rules, but we were all cocky with our successes, and now fully indoctrinated with the DO motto, "Lie, cheat and steal, but, whatever you do, don't get caught." Over many rounds of frothy drafts, we swapped stories about the trumped-up charges the FBI had used to arrest each and every one of us, with the exception of Ethan, who— planting his dead drop under the guise of jogging—somehow had outrun three Federal Agents.

We were all high on self-confidence when we arrived back at The Farm for "crisis phase." As was scripted in the mock scenario, Vaingloria would erupt into civil war. During this week, we were subject to a steady succession of searches, seizures, and roadblocks. Meanwhile, we were supposed to keep Washington constantly informed with hourly "situation reports." The idea was to up the stress ante even higher and to prohibit any student from sleeping more than two or three hours a night.

During this time, I grew concerned for Ethan. Of course, we'd had to cease our revivifying midnight bicycle jaunts, and Ethan seemed to be cracking under the strain. His eyes were always red-rimmed and he was perpetually pissed off, muttering about the "asshole collaborators" and "those fucking Vainglorian dickheads." It seemed to me he might be losing himself to the absurd construct of The Farm.

Quietly but fiercely competitive, he was also anguished by the astonishing number of lesters he'd racked up during the final few weeks of training. I had only two lesters, one for the credit-card fiasco (which was not even really my fault, I thought somewhat resentfully) and one from several weeks earlier, when I'd forgotten to provide a promising Russian walk-in a recontact number. Poor Sally must have had at least a dozen lesters. Still, everyone knew that you couldn't find a more patriotic or dedicated young woman in the entire organization, and so—no matter her failings—the instructors would surely let her pass.

No family members, spouses, or significant others were allowed to attend our graduation from The Farm. It didn't really bother me, as cut off as I had become.

CIA director George Tenet, popular at that time—especially in comparison to his disastrous predecessor, John Deutch—gave a few inspiring remarks about the courageous path upon which we were about to embark. The momentous mood was dampened slightly by the fact that the Murder Board had eliminated one of our classmates, without warning and for no evident reason, twenty-four hours prior to graduation. As the rest of us readied ourselves for celebration at the base bar, our former classmate was being escorted to the gates with her luggage in hand.

Before heading to the bar, I stopped off to see Bill, as he'd requested, in his office.

"You did very well, you know," Bill said to me. "You're graduating at the top of the class, second to Jin Suk."

That's fine, I thought. I would never want to be like Jin Suk anyway, even if it meant a slightly less burnished reputation at the Agency.

"Are you happy you stuck it out?" Bill said.

"Yeah, I am. I really am."

"Good, then. I guess I can look at you as my last successful recruitment."

"Where are you going?" I'd grown genuinely fond of Bill, to whom I looked as a symbol of hope that there were impressive, cultured, and caring people within this organization that, by turns, often seemed either like a confederacy of dunces or a school of sharks.

"I'm done." Bill rested the back of his head in the crux of his intertwined hands. "Being an instructor doesn't do it for me. I miss the streets."

But Bill wasn't going back overseas; his wife had started a home business, and he wanted to give her a chance to have a career of her own, "after all these years."

"Call me anytime," Bill said. "And you know, I may need your help. I'm going to look for a job, for the first time since I graduated from college. I haven't made a résumé in over twenty-five years. I have no idea if there's anything else I can even do."

I smiled. Within the CIA, there was nothing Bill could not do. On the outside, however, it remained to be seen. I remembered the way his eyes sparkled when he talked about the whole slew of Middle Eastern chemical engineers, Indian nuclear scientists, and Pakistani military officers he had recruited.

I wondered if I would ever feel like Bill. I wondered if there would be a time, years down the road, when I would be sitting on the instructor's side of the desk, facing a young officer such as myself, eager and skeptical all at the same time.

I hoped that I would do what Bill had done for me. I hoped that I would be truthful, and measured in my advice. I hoped that I would listen to the young case officer's concerns, and that I would consider his or her needs along with those of the organization. Most of all, I hoped that, like Bill, I would have a life to look back on, rich with rewards and unblemished by regrets.

SEVEN

Tihomir picked us up in an absurdly out-of-place, brand-spanking-new SUV, in which he has driven us several miles south through the glorious snowcapped Rila Mountains. I am back in Bulgaria with Emma and Emily. Tihomir is a Bulgarian lounge singer, commonly referred to as "the Frank Sinatra of the Balkans." A man who has relative fame, fortune, and family connections, he lacks only a wife. Unhappily single and approaching middle age, he has his eye on Emma. "American girl with blood from Bulgaria!" he declares unabashedly. "It is my perfect combination!"

Tihomir has promised to take us to his "castle in the hills." We stop first at a roadside restaurant, which (I'm pretty sure) he arranged to have constructed the day before, hoping to impress Emma. Notwithstanding the tavern's rustic ambience—the wood smells freshly cut and a fire burns in the hearth—the tables have

been set with fresh, white linens. The waiters are all got up in traditional Bulgarian folk garb and they seem to have been expecting us for hours. They jump to attention as soon as we walk in
stomping snow off our boots.

"Tihomir! Tihomir!" they shout merrily as if it were the return
of the exiled king. He shakes hands with all the waiters, slaps their
backs, then gestures grandly toward the three of us. "May I present, please . . . American girls!"

The waiters break into a short applause, after which they begin
scuttling about, proffering chairs, and decanting glasses of water
and wine.

The girls and Tihomir and I, an odd-looking quartet, sit and
consume a multicourse meal: tripe soup, pepper-and-cheese salad,
duck and venison, and—of course—carafe after carafe of Bulgarian red wine.

Some hours later, stumbling out of the tavern into the snowy
landscape, we pile again into Tihomir's SUV, which he steers not
back toward the road but—to our collective astonishment—over
the river and through the woods. Barreling along some narrow
path, the car rips branches off trees and creates a confetti shower
of snow and pine.

We switch back up the mountain, as the grade grows ever
steeper. I take mental note of the make and model of Tihomir's ex-
traordinarily capable SUV, thinking I will ask for the same kind
of car when I go overseas for good.

At the summit, just beyond an ice-covered moat, we spot a
fortress wall. We emerge from the car and our legs sink knee-deep
into snow. From a chain attached to a bridge that spans the moat,
a feral-looking German shepherd lunges forward, barking savagely

and frothing at the mouth. Tihomir tosses over a slab of meat, placating the beast long enough for us all to scurry across the bridge.

"Welcome to my castle!" He produces from his pocket an enormous iron key with which he unlocks the fortress gate.

Within the gate, we find a bona fide castle, like something out of a fairy tale, complete with a damsel-in-distress turret. For the next hour or so, he conducts a tour, pointing out the extraordinary workmanship and masonry, focusing primarily on two chambers: a master bedroom fit for a king and queen—"I am waiting for special lady into my life"—and a dank subterranean dungeon.

"A place for rival suitors," I whisper to Emily as Tihomir ushers Emma back upstairs.

"Or pesky meddlesome girlfriends who sabotage first dates," Emily whispers in return.

Emily and I are thrilled by the castle and so pretend to be oblivious to the look of mortification that's been fixed on Emma's face all afternoon. Emily is already scheming about which famous deejays to import from Amsterdam for the all-night raves she plans to host at the castle.

"After they're engaged, of course," Emily says, winking at me and causing Emma to flash her a look of death. Meanwhile, I'm wondering what shady undertakings Bulgaria's Frank Sinatra must be involved in to have gotten his hands on this piece of real estate.

As we tromp around the snowdrifted castle grounds, I silently deliberate: Will I report Tihomir as a professional or as a personal contact back at Headquarters? Already, I am viewing him as a potential recruitment, thinking I can justify it by highlighting Tihomir's probable connections to organized crime. Perhaps he's even a middleman for some nefarious Middle Eastern arms dealer *types! But what are this man's vulnerabilities? (Headquarters, of course, will want to know.) His ego perhaps and, well, Emma, for one. Could I possibly use my relationship with Emma as the in-road to a potential recruitment? Have I really become that sleazy and opportunistic?*

Tihomir interrupts my internal debate by announcing, "Now I want to make a picture!" He conducts Emma, Emily, and me to pose beneath a stained-glass window within a stone garret. We put our arms around one another and smile broadly when Tihomir shouts, "Kashkaval!"—a Bulgarian word for cheese.

Some weeks later, Tihomir will send me a copy of this photograph—the girls and me, huddled together against a backdrop of snowcapped pines and peaks. I will carry the photo in my wallet for years to come, and I'll look at it so often that its edges will fray, and layers of smudgy fingerprints will blemish the white snow. I look back on Emma, forcing a smile, and Emily, rosy-faced and giddy, and me, pensive, slightly anxious, captured on the cusp between fantastical freedom and the confining reality of a covert existence.

Upon my return from The Farm to Langley, I was enlisted by the Central Eurasian (CE) Division—no surprise, given my background and interests. I was told I would receive my overseas assignment after the New Year.

With three weeks of vacation ahead of me, I called Emma and Emily to inquire about making a trip to New York. The girls had no pressing engagements either, as both of them were between jobs, so we decided to travel, discussing the possibilities: Mexico, the Caribbean, Southeast Asia. Ultimately, we decided to return to Bulgaria, where we could stay for free in a centrally located studio apartment, recently bequeathed to Emma by her grandmother, who'd been a renowned Bulgarian sculptor. We knew it could be frigid in Bulgaria, but we'd all be together in a place that we loved, not to mention one of the most unlikely locales to be affected by the much-anticipated Y2K chaos.

While the girls readied themselves in New York, digging out dusty ski equipment and stocking up on the cartons of Marlboros we would need for bribes, I struggled to get approval for "Personal Overseas Travel" back at Headquarters.

"Why Bulgaria?" the prototypically paranoid security officer asked me.

"It's cheap, I can ski, I'm going with my *American* girlfriends." By this time, I was used to the Agency's pervasive xenophobia and knew better than to allude to any Bulgarian acquaintances, or my fondness for that country.

"Will you see your 'close and continuing'?" The security officer scanned my file as we spoke. "This Sasho Podorov."

"*Todorov,*" I said. "No, he lives in San Francisco, actually."

Every time I answered one of these questions so as to save myself from further scrutiny, I felt as if a little part of my reserve had been chipped away. Gradually, I—like many others within the organization—would find ways in which to make myself invisible and nonthreatening: I would stop speaking my mind, avoid discussion of anything personal, and keep any "leftist" political opinions to myself as well. Often I felt as if caught between the pages of some Orwellian novel.

The security officer concluded our conversation by handing me a ream of paperwork to fill out, memo upon memo justifying and cataloging the details of my trip to Bulgaria, and in which I was to report the names, addresses, and telephone numbers of each of my hosts. Emma had no idea what the address of her dead grandmother's artist studio–cum–loft was. "You know, it's on the corner of Gurko Street and Boulevard Levski," she said. She also couldn't fathom why I was intent upon knowing it: "Are you going to be receiving mail there?" Ultimately, I decided that further inquiry would cause Emma and Emily—who still didn't know where I worked—to suspect me, if not of being a spy, then of having grown annoyingly anal and uptight. I dropped the issue and reported on my paperwork that I would be staying at the Sheraton, a ludicrous prospect for anyone who knew Sofia, since the cheapest room there was three hundred dollars a night.

Approval came, I would discover later, the day *after* I left.

Back in Bulgaria, I experienced a brief—but exhilarating—return to freedom and my former self. By day, Emily and I hiked and skied on nearby Mount Vitosha, capping off each afternoon with beers and french fries at the summit hut. At dusk, we would ride down in the gondola, the lights of Sofia spread out below us, flickering to life as the pink sky gave way to night. We would convene with Emma in the studio and begin the first round of cocktails as we readied ourselves for the sequence of clubs and twenty-four-hour discotheques.

I also had the chance to reconnect with several former rock-climbing friends, a few of whom immediately demanded my assistance in getting them visas to America and almost all of whom openly challenged my claim to have become a diplomat. "How does it feel to be a spy?" they would ask with no evident compunction. I laughed off these less-than-subtle inquiries, feeling uncomfortable.

Toward the end of our visit to Bulgaria, I made a trip by myself to Plovdiv, the charming city in the middle of the country on whose outskirts Sasho's mother still lived. I'd been to Plovdiv many times with Sasho, of course, so I knew how to navigate the train and bus sequence to transport me to the small, but spotlessly clean, apartment on the far edge of town.

Sasho's mother lived there on her own now. Sasho was in San Francisco, and Kamen, her younger son, had gone off to England to pick strawberries and save enough money to pay for medical school in the West. The father was still a practicing surgeon in Libya.

Her situation broke my heart. Sitting across from Sasho's mother, watching her slowly go through the stack of photos that I'd brought, I felt my eyes begin to water.

"He's lost weight," she said, and then looked at me, worried. "He's not eating?"

"I don't know," I said. "You know I live in Washington now. California is very far."

"Aaah." Sasho's mother nodded her head. "Too far to drive?" Most Bulgarians, whose own country is about the size of Vermont, have no comprehension of how vast America is.

"Much too far to drive," I said.

"Is very hard for you and Sasho, then."

His mother put the pictures down long enough to pour me another cup of tea and slide a second serving of flaky, cheese-filled *bahnitza* pastry onto my plate.

Obviously, Sasho hadn't told his mother about our breakup. I decided to let it go. She would never understand, or forgive, my choosing a career over her son. And she probably wouldn't be pleased that now he had a Korean girlfriend—another struggling immigrant, no less—who was probably no better off than he. I think Sasho's whole family had always viewed me as some kind of miraculous symbol of salvation—the successful American girl—for their wayward boy who didn't give a damn about anything but climbing rocks. In Bulgaria, Sasho had been renowned: winner of every national competition, the first Bulgarian to summit mythical El Capitán, in *Caleeforneeyah*, U.S.A.—a place from which his many friends and family still awaited his return.

That night, I slept on the tiny twin bed in which Sasho had slept growing up. From the living room next door, I could hear his mother pulling out the sofa that had served as her and Sasho's father's bed, and that now was hers alone. My heart ached for her. How could she stand this loneliness?

Sasho's mother seemed to have looked forward to my visit, and the following morning she prepared an elaborate break-fast, prolonging my stay and causing me to miss the morning train. When I finally left, I think she had surmised, as only a mother can, that her son was no longer in my hands.

"You were good to Sasho," she said, zipping up my down jacket, shoving wax-paper packages of food in the crook of my arm. "You, Sasho will not ever forget."

As I walked through the gloomy Eastern European streets, the factory smokestacks looming against the colorless sky, I was not so sure. Perhaps Sasho had already forgotten me, as his mother eventually would, as would all the foreign people I had met and would come to meet, and into whose lives, from now on, I would make only transient forays, under false pretenses and with ulterior motives.

Emma and Emily and I threw a New Year's Eve party in the loft, with more than sixty guests, ranging from my grungy rock-climber friends, to the Frank Sinatra of Bulgaria and his mobster like entourage, to a smattering of starving artists, reverent of Emma's famous grandmother. Clustered in the tiny kitchen was also a fair representation of Sofia starlets, whom Emma and Emily knew from having worked on films in Bulgaria's version of Hollywood, a dilapidated ranch on the outskirts of town.

An hour before midnight, the whole ensemble herded out into the snowdrifted streets and commenced a staggering parade down to the National Palace of Culture, a colossal Communist relic that had been outfitted for the evening with crookedly slung strands of colored lights and an enormous digital clock, which would indicate the minutes and seconds before the New Millennium. New Year's Eve was still a far more celebratory occasion than Christmas in Bulgaria, since for years the Communists had forbidden any public tribute to or acknowledgment of religious holidays.

We spent the minutes before midnight standing in the bone-chilling cold among thousands of Bulgarians, taking swigs from open bottles of champagne that we'd carted with us for the toast. Typically Balkan, the enlarged digital clock that was intended to show the countdown of seconds malfunctioned sometime during the last minute. Everyone looked about confusedly, asking each other if it was the New Year or not. I relished the absurdity of it all, a welcome respite from the Agency rigidity that infused my life. I felt at once at home.

Flying back to Washington a few days later, I quelled the apprehension I was experiencing, knowing that never again would I travel to a foreign country unencumbered by a hidden agenda.

As it turned out, it was back to the Balkans for me; I was to be sent for an unspecified period of time to Skopje, Macedonia. My fellow classmates, dispersed all over the world, gently mocked me for being exiled to a remote outpost whose name none of them could even pronounce.

Since I already spoke rudimentary Bulgarian, a language almost identical to Macedonian, the Agency opted to train me in Serbo-Croatian, which would serve me well in any of the former Yugoslav republics. I commenced language lessons under the tutelage of a deranged, displaced Serb.

Bojana—who had pierced her tongue and dyed her hair orange in protest of the NATO bombing of Belgrade—spent her evenings trolling the Internet in search of some man to father her child, and her days drilling students in Serbian with repetition of ghastly sentences such as *All the women were raped. Some of the women were raped, but all the men were killed. A few of the houses were bombed and several of the men were killed. None of the barns was burned, but all the women were raped.*

I was in class with two other case officers slated for somewhere else in the Balkans, both big blowhards who bullied Bojana and butchered her native tongue. One of them bragged incessantly about his venerated Gestapo grandfather, who'd perished—"tragically"—in a Russian POW camp. Well aware that I was half Jewish, he arrived one day with show-and-tell photographs of the grandfather, outfitted in full Nazi regalia. I refused to look, and silently simmered, while maniacal, orange-headed Bojana oohed and aahed over the handsome young man in the photo and his *prekrassni* (beautiful) black boots.

At the onset of language lessons, I tried to establish some semblance of a normal life for myself in Washington by joining a local recreational swim team.

I'd been swimming with the team for a few weeks, in the slow lane, among a number of exceptionally fit septuagenarians, when a woman from the next lane over invited me to join a group getting together at the State of the Union club that night.

Having always been a social person, I looked forward to the chance to get to know some of the younger people from the team, but I was also oddly nervous. For more than a year, I'd pretty much restricted myself to socializing only with people inside the Agency. Occasionally, I saw Emma and Emily, but they'd given up on asking me any questions.

I decided I would drag my old college buddy Jared to the bar with me. A decidedly eccentric guy, Jared always wore Groucho Marx glasses for school portraits, routinely tried to engage waitresses in philosophical discussions, and passed out handfuls of Starburst candies from a bag he kept with him at all times. I figured that whatever I said or did would pale in comparison to Jared's behavior.

We arrived at the bar and Jared reached into his backpack to find the inevitable sack of Starbursts, which he immediately began proffering around. Through the haze and over the din and amid all the other faces—some familiar and some not—I was drawn to one man, casually standing among the other swimmers, oblivious to me, facing the band and drinking a beer. This, I would later learn, was James, the fastest swimmer on our team, a freelance photographer who had been absent the past several weeks because he was on a shoot in some Ugandan jungle.

With the exception of meeting James, it was just an ordinary evening—standing around, half listening to the band, drinking one too many beers, eventually collapsing on Jared's couch. But I couldn't sleep that night, as I excitedly dissected my first introduction to this James. Something about him had knocked the wind out of me.

The next day, at the pool, James arrived late. Crouching in the slow lane among the geriatrics, I noted his friendly smile, the easy way he greeted people, the artless confidence with which he walked past me over to the fast lane. And I allowed my heart, however disciplined it had become, to skip a beat.

One day, Bojana released us from Serbian classes early, so I headed over to the pool to swim before our regularly scheduled practice time.

The pool was empty except for a squat Asian man performing what appeared to be some form of martial arts throughout the shallow end. As I dipped my toe in the water and began to don my cap, I saw James emerge from the men's locker room. My heart began to race. I'd never said more than a few words to him, and now here we were: practically naked and practically alone, save for the strange Asian man hurling himself around the pool.

James walked over and asked how I was. I had my swimming cap half on my head, and I was sure I looked ridiculous with my hair sticking out partway.

"I came early today," I said, as if that were not totally obvious.

James smiled. Clearly, he sensed my anxiety. "Yeah, me too."

"You're a photographer, right?" I said.

"Mm-hmm."

"That's cool." I felt more idiotic with each passing second.

"And you?" I had the impression he wanted to start swimming and was just being polite.

"I, er, um, I work for the government," I said. "I'm going overseas soon."

James smirked. "A diplomat?"

"Yeah." I was encouraged that he at least had an idea what that meant.

"I was fixed up once with a so-called diplomat," James said, stretching his arms up over his head. "A political officer, or so she said. I met her when I was traveling through Costa Rica. My cousin worked at the embassy there."

"Really?" I was already jealous of this unknown woman.

"Yeah, but I think she worked at the CIA, actually."

"Oh, really?"

"Yeah, she was totally cagey and uptight," James said. "Actually, we never ended up going out, because she refused to take public transportation."

"I love public transportation!" I blurted out. James looked at me as if I were afflicted with Tourette's syndrome.

"Trains, busses, trolleys . . . you name it," I went on.

James just stared.

"Well, I better start my workout," I said. I hopped in, pushed off the wall, and, for the next hour—one monotonous lap after another—I thought of all the clever things I might have said.

I was surprised by how nervous James made me. I'd never been a particularly nervous girl. Over the weeks, I watched him from the corner of my eye and saw that he treated everyone well—from the other fast guys in his lane, to the wrinkled old people in my lane, to the black lifeguards who fished out hairballs from the drain. It impressed me, and made me think he must be a warm person. I wanted to know him. And I guess more than that, I wanted him to want to know me.

As life will have it, however, it emerged that James had some supermodel girlfriend. I met her at one of the occasional swim-team social gatherings, a tall, slender woman whose beauty was so arresting as to seem, to me, surreal. And so I wrote off the possibility of a relationship with James as something not meant to be, and continued to ready myself for my move overseas.

But over the next several months, which I now remember as nothing other than Serbian lessons and swimming, there were clues that, at the time, I was too dense, or perhaps too guarded, to notice. A smile that seemed particularly directed toward me; James jockeying for a seat next to me; him linger-ing at the end of the slow lane (my lane) for no evident reason; or his sudden interest in photographing an alpaca ranch, when I mentioned that my father had retired to one in West Vir-ginia. (The alpaca expedition never came to pass, but I did spend a considerable amount of time fantasizing about how the limited sleeping arrangements on my father's farm might have finally pushed me and James together.)

I must have willfully ignored these clues in order to keep my heart in check. Pride caused me to flit off every time James approached to start a conversation. Somehow, I knew it would be dangerous to meet his gaze, and whenever I did, I quickly looked away.

I was happy to have an excuse to leave, to go to Macedonia, a place that at least sounded romantic. I figured time and distance would free me from my fruitless girlish reverie, and James and I would go our separate ways.

The day before I left for Macedonia was sweltering and promised a storm; the outdoor pool was about to close for the impending change of season, and after practice the team held its annual end-of-summer party, with a lot of food and lots more drink.

At the end of the party, James asked me for a ride home, as he had biked to practice. We must have sat in the cab of my truck in front of his house for three or four hours that night, talking about all the things I wished we'd talked about earlier, had I not been such a basket case every time he came around. I felt my heart at once buoyed—this was someone I really could care about—and sunk: This is someone I probably will never see again.

At the end of the night, we stood awkwardly in the road, his bike hauled from the back of my truck and perched between us like a boundary marker. "Good luck in Macedonia," James said.

"Yeah, thanks. Good luck here."

He shrugged, staring off for a moment. "Macedonia, huh?"

"You're welcome to visit," I said feebly. It was an absurd notion, given that sitting in my truck for the past few hours was the closest we'd ever come to a proper date.

James was looking at me again. I could feel my brow begin to bead with sweat. When he asked if he could kiss me goodbye, I said "Sure!" way too quickly and enthusiastically, and then immediately began to hyperventilate.

Later, I lay alone on the bed in my airport hotel room (my flight left at six in the morning, a mere few hours away), reliving the moment. I cursed myself for not having offered him a ride home months earlier.

Oh well, I thought. *Que será, será.*

I would pack my memories—a few furtive glances, an unexpected kiss—in my carry-on bag, and I would head off, determined not to be held back by one more false start.

EIGHT

It's Friday night in the Balkans and I am sitting in a parked car with an older man. The windows are steamed up and rain falls in torrents around us. It's impossible to see anything outside, save the occasional blurry beam of passing headlights that always causes my heart to seize up.

The man, a Serb, smells of cigarettes and looks worn out by years of drinking and general discontent. He's squeezed himself into the passenger seat and, with his lumpy brown trench coat and mottled face, looks like a large sprouting potato you'd find forgotten at the bottom of the pantry.

A few minutes earlier, I had picked him up at the rear exit of a shopping mall a mile away. Before that, I spent two hours driving around, just like in training, to make sure I wasn't being followed. In training, they always cautioned us, "You have to be one hundred percent sure you're clean. Otherwise, abort the operation."

I've been doing this spying thing for months now, and I've realized: You can never be one hundred percent sure. Still, my eyes are trained to dart around at all times, even when I'm doing everyday errands or just out for a walk. I'm constantly on the lookout, and on a night like tonight, all my senses are on high alert. I feel less like a predator than prey. Truth be told, I am almost always terrified of getting caught.

Of course, we have our cover story, this man and I. Pretty standard. We are lovers.

"If anyone asks what we're doing together," I said to him the first time we met, a few days earlier, "we're having an affair."

The old man nodded his head as if ashamed, as if we actually were having an affair. Supposedly, he knew the routine. Supposedly—that is, according to him—he too had been an intelligence officer, for the Yugoslav Internal Security Service, otherwise known as the Secret Police. So the man didn't balk when I asked him to meet me three nights later at the rear exit of a shopping mall. And he didn't seem to find it strange the way I drove us around, taking one left turn—better for spotting cars behind you—after another, until I found a nearly empty parking lot behind some Soviet-style apartment blocks.

He probably even suspects that I'm wearing a wig, which I am. My scalp gets itchy as the humidity causes moisture to collect between the mesh lining and my own hair; I want desperately to scratch but know it might make the wig go lopsided. Even if the man has guessed that I'm in disguise, I feel we ought to maintain the charade. In any event, there's a part of me that still wonders if he's for real.

I take out a small notepad and pen—thinking: most people would be surprised to discover the primitive nature of an average spy's tools—and turn to him.

"You have information on the whereabouts of Radovan Karadzic?" I say in Serbian.

The notorious Serb dictator Slobodan Milosevic had been deposed, but the CIA was still actively pursuing many other "persons indicted for war crimes," or PIFWICS, as we called them. Among the most sought-after Balkan war criminals was the former Bosnian Serb commander Radovan Karadzic, who had been instrumental in the mass murder of hundreds of thousands of Muslims—a campaign of "ethnic cleansing." In my naive and eager state of mind, I imagined that—with the help of this disheveled old man—I would bring the modern-day monster to justice.

I'd been overseas half a year, waiting to hook such a fish, to do something—*anything*—that would make my job seem more worthwhile. I was puzzled by the pool of small-time targets that Headquarters and my CIA boss encouraged me to pursue, not to mention a bit disillusioned by the actual banality of being a spy. Turns out it was a lot of paperwork.

This man—who had volunteered information by writing anonymously to an "intelligence officer" somewhere else in the world, but who had agreed to meet me in Skopje—presented a real opportunity for me to do something good.

"It is true I have information on this guy." The man reached into the pocket of his crumpled overcoat for what I could only

hope would be a diagram of the secret bunker in which
Karadzic—and possibly even a few other PIFWICs, I thought
with mounting anticipation—were hiding. But he pulled out
a pack of second-rate Yugoslavian cigarettes.

Having thought ahead, I produced from my own pocket
some superior American-manufactured Marlboros, of which
the man contentedly partook: one to light now, a meaty fistful
more for later.

"As you know, we are greatly interested in the whereabouts
of Mr. Karadzic," I continued. "Any information you can provide that would lead us to his capture would, of course, be
duly rewarded." I was thinking of the six crisp hundred-dollar
bills practically burning a hole in my pocket. More than likely,
I would hand over this money to the man at the end of this
meeting. Six hundred dollars was a pittance to the Agency, I
knew, but it would indicate that we meant business, that there
was more where that came from. If the man really could lead
us to Karadzic, he stood to earn hundreds of thousands of dollars. We might even help him and his family relocate to the
United States, which I assumed was his ultimate goal.

"Now I am going to tell you . . ." said the man, clearing his
throat. I was on the edge of my seat, forgetting that "now," in
the Balkans, more often meant "never."

What the man wanted to tell me, as it turned out, was not
the whereabouts of one of the CIA's most wanted war criminals, but the history of modern Yugoslavia from his perspective.
From the glorious birth, industrious lifetime, and tragically
untimely death of Josip Broz Tito to the ill-fated ascent of Slo-

bodan Milosevic and the destruction that he and his cronies had wreaked upon what was once a great nation, he recited it all in excruciating detail. By the time we'd reached modern-day Serbia—its staggering inflation, rampant poverty, general lawlessness, and communal malaise—my excitement had eroded into total annoyance. I felt bleary-eyed and nearly asphyxiated by secondhand smoke.

But because there might be some light at the end of the tunnel of this man's blather, I sat and listened. For hours, in fact. A couple of times, I restarted and relocated the car—not so much in order to heighten our security, as indeed I'd been trained to do—but in the hopes that physical movement might spur the man on.

Meanwhile, I kept steering the conversation back to Karadzic: "How do you know him?" The man outlined, at great length, a convoluted family–neighbor–former colleague connection. Moments later, he conceded that he did not know Karadzic "personally" at all.

"Does Karadzic know *you*?" I asked.

He shrugged his shoulders and pondered another unlit cigarette. "It is possible yes. . . . It is also possible *no*."

"Look, sir!" I finally blurted out. "Do you have any idea where Karadzic actually is right now?"

"Ahh." He smiled, gingerly cupping one hand over the other as he lit his next cigarette. "Now I am going to tell you . . ."

My head was itching like crazy and I was finding it increasingly difficult to mask my irritation as the man sailed off on another historical tangent. If it weren't for him, I'd be driving that night to Bulgaria, where—as my tremendous good fortune would have it—both Emma and Emily were again living: Emma to work on another low-budget American film being produced there, and Emily on a Fulbright, teaching English at Sofia University. It was a three-hour drive from Skopje to Sofia, and in between skulking about the Balkans—*spying*—I tried as often as possible to see the girls. I desperately needed the reprieve that their friendship provided.

Every time I showed up at Emily's small apartment, I dropped my bags and fell into the girls' open embrace. An uncorked bottle of red wine and a platter of Bulgarian cheese and fat Greek olives awaited me on the coffee table. Emily would pour the wine while I flopped onto the couch, removed my shoes, and curled my legs up under my body. They knew better than to ask too much about what I'd been up to; questions were sure to sour my mood. It always took me several hours to unwind, but as I listened to the girls' madcap adventures and their carefree stories, I could hear the faint laughter from the belly of my former self.

Sometimes—often, in fact—work precluded these weekend visits.

Initially, I had admired the Serb in my car for bravely coming forth and volunteering information, for agreeing to travel from Belgrade to meet with me, and for refusing to accept any money at our first meeting. But I was fast growing suspicious of him.

Clearly, the man had no more clue where Karadzic was than did my ninety-five-year-old grandmother, back at her assisted-living facility in New Jersey. No doubt word had spread that the CIA was doling out big bucks for info, and the man had obviously come to cash in. As much as I hated to pay him for wasting my time, I realized that it was quite possibly the easiest way to get rid of him. I glanced at the car clock, its digits glowing red through the haze like dying embers of a fire. It was close to midnight. If I went to bed soon, I could wake early and drive to Sofia for the rest of the weekend.

"Look, I have to be honest with you," I said. "The names you provided me the other day—of your former colleagues in the Secret Police? Well, none of them checked out. You know we have records on who everyone is."

"Your records are wrong," the man said, as if the explanation were perfectly obvious. I had to admit that I probably put even less faith in the accuracy of CIA data, at that point, than this guy did. Of course, I didn't tell him that.

"The point is," I said, "my colleagues back in Washington"—in other words, my CIA boss in Skopje—"aren't convinced that you are who you say you are."

"Your colleagues in Washington are idiots!" he said, suddenly agitated.

"Perhaps, but they're not such idiots that they're going to pay for faulty information." Even as I said it, I knew it to be a blatant falsehood. The CIA, I'd been discouraged to discover, paid for faulty information all the time.

"Look, it doesn't really matter to me who you are or what you do," I said. "Either you know where Karadzic is or you don't. If you do, I'm prepared to show an offer of our good faith. . . ." I made a minor production out of thumbing through the six crisp hundred-dollar bills. "If not, I will pay you for your time and let's both be on our way."

Oddly, the man refused to even look at the bills. "I do not want your money." He cast his gaze toward the window, as if hurt or embarrassed. "I just want to do what is right."

Suddenly, I felt sorry for him. I looked at his weatherworn shoes, his face as craggy and hardened as a limestone cliff, and the tiny nub of a still-lit cigarette, pinched between his sausagelike fingers. He probably had been in the Secret Police, I thought. Now he was just some old man struggling to make ends meet.

Sadly, I realized that as much as I'd wanted the man to be *somebody*, he wanted it even more himself.

"Why don't I drive you back?" I finally said.

"Next time we meet, I am going to tell you . . ." But then his voice just trailed off.

At the rear of the shopping mall, I handed him three hundred dollars. As was standard, I had him sign a receipt using a made-up name. This money, which flowed like water through the Agency, was government money nonetheless, and thus had to be accounted for. The man scrawled something across the bottom of the scrap of paper I handed him. He folded the bills precisely in half and slid them into the pocket of his overcoat.

"I will call you when I find out some more," he said. But both of us knew he would never call.

My boss didn't care about the wasted time or even the wasted money. "It's a good experience for you," he said to me later, just as he said about every other false lead.

The money represented but a drop in the vast sea of Agency excess and incalculable waste. Anyway, I rationalized, we'd

bombed the poor guy's country just one year before. To myself, I could justify the three hundred dollars as a kind of random act of charity.

I did not watch the man walk away into the shadows of
darkness. For all I knew, he'd accomplished exactly what he set
out to do, and there was a new bounce to his step, and his face
bore a wide, self-satisfied grin. For all I knew, he would fritter
away that money on alcohol and more cigarettes. That was the
thing about being a spy: There seemed to be so little I could
ever actually know.

When I'd arrived in Skopje, months earlier, I found it a hot,
dusty, and altogether discouraging place. Unlike Bulgaria—
where the people had seemed cheerful and welcoming—
Macedonians always appeared to be angry.

The center of Skopje, albeit tiny, was somehow cacophonous and intimidating. I braced myself as I wended my way
among leering shopkeepers, hawkish street vendors, café tables
occupied by brooding thugs who would occasionally explode,
seemingly apropos of nothing, into anger—shouting at each
other or into the faces of their pouty, doe-eyed girlfriends. A
stroll through town was set to the invariable tune of blaring
car horns, outbursts of road rage, and the incessant standard
Slavic insult, "Up your mother's pussy!"

The Macedonians were angry foremost at the Albanians.
They had less disdain for the country of Albania, neighboring
Macedonia to the west, than they did for the population of
Albanian Muslims in Macedonia itself. The Macedonians

generally referred to them as "criminals," "barbarians," or "Muslim dogs."

My neighbor, a vile old woman who complained endlessly about her diminished lot in life since the fall of Yugoslavia, said, "They breed like farm animals, these Albanians. They're taking over our country and turning it into a gangster state."

As much as they despised the Albanians, Macedonians exhibited almost equal antipathy toward the Greeks. Their communal ire toward their southern neighbor seemed to me a modicum more rational, though. Following the dissolution of Yugoslavia, when Macedonia became an independent nation, Greece had refused to recognize the name "Macedonia" because a small portion of northern Greece bears the same name.

The new country thus had been forced to adopt the altogether uninspiring title "The Former Yugoslav Republic of Macedonia," or FYROM, to which most Macedonians understandably objected.

"Can you imagine?!" an enraged Macedonian cabdriver once demanded of me. "If you are from the Former British Colony Known as America? How would you feel then?!"

The only group that could enrage the Macedonians more than the Greeks or Albanians was the Bulgarians. "Bulgarian men are hoodlums," said my neighbor in a rare deviation from her theme of Albanian barbarism. "And the women? Whores!"

Macedonians' hatred of Bulgaria, so far as I could ascertain, stemmed from enduring hostility since the Second World War. Also, just as the Greeks wouldn't accept Macedonia as a name, Bulgarians refused to acknowledge the Macedonian language, which they considered to be a dialect—a bastardization, in fact—of proper Bulgarian.

To make a point, the Macedonian president, in conference with the Bulgarian prime minister, had once apparently gone so far as to insist upon a translator. The symbolic but preposterous gesture was akin to having someone interpret between George W. Bush and Tony Blair.

Ultimately, I did come to empathize somewhat with the maltreated Macedonians, encroached upon from all sides in their tiny, landlocked country. It was sad then to discover that the Macedonians didn't hold Americans in any greater esteem. For a number of reasons. America had sided with Greece over the name issue, and NATO was on the verge of accepting Bulgaria, which wounded Macedonians deeply. Moreover, during the aftermath of the Kosovo crisis, the United States government had strong-armed Macedonia into accepting hundreds of thousands of Albanian refugees, whom the Macedonians now saw as a scourge on their society.

"You are a lover of Albanians!" My neighbor lobbed this accusation through the apricot tree that separated our yards on the day she discovered that I'd employed an Albanian man, the father of seven children, to tend my garden.

"United States of Albania!" she muttered as she picked among the fallen fruits of her tree, all of which appeared to be hard and unripe—like green golf balls—or rotting and infested with maggots.

United States foreign policy in the Balkans did seem muddled at best. In Macedonia, our actions—or *inactions,* as the case may have been—indeed appeared to favor the Albanian Muslim minority, who still viewed America as their savior from Milosevic. Hero worship of Americans seemed to me a crafty strategy on the part of the Albanians, as it naturally elicited our empathy and almost guaranteed our continued support. I cannot recall the number of times an Albanian cabdriver or merchant would heartily slap me on the back and roar, "America–Albania! We are brothers!" I subsequently avoided Macedonian-owned establishments—where I was sure to receive a lecture on how I and my country had ruined theirs—but I always gave the Albanians a good tip and my continued business. The mutual lovefest between America and Macedonia's Muslim minority of course generated suspicion.

One day, I went rock climbing with two young Macedonians named Vassil and Gocé. Vassil, tall and lanky, and Gocé, short and stout, reminded me of Laurel and Hardy, but without any evident sense of humor. The two of them took obvious advantage of my vulnerable position—hanging from a cliff face with my life in their hands—to berate and taunt me about American foreign policy.

"It is well-known fact that you intend to occupy Macedonia," Vassil shouted through cupped hands from the ground below.

"With these Albanian mongrels!" barked Gocé, holding the rope from which I was suspended.

"Can you please take up the slack?" I yelled, clinging precariously to a protruding sliver of granite.

"Macedonia will take up arms!" Gocé hollered in response. "We will shoot the imperialist impostors and their cronies—like dogs in the street!"

It was, needless to say, the last time I ever went rock climbing in Macedonia.

Although I managed to make a few friends in Macedonia—and, tellingly, even considered Vassil and Gocé among them—I avoided getting too close to anyone. I was wary of every local I met, and I'm sure they were equally and rightfully suspicious of me.

During the day, I performed the duties of my altogether bogus cover job, a "diplomatic representative of the United States." By night I trolled the city for obscure locations at which to meet contacts, out-of-the-way pay phones, secluded parking lots, shady playgrounds, and abandoned huts. I wondered what my neighbors thought, and was sure they considered me dodgy at best. Sometimes, as I emerged from my car late at night, I would see the old lady, perched like an owl, peering down at me through the clothing she'd hung to dry on her balcony.

Within a few months, I was actively developing several of my own contacts and had received what seemed to me inflated and undue acclamation from Headquarters.

"Kudos to C/O Hadley" was the title of one such glowing correspondence, referring to me by my Agency pseudonym. "For her aggressive efforts against a wide variety of targets, her forward-leaning-ness and her inclination to take the necessary risks to perform the duties of a practiced C/O."

Probably written by some new trainee, I thought, as I recalled

authoring similarly hyperbolic and vaguely nonsensical correspondences to our neophyte case officers in Kazakhstan. I
appreciated the praise nonetheless. Some higher-up at Headquarters obviously had told the trainee that I was doing a good
job. As I had long hoped and trained for, I finally was becoming—at least in the eyes of the CIA—a successful spy.

In addition to my own contacts, I met with agents who had
been recruited by other case officers and then "turned over" to
me. Handling a turnover, I discovered, was a more difficult task.
It was like going out with a guy who's still hung up on his ex.

"Miss Gonzalez used to let *me* drive," complained one agent.
"And she always brought extra dollar for my benzene and some
different expense."

"Miss Gonzalez and I have a different way of doing things,"
I said.

"You must give my regards to Miss Gonzalez, then," he
said, and sighed wistfully. "She was very good lady."

My CIA boss in the field—a surprisingly amiable and laid-
back man named Scott—would check in on me periodically.
But, for the most part, I was on my own. And aside from sporadic visits to Emma and Emily, spying was all that I did. My
life, notwithstanding the perks—company car, spacious living
quarters, ample budget for my work—was stressful and lonely.
I was on the lookout all the time. *Am I being followed? Is someone following one of my agents? Whose black car with the tinted
windows is that parked in front of my house? Is my phone tapped?
Is my house bugged? Where would they have planted the video*

cameras? What if I get arrested? Worse yet, what if one of my agents gets arrested?

Each day, I varied my route to work so as to throw off potential surveillants. Some days, I left before the sun rose; other days, I puttered around until nine. During lunch hour, I ran countless errands and frequently stopped by my house in an attempt to catch someone lurking the perimeter, or in furtive consultation with my neighbor. I was sure she would have welcomed any opportunity to rat me out to the Macedonian police.

I drove infinite miles from the top of Skopje's idyllic, if not particularly awe-inspiring, Mount Vodno, to the seemingly lawless and congested center of town, to the dismal city limits, festooned with defunct factories and mountainous piles of roadside trash. I always wore dark sunglasses and used the rearview mirror to scan the road behind me.

Sometimes, I would go out on foot from my house, down the steep hill, through town, and across the ancient bridge that spanned the Vardar River and connected the Slavic and Albanian sides of Skopje. There, I wandered the winding cobblestone streets. Albanian men stood in the doorways, blowing smoke like dragons in front of their lairs, while the women shuffled along with bursting bags of groceries, their heads covered by scarves and their eyes cast down.

Occasionally, I went to the cheap outdoor shopping bazaar in the sprawling chaos of Shuto Orizari, where most of Skopje's Gypsies resided. In Shuto, for some reason, I felt at ease. There, it would have been easy to spot surveillants, and I was followed only by noisy children with mismatched clothes and dirt-caked bare feet, who ran after me begging for change.

It seemed as if my only true companion was the secret knowledge *I am a spy*. I would say it to myself sometimes as I hiked alone up the mountain trail, or as I rummaged through swaths of material that maybe I would use to make curtains, or as I sat by myself drinking espresso and garnering the disdainful looks of Skopje's youth—for being a woman sitting by herself.

My human contact was composed almost wholly of business transactions: *How much for a pound of tomatoes? Is this real leather? How would you feel about committing treason on behalf of the United States?* The handful of people with whom I spent the majority of my time—and about whom I fretted constantly—were my agents.

Maintaining an aura of professionalism, I discovered, would be my hardest task. There were few male "targets" or agents who didn't try, at least once, to introduce the idea of sex into our relationship. Sometimes, I think they hit on me more as a matter of personal pride than out of any genuine interest. Some actually seemed relieved to discover that I was after secrets, not intimacy.

Of course, the men I targeted must have wondered what I was up to at first. Regional chauvinism prevented them from suspecting my true motives: American women were more apt to be sluts than spies. This made it easy to initiate contact: "I'm intrigued by your outlook," I would say. "Can I take you to coffee so that we can talk more, and perhaps in private?"

What foreign man was going to say "no" when a young American woman asked him out? It was easy to play the ingenue, asking seemingly innocuous questions, all the while mentally outlining the cables I would write back to Headquarters. What was *not* easy was maintaining the balance of feeding a man's ego, providing a sympathetic ear, all the while making it clear that I had no intention of sleeping with him.

The most dogged of my target-cum-pursuers was Ahmet, a jovial and dapper Albanian businessman. I eventually recruited Ahmet and he ended up being a decent agent, notwithstanding my constant reminders to him to be mindful of "the professional nature of our relationship."

At that time, the CIA was very interested in the Balkans and particularly developments in Kosovo, the contentious region bordering Macedonia to the north. While leadership in Belgrade maintained that Kosovo ought to remain part of Serbia, its largely ethnic Albanian population was demanding regional autonomy. Not unlike the long-standing dispute over Palestine, both Serbs and Albanians viewed Kosovo—which seemed to me a polluted swath of post-Communist wasteland—as the cornerstone of their respective cultures.

Meanwhile, the increasingly violent and impressively organized National Liberation Army (NLA), composed of Kosovar Albanian rebels and guerrilla forces, had begun to expand its aims, infiltrating Serbia's porous southern border into hitherto peaceful Macedonia. By the spring of 2001, the NLA was initiating routine attacks on Macedonian police stations and army barracks, and claiming an increasing number of victims.

Macedonians were outraged, of course, in particular by America's refusal to do anything about the incursions, not to mention the reluctance of the U.S. government to label the NLA a terrorist group.

The Macedonian police and military were crippled by lack of funds and equipment—"When Tito fell, the Serbs took even our light switches and toilet seats!" one army officer complained to me. This, coupled with their own bumbling incompetence, left Macedonia unable to effectively fight back. The small country once heralded as a paradigm of peace in the Balkans now teetered on the brink of civil war.

I'd originally spotted Ahmet at an "interethnic symposium," which took place at a poorly lit and outmoded hotel in the middle of nowhere. He was well connected to a number of allegedly significant Kosovar and Macedonian Albanians. The former of his cohorts all seemed like mobsters to me, and the latter hapless and inexperienced politicians who—like the Macedonian Slavs—were bewildered by their Kosovar brethren's unprecedented triumphs.

When I first started developing Ahmet, we would meet at an out-of-the-way and unpopulated Albanian-owned pizzeria. With its peach-colored curtains and Norman Rockwell reprints, the tiny basement restaurant seemed more like a place to get a root canal than something to eat. Although he claimed to be a devout Muslim, Ahmet always ordered vodka and ate pizza with sausage on top. Like everyone else in the Balkans, he would smoke through the meal, taking a dozen calls on his mobile phone. You'd think he had his finger on the pulse of the world.

Despite my protestations, Ahmet would cut my pizza into small bite-size pieces for me. Once he even tried to feed me, as if I were some overgrown infant. No matter that I didn't smoke, Ahmet would wear me down with incessant offers of his cigarettes. I felt like the uncool kid in high school, pressured to try pot, and I usually took one or two just to appease him and get the conversation going in some other, more relevant direction.

Ahmet had a wife and a bevy of kids at home, but that didn't prevent him from constantly imploring me to go "nightclubbing" with him in Bulgaria. I could only imagine Emma and Emily's total amusement were I to show up in Sofia with what appeared to be an Albanian gangster in tow.

Months into our relationship, when I finally "broke cover," Ahmet's respect for me seemed to increase manifold.

"I love CIA!" he exclaimed loudly. We were sitting in his Mercedes next to what appeared to be a city dump, miles from downtown. Weeks earlier, I'd cautioned Ahmet that it was too risky for us to meet publicly; not surprisingly, he'd raised no objections to more discreet venues. "We can use my friend's apartment!" Ahmet had suggested.

"Your car will do," I'd said, to his manifest disappointment.

"How would you like to work for the CIA too?" I now asked. I had written up a careful "pitch proposal" and sent it back to Headquarters, outlining how I thought the recruitment meeting would play out.

"C/O Hadley anticipates little risk of blowback in executing the pitch," I'd written, referring to myself in the third person, as is characteristic of CIA case officers and also, I often considered, insane people. "C/O Hadley doubts that Subject ever would report the pitch or C/O's true affiliation to the local police or security services. Subject already is aware that he is taking considerable risk by meeting with C/O."

Ahmet—after a nanosecond of consideration about the implications of committing espionage—shrugged and said, "Okay, no problem."

At The Farm, they'd never said recruiting an agent could be this easy.

"You cannot tell anyone about it," I cautioned Ahmet. "Not even your wife."

"I never tell my wife anything." Ahmet winked at me.

"And if anyone catches us together, or asks how you know me . . ." I braced myself. "You should tell them we're having an affair."

"No problem, no problem." Ahmet, I could tell, was nearly beside himself with enthusiasm. "If we must to do it, then we will make sex."

"No, Ahmet! We don't *actually* have an affair. That's only our cover story—for if we get caught."

"No sex?" Ahmet said, simultaneously hopeful and disappointed.

"No sex," I said. "I give you money and you give me information. Just like you've been doing. Only now we're going to formalize our relationship. So that you will be protected and also *paid.*"

"No holding hands?"

"No, Ahmet. It's business. Serious business, okay? Because if you get caught, you could go to jail."

"Bah!" Ahmet waved his hand. "We will not get caught. I will tell everyone we are making sex."

"No, don't," I said, picturing Ahmet bragging about his young American concubine to a rapt audience at the Albanian pizzeria. "Don't tell anyone anything."

"Okay, okay." Ahmet rolled his eyes as if I were a huge bore. "It is no problem for me."

And with that, I pulled out a secrecy agreement for Ahmet to sign, as well as ten crisp one-hundred-dollar bills. It was a modest—by Agency standards—signing bonus.

While Ahmet had been relatively easy to recruit—resulting in a slew of accolades for me from Headquarters—he continued to be somewhat difficult to handle.

"Why can we not have relations?" Ahmet again pleaded as he drove us along some mountainous southern Macedonian thoroughfare. *I don't get paid nearly enough to deal with this shit*, I thought to myself. Hours earlier we'd met at a café along the road that bordered Lake Ohrid, about 160 miles south of Skopje.

Ahmet looked beseechingly at me from behind the steering wheel. "Keep your eyes on the road," I said. "I told you last time: Our relationship is business. Anyway, Ahmet, do I have to remind you? You're married."

"Ach!" Ahmet groaned. "Here, it is normal to be married and have some other girlfriends too."

"Anyway, I have a boyfriend," I lied. "And for me it's not normal to have more than one."

"What boyfriend?!" Ahmet demanded.

"In America," I lied again, feeling pathetic for resorting to inventing a boyfriend just to get Ahmet off my back. "He's American."

"American men, bad lovers," Ahmet announced authoritatively. "What is his business?"

"He's, er, a . . . photographer," I was thinking—absurdly, I realized—of James.

"Photographer!" Ahmet practically guffawed. "You will starve with this man."

"Pull in there." I pointed, as we approached what appeared to be a rarely frequented scenic overlook. Ahmet parked amid a patch of pine trees through which peeked the brilliant orange rays of a rapidly setting sun.

"Okay, what do you have for me?" I said. Ahmet reached into his jacket and pulled out a small stack of notes—in tiny writing—that he'd prepared. For the next hour or so, Ahmet diligently went over everything he'd recorded since we'd last met, a month earlier.

At the end of our meeting, I handed Ahmet his monthly salary, four hundred dollars carefully folded in a newspaper. He signed a small slip of paper with the alias name he'd selected himself, with a certain measure of pride: Bobby.

I worried less about Ahmet's amorous intentions than I did about his getting caught. He didn't pay much attention to the security measures in which I had diligently trained him.

"Never call me on the phone," I'd said to Ahmet countless times. "We'll just meet at the time and place we agreed upon, and if one of us doesn't show up, we go to Plan B, okay?"

"Of course!" Ahmet appeared visibly offended that I felt the need to remind him.

Inevitably, I would be midway through my surveillance-detection route to one of our prearranged meeting sites when my mobile phone would ring. From the caller ID, I could see that Ahmet was not even using a pay phone, as I'd instructed him to do if ever he *really* needed to call me, "but only in case of emergency."

I would debate momentarily whether or not to answer. Often, I just let the phone ring. But occasionally, worried that indeed something had happened to Ahmet, I would answer, "Yes?," hoping that my voice conveyed my exasperation.

"Lisssaaaaa!" Ahmet would shout, no matter the number of times I'd instructed him not to use my name, even though it was an alias. "I am on my way to . . . *the place* . . . now. Is okay?"

"Fine," I would say, steaming mad and thinking ahead to how I would chastise Ahmet when we finally met.

Sometimes I arrived at the designated meeting spot, where Ahmet was supposed to be skulking imperceptibly among the shadows, to find him standing in the middle of the road, chatting away on his mobile phone. When he saw me, he would begin waving wildly. Once he even had a bouquet of vibrant flowers that he used to flag me down, like an aircraft router guiding a plane to its gate.

• • •

I also handled agents out of country, meaning I met them periodically in other parts of the world. I traveled in alias, an ordeal that required significant advance planning as well as endless consultations with Headquarters and other CIA offices. Before I even could begin an operational trip, I always had to travel first to some country outside of the Balkans to pick up my alias documents from another CIA officer in the field.

The first time I was to travel in what was called "operational alias," Headquarters informed me that I should fly to Vienna to obtain my documents from Case Officer Cecelia H. Abington: "C/O Abington will forward soonest contact instructions and short description of herself to C/O Hadley, for meeting to take place 24 December."

I wasn't thrilled about the prospect of working over Christmas, but I figured staying in Macedonia and celebrating by myself—with a roasted chicken and some mashed potatoes— would have been just as grim a prospect. Emma and Emily were off on some holiday jaunt to which I'd been invited, but when I broached the idea with my boss, Scott, he sighed and said, "With Macedonia in the state it is, I can't afford to have anyone leave . . . unless, of course, it's related to an operation."

I liked Scott immensely and was eager to please him, so I didn't press the issue. I never complained about the toll I felt the job was taking on me, knowing my concerns would sound petty and inconsequential—wanting to spend time with friends, feeling lonely, hoping at some point to have a date. Scott's parents had worked for the Agency, his wife worked for the Agency, the Agency was the only thing Scott knew. In his view, the opportunity to spend Christmas working was an honor.

I had not met with the agent—a dour and perpetually malcontented Bosnian woman—since she'd first been turned over to me. Scott was afraid the woman might be feeling "left out in the cold." And December was a good time to go: It would not raise anybody's suspicions if either I or the woman traveled at Christmastime, and my absence would give my other agents a much-needed break. Ahmet, for one, had been grouchy and unreliable since the start of Ramadan. In addition to fasting, he'd also given up smoking and drinking. The last time I saw him, he looked haggard and thin, and hadn't even made any attempt to hit on me.

Holidays were a time to spend with family and friends, but I put that out of my mind. I figured my family had all but written me off as dead; my letters to them were so obscure, and surely alarming. And aside from Emma and Emily, my circle of friends had dwindled to a tiny black point. I'd received some Agency internal e-mails: from Ethan, who was based in the States but seemed to be traveling the world; Alec, serving in Latin America; Ophelia, posted to a posh Western European capital; and even Jin Suk, stationed somewhere in the Middle East. Jin Suk, like me, was the only other person *not* to have planned some fabulous holiday for the month of December. She would work over Christmas too. "I can't get enough of this job," she wrote to me. "It's so cool to actually be doing everything we trained for. I'm wondering if you feel the same?"

"Absolutely!" was my terse reply. No sense in providing ammunition she could use against me, I thought, all the while dismayed by what a distrustful and hard-boiled person I'd become.

Working or not, perhaps the operational trip would enable me some downtime, during which I could think about my life and where it was heading.

C/O Cecelia H. Abington sent word that I should meet her at the rearmost pew of a cathedral just within the city limits of Vienna. "C/O Abington is petite and blond," her cable read. "And will be wearing dark, mirrored sunglasses."

I thought it potentially alerting that C/O Abington would be wearing sunglasses in the interior of a church, but I knew better than to question the judgment of another case officer. I sent C/O Abington a description of my planned attire: wool coat with a fake-fur collar, black leather gloves. "No eyewear for C/O Hadley," I wrote, hoping that C/O Abington would take the hint.

Weeks later, I arrived at the cathedral after weaving a bone-chilling path through the labyrinth of Vienna. The streets were covered with ice and frost, and I kept thinking, *If I'm under surveillance, they're about to see me wipe out on my ass.* When at last I pushed open the weighty timber door into the church, I was at once dismayed to realize that an evening service was taking place. This was poor planning on the part of C/O Abington, the kind of move that would have garnered someone a slew of lesters at The Farm.

The rear pews, where we were supposed to meet, were filled with caroling Austrians. One of the parishioners wore dark, mirrored sunglasses and didn't appear to be singing with the others.

Could it really be her, though? First of all, the figure was of totally indeterminate gender. It could be a woman, I finally decided. And while certainly she was petite—Lilliputian even—her close-cropped hair, rather than blond, was in fact *shockingly* white. C/O Abington might have been blond fifty years ago, but she now had the kind of white hair you'd expect to find on the head of Little Red Riding Hood's grandmother, or Father Time. I gingerly approached.

"Excuse me, ma'am," I said in English. "Can you tell me at what time I might hear the Gregorian chants?" Abington had clearly gone out of her way to come up with the most ridiculous "verbal recognition" exchange she could. She cocked her forehead down and peered out above the rims of her mirrored Ray-Bans.

"You must mean the eunuchs' choir," she stage-whispered, the agreed-upon response. One of the Austrian carolers turned around, scowling, and shushed us. I slid in next to C/O Abington, and as we wordlessly faced the cathedral's ornate front, she slipped me a small plastic zip-lock bag containing my alias documents. I waited until the end of the yuletide hymn, then left the cathedral, glad to be rid of her.

From there, I commenced what would be the first of many long and circuitous journeys as Isabel Hartlet from Lander, Wyoming. I'd chosen Lander as my alias origin because, years earlier, I'd spent a few weeks rock climbing near this small

western town. My memories of dusty Lander and its surrounding environs were as vivid as if I'd lived there all my life. I could
still picture the sprawling Wind River Indian reservation; the
craggy, imposing mountains, in which were embedded crystal-
cold alpine oases; and the dense, nearly impenetrable woods,
through which myriad babbling brooks and fish-filled rivers
carved their winding paths. Whenever I felt lost or disillusioned,
I conjured these images and recalled the simple truths that the
nature near Lander had seemed to provide me.

I spent the next hour poring over my documents, hunkered
down on a bench in the dark corner of a Vienna wine cellar. I
drank chardonnay diluted with sparkling water, and ate chunks
of fatty sausage and crumbly yellow cheese. I repeated to myself over and over again my new name and birth date, my Social
Security number, my parents' names—Harold and Agnes—
and their birth dates. I knew the details of my new astrological sign, Libra, and I invented for myself a new job: I would be
a fledgling travel writer, I decided. I reveled in temporarily recreating myself.

If anyone asked, I was working on a book called "The
Women's Guide to Traveling Alone Around the World." Why
and how I managed to commence my tour in Vienna, Austria,
with a hitherto totally unadulterated passport, I hoped wouldn't
come up.

I looked around and noticed that the wine bar had filled up
with fashionable and attractive Viennese youth. I envied their
easy camaraderie and carefree laughter as they shared carafes of
wine and mountains of fried potatoes. The men removed their

ties and unbuttoned their collars. The women let their hair down.

What if someone approaches me, I wondered. Obviously, I would stick to my story. Even if it was a guy and I liked him, I would be necessarily aloof, I told myself.

I recalled Ethan e-mailing me once to say that he'd "hooked up" with a woman while traveling in alias. The woman later attempted to track him down and, based on her difficulty in doing so, finally ascertained that Ethan had given her a fake name. Enraged, she somehow found him back in the States, and commenced a campaign to smear his reputation. Ethan ultimately was forced to confess the whole sordid and embarrassing situation to his CIA boss. "The long and the short of it is," Ethan wrote, "that it was a big, fucking mess and now I have about ten new pages in my security file."

In any event, no guy approached. In fact, no one paid a whit of attention to me and, much later, I stumbled out into the wintry night alone. The cathedral square was strung with white lights, and even more alive with revelers than the crowded wine bar. Classical music blared from loudspeakers attached to lampposts, and rosy-cheeked people thronged around canopied stands from which vendors sold spicy sausages and hot mulled wine.

Vienna seemed to me preternaturally clean and bright after gritty Skopje, with its perpetually busted streetlamps. Already tipsy, I figured I might as well have a bit of the mulled wine, and cupped my steaming mug with both hands near a laughing group of people about my age. I looked down at my feet and noticed that a long strand of toilet paper extended like a streamer from one shoe. I wondered how long the toilet paper had been there—*no doubt through the entirety of my surveillance-detection route*—and if this was the source of the Austrians' great mirth. Suddenly, I felt anything but free and anonymous, and more like drunk and alone.

Using the unembellished foot to remove the strand, I shuffled toward a new spot in the crowd. But the longer I watched the bustling nightlife, the more desolate I grew. Eventually, I made my way to the underground and back to the dingy hotel in which I would be spending the night. C/O Abington had recommended the Hotel Majestic—a misnomer of tragic proportions—to me as "appropriate, out of the way, and secure."

"Hotel staff unlikely to make inquiries," she had written.

In fact, C/O Abington could not have been more wrong. The front desk was staffed by a jaunty little Indian who wanted to know all about me and my travels. Rupesh—"meaning Lord of Beauty," he proudly informed me—asked me countless questions. Was Lander, Wyoming, anywhere near Cherry Hill, New Jersey, where he had "too many relatives"? And why was a young woman such as myself traveling around all by her lonesome? And what on earth had possessed me to come to Vienna, where the people were "so colorless and mean"? But since I was here, would I consider staying a few days longer so that Rupesh could show me the best place to get a curry in all of Austria?

No matter how I tried to circumvent Rupesh, he seemed always to be at hand or underfoot. In the morning, I rose at five to catch an early bus to Budapest. He was up already, busily manning the front desk—scrutinizing passports, stapling receipts, arranging the room keys in their cubbyholes—just as he had been the night before. Trained to be highly suspicious, I also wondered why Rupesh was taking such an interest in me. As I searched in my bag for my wallet, I asked—to Rupesh's delight—if I might have his last name.

"In case I ever return," I said, tracing my finger over the embossed business card he readily offered. I would check him out through the Headquarters database, which—albeit outdated and flawed—occasionally yielded some useful information. *You can never be too careful,* I thought as I slipped the card into my pocket.

"You are most welcome every time you are returning!" Rupesh said, waving gaily as I backed out the smudgy glass door.

From Vienna to Budapest to Prague to a remote wooded spa in Bavaria, I took planes, trains, busses, and automobiles hither and fro, sometimes backtracking on myself, so that it would have been nearly impossible to follow Isabel Hartlet's route. Nearly half of my travel was designed simply to obscure the real purpose of my trip, which meant a lot of sightseeing, shopping, and eating on my own. Occasionally, someone would strike up a conversation, but I always cut him off pretty quickly.

When I finally reached the posh Bavarian resort, I couldn't really enjoy my luxurious surroundings. I was, for the most part, sequestered in a hotel room with Jasna, my agent, who spent much of our meetings complaining about her domineering mother-in-law, her good-for-nothing husband, her slutty stepdaughter, and her generally miserable life. It had cost thousands of American taxpayer dollars for me to travel all over God's green earth to meet this woman; not to mention the astronomical salary we paid her, which—I was loath to discover—far exceeded my own.

Jasna had come to the attention of the Agency years earlier when she'd claimed to her recruiting case officer—falsely, so far as I could tell—that she'd been a schoolmate and close friend of then Bosnian Serb president, and later notorious war criminal, Biljana Plavsic. Plavsic had distinguished herself even among the most brutal of Serb dictators and military commanders by openly characterizing ethnic cleansing as "a natural phenomenon." She was even famously photographed stepping over the body of a dead Muslim civilian to plant a kiss on the cheek of a murderous Serbian warlord known as Arkan.

I didn't find it implausible that Jasna and Plavsic could have once been friends, but I had begun to doubt Jasna's claim of continued access to the woman, since she rarely had any information for us.

"My friend has been very busy," Jasna said when I asked about Plavsic. "She has no time for talking anymore." After espousing some vague and unsubstantiated theories about the future of Republika Srbska, Jasna was back to lamenting about her family.

Although I knew that one purpose of these face-to-face meetings was to "build rapport"—so that Jasna wouldn't feel abandoned during the intervening months when we didn't see each other—I hated every minute of it and knew that she, likewise, would have preferred to just collect her money and be on her way.

I generally dismissed Jasna at seven o'clock every night. She was glad to be able to eat tomato sandwiches for dinner and pocket the rest of her generous food allowance. Unlike Ahmet and most other agents, Jasna didn't need to be constantly cautioned against using her CIA salary to make large or extravagant purchases, which surely would arouse the suspicions of her colleagues and neighbors. She happened to be an uncommon miser, and even steadfastly refused to let me set up a bank account for her, though I'd explained that not only would the money be far safer overseas, it would also generate interest. Jasna instead stockpiled cash in tinfoil-wrapped packages that she stored in her freezer. I think there was a part of Jasna that couldn't believe her profound good fortune and feared that, any day now, the CIA would wise up to the scam.

Once I'd released Jasna for the evening, I would hit the minibar, order room service, and then start going over my notes, struggling to garner tidbits of information that might be of interest to Headquarters amid all the boring melodrama of Jasna's life.

At the end of a couple of days of the same routine, I paid Jasna. Since we hadn't seen each other in months, the money amounted to a stack as high as a cinder block.

"What about my taxi to the airport?" Jasna demanded after meticulously counting the money twice. Although I knew that she always got someone to drive her, I peeled off a few extra bills. There was no sense in inciting Jasna. *Anyway,* I reminded myself, *she* is *risking her life.*

I made my way back toward Vienna, where I would retrieve my true-name documents from C/O Abington, anticipating the relief I'd feel when I was Lindsay Moran again. Harrowed and exhausted from operating in alias, I'd given little thought to returning to Eastern Europe.

The ride from the Skopje airport to my house traversed a predictably bleak Balkan landscape—grim architecture; roadside glaciers of blackening snow; Gypsy children swathed in stolen blankets, lighting matches under the frost-covered piles of frozen trash. Inhospitable as it was, Skopje still seemed a welcome respite from the relentless gaiety of Vienna. Here, at least, it was okay to feel miserable and alone.

Once I'd written up the few shoddy intels I was able to garner from Jasna's rambling diatribes, as well as a slew of mundane operational cables documenting all my travel, I decided to head to Sofia. The girls would be returning from vacation the following day and Emily had left me the key to her apartment, in case I wanted to surprise them for New Year's.

As my car barreled across unlit miles, occasionally broken up by the red lights and smokestacks of some gargantuan industrial plant, my mind wandered back, across the ocean, to James.

My love life had been fairly nonexistent since our long-faded farewell kiss. I'd occasionally craft some hopefully informative and amusing letter, sending it in the guise of a group e-mail—in reality, hoping to impress James.

In writing, it was easy to disguise the loneliness that seemed to plague me, and since I wasn't permitted to disclose anything about my work, I never complained about the sense of purposelessness I felt. There also was no mention of any stress. I read and reread each missive before I sent it, satisfied with the illusion I could create—to everyone, but most importantly to James—that I was carefree and contentedly living in my exotic new home.

"I generally delete group e-mails," James confessed in a letter I found waiting for me when I returned from my operational trip. "But I save yours to read when I'm alone. I like your writing. Why don't you just quit whatever it is that you're up to over there," James concluded, "and go on the lecture circuit?"

This letter gave me such an inner thrill, I read it again and again, scrutinizing the words for some hint of his deeper meaning. The only thing I could infer, however, was that James somehow had read between the lines of my messages and sensed my ambivalence toward my job. I had to chuckle, picturing myself announcing to Scott and the rest of the CIA that I intended to "go on the lecture circuit."

I envied James for living seemingly entirely on his own terms. Before I'd left for Macedonia, James had told me that for years he'd been a medical drug rep. "Hating it!" he'd said. At the age of thirty-one—the same age I was now—he'd suddenly quit to travel around the world. He supported himself by winning international swim marathons—granted, *not* an option for me—and he started taking pictures.

"I had no experience as a photographer," James said on the night we'd sat for hours, willing time to stand still in the cab of my truck. "But I found out I liked it, and so that was that."

James's confession had inspired me, albeit a little late—I was leaving for Macedonia the next day to embark upon my life as a spook. Still, I occasionally thought, *I could do something else, couldn't I?*

After rereading James's letter for the umpteenth time, I decided that indeed I would write more—although about *what* exactly, I had no clue—and also that I would start swimming again, which would link me to James.

In a futile attempt to curry favor, I asked my Macedonian neighbor about the public swimming pool. "That place is fill with vermin and disease," she said. "Is all *tsigani* there," using the common derogatory term for Gypsies. "They are using pool as public toilet."

While I hated to submit to my neighbor's prejudices, I decided to wait until I arrived in Sofia to commence my swimming career. There the public pools, if not luxurious, were at least a known entity.

I was thinking about swimming and about writing and about James when, suddenly, the lights of Sofia shone up to greet me as I rounded the final hill. This city seemed like Paris to me and, as I drew ever nearer to Emily's apartment, the closest thing to home.

NINE

No one can find me at Venci's hideaway in the hillside village of Svoge in northwestern Bulgaria. The town is famous for its chocolate, which only adds to the fairy-tale allure of this place I have come to escape.

Hours earlier, I met Venci at the Sofia Central train station, crawling with every strain of mankind's misfortunate: hardened old babas toting bulging bags of cucumbers, Gypsy kids sniffing glue from bags, a chorus line of addict-thin prostitutes pulling at their stockings. After the unsettling scenes at the train station, the countryside seems, in a word, enchanted. The train tracks follow a gently winding river that carves its way through jagged limestone cliffs, all of which seem subdued by the sweet smell of a still-distant spring wafting into the open caboose.

In Svoge itself, there's a similar sense of calm. Venci hikes up a steep hill from the edge of the tiny town and stops to buy bread and chocolate, canned fish, some pasta and tea, a few warm beers, juice for the morning, as well as four eggs and some cheese. Holding up the sack of eggs, he tries out his English on me: "Lately, we will make each other breakfast."

I am still charmed by his mistakes, and as we continue hiking upward, I am seduced by the setting sun, the whipping wind, the little villas lighting up along the darkened hillside, like ornaments on some enormous Christmas tree. Venci's family's villa is the highest on the hill, boarded up on all sides against the winter.

As he fumbles to produce the key, the mobile phone in my pocket startles both of us with its shrill and sudden ring. It's dark and I can't tell who is calling, but the shocking fluke that my phone would actually work in these elevated sticks leads me to suspect it must be important. I answer.

"May I speak to Elisaveta?" Scott's voice crackles over the line. It's code for an emergency, meaning he wants to meet immediately at a predesignated street corner back in Skopje.

"Wrong number," I say reflexively, and hang up.

As soon as the line goes dead, I realize how much trouble I'm in. Embarrassed to ask again for permission to travel to Bulgaria, I just went, without authorization from Headquarters. I didn't even tell Scott. Now he'll be expecting to see me in thirty minutes, and I'm a two-hour train ride, followed by a three-hour drive, not to mention an entire country away from our meeting spot.

Venci looks at me as if I'm crazy when I say, "I need to find a pay phone, and I need to go home."

"Now?"

"Yeah, now."

"But we just got here. There are no trains tonight."

"What about a pay phone?"

Venci must see the desperation in my eyes.

"Maybe in Svoge center," he says, scratching his head like a confused cartoon character. This episode will only confirm Venci's suspicion that I'm a spy.

As we stumble down the hill in the now consummate darkness, the air grows colder, the wind picks up, and my anxiety continues to mount. It sinks in to me that Venci and I are in the middle of nowhere and that I, for one, am up a proverbial creek.

Of course, the single pay phone back at Svoge's "center"—which itself is nearly imperceptible to the human eye—does not function. In fact, there's a gaping, cavernous hole in the booth right where the telephone should be.

Venci's not asked me any more questions, but he's gone through half a pack of cigarettes by the time I punch Scott's number into my own mobile phone. Calling Scott directly constitutes an even bigger no-no than disappearing from the country without a trace. Scott's and my mobile phone numbers should never be linked. But at this point, I don't know what else to do.

"You called for Elisaveta?" I manage to croak out when Scott answers.

"Yesssss?" His irritation seeps through the phone like a noxious gas leak.

"Well, er, she's in Bulgaria right now."

"I see," Scott's terse reply is followed by a long, interminable pause. "Well, tell her to get back as soon as she can. The shit is hitting the fan in Macedonia, and the border might be closed soon."

When I hang up, I realize my eyes have filled up. Venci's look-ing at me as if someone has died.

"I have to get back across the border." My mouth quivers as I speak. "As soon as I can."

"I'll go with you." Venci reaches for my hand.

"No, it's okay." I step back. "Look, Venci, I don't know even if this, I mean us, can work."

He's looking at me skeptically, searching my face.

"It's not you, it's me," I say, wondering if this sounds cliché in Bulgarian as well as English. "It's complicated. I can't explain. I just have to go."

"Wait until morning?" Venci reaches again for my hand.

There are no more trains back to Sofia tonight anyway. I give him my hand and together we hike back up the hill in silence. Later, I will fall asleep on the floor in front of the wood-burning stove into which Venci has stoked a blazing fire.

By morning, I am slathered in my own sweat. My head aches as I try to remember if my conversation with Scott was a dream or for real. I wash my face with water from a bucket and then step gin-gerly toward the door. By the time Venci wakes up, I will be gone.

I'd first run into him one morning, while Emma and Emily slept in, after swimming at the Sofia public pool. Venci, whom I'd originally met when I'd come to Bulgaria to teach years be-fore, must have known I'd be there, because he was waiting for me when I emerged onto Vasil Levski Boulevard. Shaking out my wet hair and blinking into the sun, I spotted him leaning against a half-crumbled concrete pillar, smoking a cigarette, and looking more like a movie star than a security guard at a Bulgarian Bingo Hall.

Venci was not what anyone would have envisioned or wanted for me. In his spare time, he did nothing but smoke and manufacture tiny ashtrays out of whatever happened to be lying around: a bottle cap, a shard of glass, a sliver of orange rind, an Odor-Eaters lining that'd fallen out of some old shoe. My mother, aghast over my having settled down with such a seemingly shiftless—and another *Bulgarian,* no less—boyfriend, wondered in her last letter, "What do his parents do?"

I didn't have the heart tell her that the father was a similarly rudderless, shriveled-up, and toothless version of Venci himself. I had met his mother only once, the first time and last time I spent the night at the apartment Venci shared with her in Lyulin, by far the most discouraging of Sofia's sprawling suburban slums. I'd been mesmerized by its wretchedness as Venci and I passed through a door with no knob into a pitch-black entryway that smelled like a shallow grave. Later, whenever I was upset with Venci, I imagined him at home on a rainy Sunday and my anger dissolved at once into pity.

Venci had the back room where there was no space for a proper bed, just some kind of fold-out contraption that looked like a piece of lawn furniture. Through the window, the moon illuminated clutter: water-warped algebra books, broken Christmas-tree ornaments, a stack of *Time* magazines fifteen years old, the pages of which must have been thumbed through a thousand times.

When morning came, I was half afraid of the light, the noises: running water, his mother—*oh, Jesus*—making coffee, clanging pots, the telephone ringing, and voices so clear it sounded as if all the apartment dwellers had convened at the foot of the fold-out bed. With each intrusion, Venci drew me closer and said, "Sleep a little longer."

The birds outside started slamming themselves against the glass, looking for a fight, but somehow I felt insulated in the pathetic little place. Sun streamed through the window and particles of dust floated like tiny angels in its beams. On the floor, I spotted a Tom Robbins novel I'd given Venci years before, when we first met, when I was an English teacher in Bulgaria and Venci was a handsome young university student, before I became a spy and he dropped out to work at the Bingo Hall. The book, as far as I recalled, was a love story that took place inside a carton of cigarettes, which now somehow seemed appropriate.

When Venci left the room, I pulled on one of his T-shirts and moved to the window. The scene outside was about as miserable as one could imagine, the brilliantly shining sun almost mocking the ugliness below. There was nothing but barren ground, scavenging dogs, a battalion of battered-looking *bloks*, and women in housedresses beating the bejeezus out of rugs—as if their sorry lot in life were the fault of the floor coverings. Some of them just stared from the balconies like guards perched in towers, overseeing a dusty prison yard below. Across the way, an old man in a white wife-beater tank top looked at me and spat seeds onto the ground. I imagined myself from his perspective. *Doesn't she have some rug to beat*, he must have wondered. *Or some rice and meat to roll up in a cabbage leaf?*

When Venci came back, he laughed at me.

"You are spying?" he said. I'd never told Venci what I did; he just assumed that all foreigners were spies. In Venci's mind, Emma, Emily, and I were all part of an elaborate female espionage network.

He could read the mortification in my eyes as I looked out upon his neighborhood.

"I gotta go," I said.

"I know." Venci gave me a towel for the bathroom, which he warned me was "not so nice."

We were almost out the door when his mother shouted in a high-pitched squeaky voice, *"Venciey! Venciey!"* She emerged from the kitchen waving a fifty-leva note for Venci to buy more coffee with while he was out. I couldn't tell who among us was most mortified when she came upon me, but once she heard my credentials, *"amerikanska diplomatka,"* she was much more welcoming—stroking my hair and telling me how lovely I was, berating Venci for not inviting me to stay for coffee. Thank God, he had the wherewithal to know that I would rather go tumbling from the tenth-floor balcony.

"A prostitute lives there." Venci pointed nonchalantly to the neighbor's door as we stepped into the elevator. "She comes over for coffee sometimes." This was his way of trying to make me jealous.

In the stark light of early-morning Lyulin, Venci and I might as well have been the last two survivors of a nuclear holocaust. We plodded across what seemed like an uninhabited lunar ghetto. The children's playground equipment—metallic skeletons petrified in concrete—looked as if they hadn't been used in years. Plunked amid these colorless Bulgarian badlands was an utterly puzzling stretch of pastoral land: farmhouses with sagging rooftops, smoky stoves in the middle of the yards, chickens and roosters strutting about as if the city's edge were their natural habitat. Venci took my arm and guided me toward a gravel heap that I never would have recognized as the bus stop. A mangy-looking dog wandered over to join us.

"He's got to get into town for an appointment," he joked as the matted, boil-covered canine stationed himself by our side.

That day, Sofia's city center had never looked so promising: the regal old buildings with ornate trim, etched windows, and fantastical gargoyles perched atop their corner spires; flashing neon signs over bustling new cafés; cascading fountains in whose mist the sun formed dazzling miniature rainbows. I stood in the spray and let the sun warm my face. Venci kissed me, and I thought we must have appeared very much in love.

In front of the National Theater, we stopped to gaze at a statue of a ballet dancer with disproportionately large feet.

"Sasquatch!" Venci said. I could not take my eyes from the statue: this elegant woman frozen in a gesture that yearned toward an utterly elusive freedom. It was as if the mammoth feet fixed her otherwise graceful body to the ground.

I probably could have stood staring at that statue for hours, but I was anxious to get back to Emily's apartment. I had plans with the girls to eat eggs Benedict at the Sheraton, an establishment that Venci regarded with envy and disdain.

"Only *mootrité* go there," he said, referring to the thick-necked professional wrestlers–turned–mobsters who, having

purloined all of Bulgaria's public funds, had declared themselves the country's emerging aristocracy.

"*Mootrité,*" he said. The disgust in his voice was palpable.
"And Americans."

Mootrité notwithstanding, I liked the Sheraton. I couldn't
count the number of hours I'd spent in Capitol, the hotel's elegant, high-ceilinged restaurant, on Sunday afternoons with
the girls, wishing I would never have to get up and leave.

When Venci and I stopped at last in front of Emily's apartment building, he leaned over to kiss my forehead and said,
somewhat wryly, "Give my regards to the *team.*" Venci was
jealous and suspicious of the girls, and the feeling was mutual.
He would become another part of my life that I couldn't really
share.

From that first date—if you could call it that—he and I
spent the next several weekends together, either in Sofia or in
Skopje: walking around arm in arm, sharing plates of fried
potatoes with cheese, drinking cups of espresso into which
Venci would carefully stir six thimblefuls of cream. At some
point, I realized: *I've got a boyfriend.* I didn't care that everyone
thought Venci was wrong for me. To me, he represented a
quiet form of rebellion. I even relished the opportunity to fill
out the CIA-required paperwork.

"Is it serious?" Scott asked me when I handed him the form
on which I'd designated my relationship with Venci as "intimate," hoping that Scott would not expect me to further
elaborate.

"Not really," I said, and—as if I needed to better justify myself—"He's more like a friend. I've known him for years."

"You've got a thing for Bulgarians?" Scott's friendly smile prevented me from taking offense. I was only half joking when I said, "Well, sir, we're not *allowed* to date Russians." Scott, who had served in Moscow during the Cold War, considered anyone from the Eastern bloc to be evil incarnate, and as Agency officers, we were in fact explicitly forbidden from having personal relationships with Russians.

"I'll send this in to Headquarters." Scott slipped my Close and Continuing Contact Form into a folder marked "Top Secret," although I was well aware that information on our personal lives was anything but top secret. "And we'll see what they say."

Scott had less of a problem with Venci than did Emma and Emily, both of whom found him toxic, depressive, and too demanding of my time. I started to split my weekends in Sofia: Saturdays with Venci, Sundays with the girls. His companionship was something I came to need. The simplicity of Venci's life seemed in such stark contrast to the increasing complexity of my own, and in that I found some small, inexplicable comfort.

The weekend Venci and I had gone to Svoge, I'd been away for all of half a day when Scott had called to beckon me home. The border did not close after all, and the following morning I made it back to Macedonia, where tensions were high on account of the Albanian rebels acting up again. A bomb had exploded at another Macedonian police station, claiming five more victims. Scott, when I finally met with him, said he wanted me to call out Ahmet for an emergency meeting.

"The seventh floor is on my case about the situation over here," Scott said. He always referred to Headquarters as if it were his meddlesome mother-in-law. "See if your guy has any intel on what the NLA's next move will be?"

Scott must have known, as I already did, that Ahmet was not intimate enough with the hard-core rebels to have so much as a clue as to their proposed plan of attack. Part of me suspected that Scott, or someone back at Headquarters, had guessed I was in Bulgaria with my new boyfriend, and summoned me just as a means of exerting control.

Macedonia had been teetering on the precipice of civil war for weeks now, a simmering pot we were all waiting to boil over. As spring approached, the attacks multiplied and the number of casualties mounted. The NLA even managed to completely overtake the village of Aracinivo, just on the outskirts of Skopje. I often fell asleep at night to the sound of gunfire and shelling in the not-too-distant hills.

Soon nearly all official American personnel were recalled; only officers deemed "essential to the mission" were permitted to stay. Those of us who worked for the CIA, of course, remained.

It was becoming less and less comfortable to exist as an American in Macedonia, where most of the population reviled us. The U.S. government's refusal to intervene in what Macedonian Slavs saw as a terrorist-driven plot to overtake their country represented the ultimate affront. The Macedonian leadership thought we owed them after they had agreed to construction of a U.S. Army base within the borders of FYROM. Not to mention that, at the behest of our government during and after the Kosovo crisis, Macedonia had taken in countless Albanian refugees.

"No good deed goes unpunished, eh?" an ever-more-belligerent Vassil, the rock climber, complained to me in one of our last phone conversations. "Isn't that how you guys say it in American?"

The American Embassy in Skopje had been attacked twice by mobs of angry Macedonians—rocks thrown through windows, diplomat-plated vehicles set ablaze, swastikas and "NATO = Nazi" scrawled in black and red spray paint across the embassy's once pristine white stucco walls.

After the second attack, an entire battalion of upright, close-cropped, and freshly scrubbed Marines arrived to protect the embassy. Whenever I passed the now heavily guarded compound, I would greet whichever young man happened to be on perimeter duty. Inevitably, the marine would nod curtly and say, "Morning, ma'am." This interaction with the marine guards soon became my singular daily encounter with civility.

In Skopje, I refrained from speaking English in public and I visited less and less frequently with the scant few Macedonian friends I had. Vassil and Gocé both were particularly bitter about the fact that rock climbing was now totally out of the question. The mountainous regions surrounding Skopje had been overrun by gun-toting Albanian guerrillas.

"They have ruined our country," Gocé said bitterly when we ran into each other one day, after weeks of not speaking. "And it is with the help of people like *you*."

I never knew how to respond to such accusations, especially given the nagging sense that the allegations might be true. Instinctually, I empathized with the Albanian rebels. But intellectually, I realized my affinity for the presumed underdogs had resulted from their almost innate skill at flattery and manipulation. While the Macedonians took every opportunity to rant against Americans, the Albanians were constantly blowing sunshine up our asses; it was natural to side with them over the Slavs.

Eventually, however, I was so hard-pressed to defend U.S. policy in Macedonia that I ceased almost entirely to develop Slav contacts. This frustrated Scott, who was under increasing pressure from Headquarters to obtain advance knowledge of both sides of the story.

Luckily, I looked and dressed enough like the local women that—as long as I kept my mouth shut—I was able to blend in. That said, my hostile neighbor never forgot where I came from, and by summertime she'd ceased speaking to me altogether.

About two weeks after the stray calico cat that I'd adopted gave birth to a litter, I came home to find the mother cat dead. The kittens were scattered about the yard, in various stages of expiring. Horrified, I watched the one kitten that was still gasping for life die, cupped in my hands. With a torrent of tears streaming down my face, I scooped each of the dead kittens and their mother into a garbage sack to dispose of.

"They were poisoned," Scott said the next day when I told him what had happened. "Our dog suffered a similar fate."

Sure enough, the Albanian gardener later discovered remnants of rat poison in and around the dish I had used for the mother cat's food. Outraged on my behalf by the cat massacre, he almost proudly presented me with the corroborating evidence: a powdery white substance sprinkled around the few remaining morsels of soggy cat food. As the gardener held up the small plastic bowl for my examination, I could not help but notice him casting a wary eye toward the neighbor's house.

After a while, the near-constant threat of violence in Macedonia became monotonous—like a noise that's grating at first but settles into dull, droning background. There was always another bombing, a roadside skirmish, a truck blown up by a land mine, a random firefight in the hills, more shelling of villages near the border.

Walking around Skopje—never a particularly pleasant pastime for me—grew into an eerily solitary endeavor. I almost missed the once-constant cacophony of the city and the affected aggression of its inhabitants. I figured that while the rest of Skopje hibernated, the few people who continued to venture out must be like me: up to no good.

As the security situation in Macedonia deteriorated, I had to be much more careful about surveillance detection. Even the urban streets were lined with sandbag dugouts, behind which the Macedonian military would hide from view. Teenage soldiers roved the city, carelessly swinging about their AK-47s. A drive into the hills was unthinkable; one was sure to be stopped, if not by the hapless Macedonian police or military, then at random roadside checkpoints manned by the more professional and intimidating-looking members of the

NLA. Once, when Emily visited me from Sofia, we watched a news report featuring a division of the Albanian guerrillas, marching in crisp and perfect formation through the abandoned center of a Macedonian town.

"My God, they're *hot*!" Emily exclaimed of the fit young men with their sharp features and piercing blue eyes. "I had no idea!"

Truly, the vigor and discipline of the NLA only made the Macedonian regiments—with their ill-fitting uniforms and shaggy-dog looks of surrender—seem all the more hopeless.

One unusually blustery Sunday, I spent the morning preparing to service a signal site. The site was at Panteleimon, an ancient monastery perched high on the western side of Mount Vodno, now home to a restaurant that boasted a spectacular view of the otherwise unspectacular city.

During training, I had considered the signal site exercises a waste of our time. "We'll never use this crap in real life," I remember complaining to Ethan after I'd spent two hours slogging around Colonial Williamsburg, looking for a place to plant a fake rock. The technique of communicating with agents—via chalk marks, discarded bricks, and scattered sunflower seeds—seemed to me archaic, not to mention inappropriate to any place except Moscow or Beijing, where the foreign intelligence services were so aggressive that it was impossibly risky to hold face-to-face meetings. But Scott had asked each of us to develop a signal site system for use with one of our agents: "All of you are relying way too much on telephone communication," he cautioned during a monthly convening of his small cadre of case officers.

My sign would be a charcoal slash mark on a concrete water well, situated in the parking lot behind the hilltop restaurant. This would alert the agent that I wanted to hold a meeting within twenty-four hours. The agent passed the site every Sunday at dusk, under the pretense of taking a diversionary drive up to the monastery. Upon seeing the charcoal slash mark, he would know to meet me the following day at five in the morning, at our usual spot.

I decided to ride my bike to the site, thinking I would create the appearance of someone out recreating on a Sunday afternoon. First, I would conduct a "bicyclical" surveillance-detection route through town. I slipped a charcoal briquette from the sack stored under the sink into my pocket, and went out the door. For almost two hours, I rolled aimlessly around the nearly abandoned city. A memorial service for some slain Macedonian soldiers had taken place the day before, and Skopje seemed even more somber and empty than usual.

Relatively sure that I had not been followed, I started up the incline toward Panteleimon. Just then, a Macedonian fighter jet—I'd been amazed to discover the country actually possessed a few—soared deafeningly, and it seemed to me dangerously close, overhead, causing me to veer headlong into the bushes. Collapsed under the frame of my ridiculously outmoded bicycle, I was sure that I looked something like Inspector Clouseau.

I struggled to my feet and started cycling again. Eventually, I reached the police checkpoint in front of the Hotel Panorama. The usual cadre of guards—seated around a poker table, eating grilled sausages and drinking coffee from a thermos—nonchalantly waved me on.

My legs burned as I pumped up the zigzag road. Soon the air seemed fresh and silent. I realized that I was blissfully alone, miles up and away from the gloomy city. As I neared the steep ascent that briefly plateaued at Sredna Vodno, Middle Vodno, I perceived three camouflage-clad, heavily armed soldiers swaggering toward me in the middle of the road. Their disorderly appearance would lead anyone unfamiliar with the terrain to believe they were guerrilla insurgents. To me, they looked like the riffraff of which the Macedonian Army was generally composed, except that these guys appeared ready and poised to conduct an attack. One was tall, dark, and lanky; another could not have been more than seventeen years old; the third was the most frightening looking—a short, unshaven man with a barrel belly and a camouflage bandanna tied backward, à la Che Guevara, around his head. As the distance between us narrowed, I noticed that the tall, lanky one had a small Macedonian flag sewn on the side of his jacket, and the short guy had a similar patch pinned to the front of his bandanna.

Judging by the trio's willful gait and aggressive air—highly uncharacteristic of the generally submissive Macedonian military—I seriously considered the possibility that these were NLA rebels who had ambushed and killed three Macedonian soldiers, disguised themselves in their victims' uniforms, and set about taking the mountain by surprise. Unsure of the men's allegiances, I decided to ride by them without a word. As I pedaled by, the youngest guy said something to me, which I did not understand, and the others broke into derisive laughter.

About half an hour later, I arrived at the Panteleimon parking lot, where I paused at the well to drink some water and slip the chunk of charcoal from my pocket. Quickly, I made a long, firm slash across the concrete. With the signal in place, I turned around to head back home.

The trio of armed soldiers was all but forgotten by the time I'd descended to Sredno Vodno. Rounding a turn, though, I suddenly caught a fleeting glimpse of the short one—obviously galvanized by my approach—leaping into the brush at the side of the road.

Holy shit! These guys are going to kill me, I thought as my tires screeched to a halt. My body was shaking, and I was quite sure that my heart lay beating wildly of its own accord somewhere on the pavement.

"Excuse me," I called—absurdly politely—into the shrubbery. When I heard nothing but rustling leaves and the click of a trigger being cocked, I abandoned any pretense of civility.

"Yebe ti maika!" I shouted, knowing that "Fuck your mother" was one of those remarkable Macedonian expressions that, notwithstanding its literal meaning, actually could impart a sense of camaraderie. "What the hell are you guys doing?"

Much to my surprise and relief, the three motley musketeers—led by the short, scary guy—filed sheepishly out of the bushes. They appeared embarrassed to have come close to launching an all-out assault on a girl on her bicycle.

"Se izvinuvam, se izvinuvam," they all excused themselves repeatedly. But their evident compunction only fortified my anger.

"Do I look like I'm *Ooo Che Kah*?" I demanded, using the Macedonian acronym for the NLA, while gesturing at my bicycle, Minnie Mouse T-shirt, and braided pigtails, to emphasize the ridiculousness of their aborted ambush.

The short, scary guy spoke. "Are you one of us?"

"No, I'm American," I said, though I realized that I was going out on a bit of a limb.

"But your parents are Macedonian, then?" he said.

"No, my parents are American."

The tall, lanky one who had been hanging back now sauntered up.

"I am Tony," he said in English, thrusting out his hand. Noticing that Tony wore a small earring, I suddenly felt inexplicably better. It was as if the little silver hoop were some sort of indication that these guys were just confused kids.

"Nice to meet you, Tony," I said, aware that our introduction was probably the first and last human interaction I would experience during the entire weekend. "I thought you guys were going to kill me."

Tony introduced the other two as Dragon—an apt name, I thought, for the short, scary guy—and the youngest one as Mitko. We all shook hands as if we'd just met at a cocktail party, as opposed to stalking through the bushes with AK-47s.

"I used to work for an American," Tony said. "Do you know Mr. Joe Forzani?"

I shook my head no.

"Oh." He looked somewhat surprised and disappointed. "Anyway. What are you?"

"A diplomat," I said uneasily.

"I mean, you don't look American," Tony said. "Like you should be taller and have blond hair or something."

"You've been watching too much *Baywatch*," I said, laughing. At the mention of *Baywatch*, Dragon and Mitko came to life, high-fived each other, and gave me the thumbs-up.

"*Baywatch*—super!" Dragon cried out, grinning from ear to ear.

"So you are not Macedonian at all?" Tony looked at me skeptically.

"My father's family came from Ireland and my mother's family came from Russia," I said, thinking I might use the opportunity to enlighten the young men about American multiculturalism. "I am half Catholic and half Jewish."

"See!" Tony shouted righteously at the other two, as if he'd just won a bet. "This is typical American—Irish Jew."

Meanwhile, I was wondering if the three of them had been among the demonstrators who had recently thrown rocks at the U.S. Embassy and set diplomatic cars on fire.

All of a sudden, Dragon shouted out and they all dove back into the brush. I was left standing with my bicycle, glancing around and wondering what wayward shepherd or picnicker would be targeted next. Not wanting to get caught in the cross fire, I waved once in their general direction and started to coast downhill.

"Hey, lady, can you wait?" It took Tony only a few seconds to abandon his post and jog up beside me. "When this thing is all over . . ." he gestured expansively at the surrounding hills, "I would like to get a visa to come to America."

"I also am half Greek, half Romanian," he said, as if evidence of mixed heritage would have particular sway. "But I am from Macedonia."

"You've got to go to the U.S. Embassy," I said. "Although after the attacks, I'm not sure they're doling out visas these days."

"You know, I used to work with Albanians," Tony said. "We worked with them in Kosovo. I had so many Muslim friends."

"And now?"

"Now I am a soldier. Now they are killing us, and so we must kill them," Tony said.

"What are you guys doing here on Vodno?" I said, recalling Scott's recent request that I develop more contacts among the emerging cadre of Macedonian extremists. "I mean, are you all expecting something to happen?"

"We are always expecting something," Tony said. "We are always prepared!" He paused before looking at me expectantly. "Anyway, what do you think? About the visa?"

"Meet me in this exact spot at the same time tomorrow," I said, already thinking about how I would race down to my office and write to Headquarters about this promising new contact.

TEN

My car has broken down in Bulgaria and I've got to get back to Macedonia for a meeting with Tony, my new developmental contact, so I'm taking the bus. Emily, thirsting for adventure, has decided to come with me.

Sofia's central bus station seems to accommodate the overflow of human misery from the train station about one hundred yards away. A Macedonian company called Nedezhda—meaning, ironically it appears, "hope"—operates the Sofia–Skopje run. By the looks of the bus, which we find parked at the far end of a muddy lot, one might assume this to be a retired vehicle: exterior paint entirely chipped off, doors rusted half shut, tires sagging under the weight of its passenger-packed frame. Inside is no better; the windows are so dirty you can't see out, and the smell of body odor could knock you over like a twenty-foot wave.

As Emily and I settle into a seat close to the rear, an enormous lady lugging an overstuffed sack walks back to the row opposite ours and, with a quick nod of acknowledgment, proceeds to take off her clothes. Within seconds, the lady is standing there in her enormous black bra and enormous black panties. She begins removing clothes from her sack and putting them on her body—one item after another.

By the time she's finished, the lady is wearing about ten blouses, four or five leather vests, a similar number of sweaters, and several pairs of pants. Now even more enormous than before, the lady can barely fit in the aisle as she waddles toward the front, her enormous rear end shimmying between the seats.

Emily and I look at each other, realizing at once that what we've witnessed is the groundwork laid by a small-time smuggler.

As it turned out, Emily and I were the only people on board the bus, aside from the driver, who were *not* small-time smugglers. All of the other passengers began pulling out their wares, trading them among one another, so that each person was smuggling the same amount of goods but had distributed them evenly enough among his compatriots so that he didn't have an overly suspicious quantity of any one item. The border guards would have to be deaf, dumb, and blind not to know what was going on, and I imagined most of them were routinely bribed, so this ritual, I supposed, was more symbolic than practical.

Shortly before we arrived at Kyustendil, the western Bulgarian border town, the bus ground to a hasty, gravel-spraying halt by the side of the road, the doors were flung open, and a whole slew of rowdy new passengers boarded. The newcomers were greeted warmly and familiarly with hearty hellos and slaps on the back.

Among the new group was a lady who seemed to be a ringleader of sorts. With her frosted blond bob falling over furtive eyes, she made quick work out of stashing various bottles of hard liquor in and around Emily and me. Natasha—she paused briefly to introduce herself—turned out to be the real pro. Once she'd finished sequestering the booze, she began tucking away vials of rip-off designer perfumes into the snug crevices between the seats and seat backs. Two subordinates aided Natasha in her labors: a somewhat less industrious woman with frizzy red hair and a scruffy, stubbly man who appeared to be totally drunk.

Their work at last complete, the redheaded woman and Natasha took a seat in front of us while the man collapsed in the row behind Emily and me, enveloping us in a cloud of alcohol fumes. For a large part of the trip, the man muttered angrily to an imaginary companion at his side. Every once in a while, he pulled himself up and made a point out of creating a certain amount of friction between his crotch and Emily's shoulder as he stumbled up and down the aisle. Occasionally, he'd break into song, a ditty he had evidently composed himself, the only line of which was *"Natasha, Natasha ot pet do dva"*—"Natasha, Natasha from five until two." Natasha totally ignored him, too busy trying to cajole Emily and me into hiding more moonshine in our overhead baggage. Emily pretended to be asleep and I feigned incomprehension until Natasha threw her hands up in disgust.

The driver soon stopped again, at a duty-free stand by the side of the road—well within earshot and eyesight of the border police—in order to facilitate the purchase of more bootleg liquor and a whole new hoard of goodies that the small-time smugglers efficiently squirreled away as soon as they were back on board.

We sat for close to an hour on the Bulgarian side of the border, waiting for our passports to be checked. When the border gendarme finally returned, he handed over the whole stack of documents to some random person seated in the front row. During the ensuing disorderly redistribution of the passports, there was a stir of disbelief among the smugglers when Emily and I were exposed as Americans. A mob formed around the person who'd made the discovery, and every other passenger then pawed and scrutinized our passports, admiring their superior quality and appearance. Natasha even held our documents up to the light as if to determine if they were counterfeit.

As I dejectedly skimmed through the little blue book that had been returned to me smudged and tattered, Emily nudged me and nodded toward a hitherto unnoticed gentleman gaping maniacally through the space between two seats. With his shaved head, wild eyes, and flaring nostrils—one of which he was busily excavating—the man bore the closest resemblance to complete lunacy I'd ever seen. When we all disembarked in order to have our luggage searched, I half expected to see him in shackles.

After an outrageously cursory luggage inspection, our bus inched forward, only to be caught in the no-man's-land between the Bulgarian and Macedonian borders for another two hours, during which time the lunatic continued to gawk at us and the raving drunk got drunker and louder. Emily's patience wore so thin that she begged me to make use of my diplomatic status to get us through the border.

I was traveling on a tourist passport so as not to draw attention to myself, but I did have my diplomatic passport, concealed in a secret compartment within my purse—just in case. I was glad of that, at least, since it seemed there was a good chance Emily and I would be arrested for whatever crap we were unwittingly transporting across the border.

"You could pretend that you're doing some sort of frontier security check," said Emily, brimming with ideas. "Or you could say you have an important meeting with the ambassador tonight!"

I wished that I could tell Emily that I wasn't even really a diplomat. It was late and, at this rate, we didn't stand to roll into Skopje until midnight, well after my scheduled meeting with Tony. I was just as anxious as Emily to get moving. Finally, I marched to the front of the bus, where I woke up the heavily snoring driver: "What is the problem here?"

The driver rubbed his knuckles into his eye sockets and yawned. "The police."

"I am a diplomat." I flashed the black document that I'd recovered from its secret compartment. "Do you think I could go talk to them and we could get across the border faster?"

The driver shrugged and sighed heavily. "They just don't understand us," he said, as if we were all a bunch of troubled adolescents.

Meanwhile, several of the small-time smugglers, curious to know what I was up to, encroached upon me from behind. Eventually, everyone agreed that there was no hope of wielding any sort of influence over the border police. They broke into a mumbling chorus about the injustice of our shared lot in life. Emily and I, it seemed, had become honorary members of their corps.

Later, when we were at long last on the Macedonian side of the border, another border gendarme arrived to demand our passports. This time, I immediately handed over my diplomatic passport, which impressed the border gendarme so much that he allowed Emily and me the special privilege of remaining on the bus, as opposed to standing out in the cold, while the superficial customs inspection took place. On the bus, Emily and I watched a trio of customs inspectors' eyes graze over the many bottles, like poorly hidden Easter eggs amid the luggage rack and between the seats.

Once everyone reboarded, we discovered how much of a pro Natasha actually was as she started pulling one after another bottle out from around Emily and me, none of which we'd even seen her stash. I half expected to find a flask of Jack Daniel's in my own butt crack when I went to bed that night.

But, at that point, we'd just crossed the border and bed was still hours away. The driver, suddenly anxious to get to Skopje, was accelerating so fast that I worried perhaps he'd fallen asleep at the wheel; the way we careened around each hairpin turn along this mountainous road was the only evidence to the contrary.

The drunken man, meanwhile, had become agitated and was shouting at Natasha's redheaded friend in Serbian, which unfortunately I could understand. The litany of insults was linked thematically by repetition of the phrase "up your mother's pussy." Shortly thereafter, his attention turned from Natasha's friend (and her mother's pussy) to Emily and me. Having stumbled up a few rows, he consorted with the escaped lunatic, trying to convince him that the two of them stood a chance with us, and cataloging our many fetching attributes. Depressed that these two considered us not only in their league, but also the most likely potential conquests on the bus, Emily and I leaned into each other and pretended to be asleep.

The drunken man finally gave up and lurched his way back to the seat in front of us, where—in an evident fit of remorse—he flopped onto the redhead and began to stroke her head as if she were a dying pet. At first, the redhead swatted at him as if shooing away a horsefly, but then she seemed to lose the energy to object and so snuggled into his shoulder.

The bus driver had forgone the routine dinner stop— probably on account of my "urgent meeting with the American ambassador"—so by the time we pulled into Skopje, we were starving. We reached the downtown McDonald's just on the verge of closing for the night and spurred an immediate flurry of activity. The cheerful staff started heating up the deep fryers and plugging back in the milk-shake machine, whose familiar purr soothed my soul. In Skopje, McDonald's—I'd come to realize—was much more of a friendly haven than even the American Embassy. With Emily by my side and a hamburger poised in front of my mouth, my shoulders began to relax and I felt just a little bit less lost. *Now, what to do about Tony?*

American intervention finally came to Macedonia in the form of a hard-charging, no-nonsense "special envoy" named James Pardew. During the long, dry summer, Ambassador Pardew presided over several days of heated debate between Macedonia's Slav and Albanian leaders at a posh presidential compound alongside Lake Ohrid, where he finally brokered an albeit tenuous peace agreement between the Macedonian government and the NLA. The summer of 2001 brought to Skopje an eerie and unexpected sense of calm.

The consensus among the CIA's Balkan analysts was that if violence erupted again in Macedonia, it would be *not* on account of the NLA or any other Albanian rebel group, but of the Lions, a rogue police force composed of Macedonian ultranationalists, many of whom were former criminals. The Lions' chief mandate—as dictated by their xenophobic leader, Macedonian minster of internal affairs Ljube Boskovski—was the nebulous charge of protecting Macedonia *for Macedonians*. Dubbed "Mini Milosevic," Boskovski condoned the group's thuggish antics, which included marauding about Skopje—fueled by bitterness and booze—beating up ordinary citizens.

Having personally sanctioned this assemblage of hooligans and convicts, Boskovski also saw to it that the Lions were better paid and better armed than the other quasi-valid paramili-tary forces: the Tigers, another component of the Macedonian police; the Wolves, the Macedonian Army's elite special forces unit; and the Scorpions, a group whose responsibilities no one was quite sure about. All these childish animal kingdom names seemed only to highlight the amateurism of the country's en-tire security apparatus.

Still, Scott was anxious for me to recruit someone from one of these groups. "We've got a handle on the Albanians," he said. "But the Slav nationalists are a real unknown."

As my unfathomable good luck would have it, Tony—the visa-seeking combatant from Mount Vodno—had a close friend who was a Lion.

"I'd like to meet him," I told Tony over a middle-of-the-night whiskey when he mentioned his radical friend Dimé. "We know the Lions orchestrated the attack on the American Embassy," I said. "And that they pretty much hate us. But it would be helpful to understand *why*."

"No problem," said Tony, forever focused on obtaining a visa. "We will go make party on the weekend."

That Saturday night, I met Tony and Dimé—as well as Dimé's visibly pregnant wife, Snežna—in front of the Trgovski Centar, the strip mall that formed Skopje's social nucleus. Paunchy and greasy, Dimé sported a scraggly goatee, slicked-back hair, a few gold chains, and a large platinum ring—adorned with, I noted, the Lion insignia. Snežna looked as if she might give birth any minute.

There was the usual hemming and hawing about which of

the three totally identical Trgovski Centar bars we would go to, until Dimé and Tony finally agreed on a pizzeria called Rimi-Parigi, Rome-Paris—yet another example of almost poignant wishful thinking on the part of Macedonian management.

Dimé, Tony, and I all ordered beers while Snežna lit up a cigarette and demanded a double vodka. Dimé seemed pleased to no end that an American was interested in hearing his point of view. He proudly informed me that he headed the Lions' unit in his neighborhood of Kisela Voda—literally, "Sour Water"—and he was more than happy to share his life story, which included a brief foray behind bars for "making the wrong guys angry." Boskovski had personally offered Dimé the opportunity to redeem himself by becoming a certified police officer with a newly formed regiment called the Lions. Dimé naturally felt deep gratitude for this break.

"I already had some expertise, you know," he said. "Anyway, Tony mentioned to me you are a diplomat and you are interested in what we are thinking about Americans."

"Yes," I said. "A lot of Macedonians are unwilling to meet with someone like me."

"Well, lemme tell you." Dimé leaned forward. "You guys are making a big mess of everything in this country."

Tony reclined in his chair with a look of smug satisfaction, as if Dimé had just articulated everything he'd been dying to say himself but couldn't—not without jeopardizing his chances of obtaining a visa.

"When you give help to these Albanians," Dimé said, "is like sending money directly to Usama bin Laden."

I was impressed that Dimé had any idea who bin Laden was, since at the time most Americans didn't. But in the Balkans, there'd already been much speculation about the Saudi fugitive, his alleged support of the Kosovo Liberation Army, and Albanian rebels who'd supposedly trained at Al-Qa'ida-run terrorist camps. Long before Usama bin Laden would become a household name at home, a few wary Macedonians, like Dimé, obviously viewed him as a significant threat.

Dimé ranted through our second round of drinks, after which I felt as if I ought to engage Snežna. She'd been sitting there silently, using her front teeth to peel away minuscule slivers of her thumbnail.

"So when are you due?" I said.

"Any day now." Snežna smiled and downed the last gulp of her second double vodka. It was disconcerting to be chatting with a pregnant woman obviously on the verge of a total bender.

"Will you go to the Centralna Bolnica?" I asked, referring to Skopje's main hospital, a sprawling cluster of buildings that looked more like an industrial plant than a place of healing. The children's ward, in particular, I recalled as an awful asylum like something out of *Oliver Twist*.

"No, I will go to new private hospital." Snežna spoke in heavily accented English. "It is, by our standards, how do you say . . . steak of the ark."

"This place for Snežna is very expensive," Dimé chimed in, obviously annoyed that attention had been diverted away from him.

"Well I am sure it's well worth it." I nodded cheerfully.

"Dimé thinks it's a waste of money," Snežna said, and threw her husband a malicious glare.

Not wanting to become embroiled in domestic discord, I excused myself to use the ladies' room. When I returned, Dimé was paying the bill and a plan was under way to transfer our party to a place "more like a discotheque."

When I proffered that such an establishment might not be so appealing to "the baby"—really I was thinking of Snežna—she patted her stomach and said, "It's okay. He's sleeping now."

We moved onward in typical Skopje style: all of us piling into Dimé's car to drive a single city block.

The next bar was not so much a discotheque as a smoky, loud, cavernous basement, populated by clusters of patrons ranging in age from about fifteen to fifty-five. Dimé knew the owner, and so we were seated instantly at the one unoccupied table, that had been cordoned off with a thick rope. A small "reserved" card in its center bore Dimé's name and—yet again—the Lion insignia.

As the night wore on, it became increasingly difficult for me to hear what Dimé was saying, though I assumed it to be mere variations on his earlier themes. Friends of Dimé had joined us: a few more Lions, a Tiger, two Wolves, and one Scorpion. *Scott will be so proud!*

"This guy is part of our Rapid Reaction Force," Dimé said admiringly of the Scorpion, a big oafish fellow.

The cadre was composed entirely of enormous guys, many with lots of tattoos and a gnarly selection of teeth. They all knew each other and Dimé well, but seemed a bit perplexed by me.

In time, the owner of the establishment also joined us. Dimé introduced him as "Freddy . . . an important businessman."

"How much money for American visa?" Freddy said, grimacing. "I pay big!" He rubbed his thumb and forefinger together in the air.

The blaring techno music prevented me from hearing most of what was being said, but I did comprehend that Freddy also owned a restaurant, to which I was invited the following week for dinner.

"Great," I said, already anticipating how pleased Scott, not to mention Headquarters, would be when I reported back on my newfound social circle.

Just as I was starting to lose interest in the scene altogether—not to mention growing ever more concerned about pregnant Snežna, who, despite the din, somehow had managed to doze off under a cloud of cigarette smoke—a dozen police officers stormed through the front door. The music was turned off at once, and all of the lights switched on. Everybody was shouting at each other in the sudden silence and blinking their eyes to adjust to the light.

"Identification cards out!" one of the storm troopers shouted. "And if you're carrying a weapon, put it on the table!"

Everyone—including my brutish company—dutifully followed the police officer's directive. Each guy reached into his leather jacket to produce a gun. Evidently, I was one of the few people in the establishment *not* packing heat. I found myself facing an array of weaponry—including a small cluster of hand grenades—on our tabletop, as well as nearly every other tabletop.

The storm troopers made the rounds, checking ID cards and inspecting all—but not confiscating any—of the weapons. At our table, they merely shook hands with everyone, including me, and didn't take a look at any of our IDs, or bat an eye at the centerpiece of artillery.

Their work evidently done, the cadre of storm troopers began to filter out the door. As the lights were turned back off and the music back on, Dimé leaned over to me and whispered, "These guys are undercover Lions. They work for me." I found it infinitely amusing that the undercover Lions' means of disguise was to alter their dress from biker gang to that of ordinary cops.

"I'm outta here," I finally said, but not before slipping Dimé my card. "Here's my number. Give me a call. I think we should meet again."

The day after Snežna gave birth to a *healthy*—I was pleased and shocked to discover—baby girl, Dimé called me in order to arrange dinner at Freddy's restaurant for the following Friday night. Emily had gone back to Bulgaria, but Emma would be staying with me that weekend and, since it was only an exploratory meeting, I said I would bring her along.

"Super," Dimé said. "I will leave my wife at home."

"Are these guys friends of yours?" Emma asked when I told her about the plan to meet Dimé for dinner at Freddy's restaurant.

"Not really," I said. "It's just kind of good for me to branch out."

"I wish I had a clue what exactly you do," Emma said, and laughed.

We met Dimé in front of the Trgovski Centar, from which we all set out in his brand-spanking-new BMW for Freddy's restaurant. "Restaurant" turned out to be a bit of an exaggeration. Dimé pulled into a deserted lot on the outskirts of town—where, coincidentally, I'd once held an agent meeting—and we stomped across the gravel toward a seedy-looking structure with a large red and yellow Macedonian flag hung over the single window.

Inside, we found four tables arranged symmetrically around a smoke-filled, brightly lit chamber. Huddles of men in red workers' jumpsuits sat hunched over a menagerie of empty shot glasses and beer bottles. An enormous map of "ancient Macedonia," which of course had occupied a considerably grander area than the country does today, adorned the wall behind the "bar," a water-warped linoleum countertop.

Freddy—his arms flung open expansively—strode over to greet us and, with a salacious glance toward Emma, took her arm and led our party to the one free table. He motioned to a pallid waiter to come over and take our order.

I followed Dimé's example and ordered *rakija*, while Emma, much to the silent derision of the others, asked for a glass of white wine. Freddy joined our table, as did another man who introduced himself as "Herr Direk-*tor* of the Skopje Zoo." It was hard to greet him warmly after my one and only visit there with Venci. The creatures, it was plain to see, received no nourishment aside from peanuts and candy that passersby would slip through gaps in a chain-link fence. They appeared uniformly weak with hunger and visibly malnourished. In the reptile house, we'd come upon a glass terrarium with a huge shattered hole in its side, from which whatever snake once resided there obviously had long since slithered out. The monkey house had been in a similar state of shameful neglect: With no trees from which to swing or leaves on which to nibble, the chimps squatted amid trash in the corners of their cells, with expressions of depressed resignation. I'd wanted to leave immediately after that, but Venci had insisted we visit the "aviary." In the single gargantuan cage lay a dead, headless buzzard, belly-down on the floor. Ironically, I reflected, the lions were no better cared for: housed in a stinky little shack in which half a dozen breeds of emaciated felines paced restlessly.

My reverie about the Skopje Zoo—which in fact was more like an animal concentration camp—was broken when Freddy suddenly shouted, "Motherfuckers!" The conversation at the table had evidently turned to politics, and Freddy was animatedly explaining to Emma how Albanian culture was the root of all evil, with American culture running a close second. Emma, as a native Bulgarian, could comprehend his Macedonian perfectly well, but she wisely pretended not to understand, prompting him to shout in English, "Muslim is shit!" He made a loud farting noise with his lips and then pantomimed two cupped palms to indicate an imaginary dump. Emma was looking at me, obviously baffled by my choice of new acquaintances.

"You can tell Albanians by their smell," Freddy bellowed

across the table, prompting the zookeeper to nod his head in agreement.

"Is awful smell like burning fat," he went on. "Like the burning fat of a pig, you know, when you cook this pig."

An ever more agitated Emma whispered to me, "Um, how long are we thinking of hanging out here?" I felt bad that I had brought her along at all.

"It is not precisely the smell of burning fat," the zookeeper ventured in an almost clinical, scientific tone. He paused while the waiter delivered dinner: an oval-shaped platter with a few slices of cucumber, a smattering of cherry tomatoes, and some chunks of white cheese.

"They have the smell of animals," the zookeeper continued. "I should know."

"And the Albanian woman!" Freddy erupted again, throwing his arms into the air. "Their breath!"

Making a long sweeping hand gesture from his gaping mouth, he exhaled gutturally to indicate something like a fire-breathing dragon.

Again the zookeeper weighed in: "These people stink because of their diet. Not like us." He nodded at the somewhat pitiable platter of crudités. "The Macedonian salad is good for digestive. The best in the world."

This gave me an idea for a means of escape. I clutched my stomach and croaked to Freddy, "Toilet?!"

"No toilet," he said merrily. "Bucket out back."

I made an exaggerated performance of lurching toward the door, and by the time I returned, Dimé had discovered Emma's Bulgarian heritage.

"You grandfather probably raped my grandmother in Second War," he morbidly joked with her.

"Emma and I have to go," I said to Dimé. "I'm not feeling well." Unfortunately, I could already foresee that Scott would be beside himself with excitement over Dimé, whom he'd surely want me to pursue. I glanced at Freddy, his face planted on the table. The buzz of Emma's and my imminent departure enlivened him, and he suddenly sprang to life, jumping up and roaring, "We go now listen Macedonian national music!"

When at last we had extricated ourselves from the smoky shack, Emma and I ran toward the street and let loose with howls of laughter.

"How do you deal with that shit?!" Emma said as we stood panting by the side of the road.

"I don't know."

"I mean, is it your job to meet with people like Dimé and Freddy? Because I can't imagine why else you would hang out with these jokers!"

"I know," I said. "It's crazy."

"I hope it's all worth it." Emma had turned from me and was looking out toward the misty, rain-slicked street. "I mean, you would know. I am just counting on that fact—that you, and *whoever* it is you work for, that you guys know more than someone like me."

As it turned out, neither I nor the people I worked for knew any more than Emma. The myth of the all-knowing, omnipotent Central Intelligence Agency turned out to be just that—a myth. And it was shattered not just for all its employees, but also for all the Americans whom we failed, in a single day.

. . .

A few weeks later, I went for a routine appointment at the Macedonian gynecologist. I liked Dr. Tuporkovski, though I had some reservations about her expertise—ever since she'd warned me I could get chlamydia from swimming in Lake Ohrid, and other sexually transmitted diseases from Western-style toilet seats. Dr. Tuporkovski always performed a mercifully cursory gynecological exam, and spent the rest of the time regaling me with stories about her own remarkably active and varied sex life. I visited her less for any health-related purposes than because I got a kick out of her racy narratives and harebrained medical theories. In addition to her other warnings, she routinely cautioned me against dating Balkan men.

"The man are having stronger sperm over here," she said, peeking her head over the white sheet draped like a theater curtain between my knees. "Not the weak sperm like in America. You must to be careful or you will end up with baby."

"Thanks for the advice," I said.

"And I am telling you, this guy will never take care for this baby," she went on. "Our men are having the strong sperm, but they are all bums."

"Good! You are not swimming in the Lake Ohrid, I see," she said, shedding her rubber gloves with a sigh of satisfaction. "And I hope you are finished with that *Bulgarian*." Dr. Tuporkovski always mispronounced the word, saying "that Vulgarian."

"Venci?" I supposed I was done with him. We'd spent half a year together doing nothing. During all of the turmoil,

Venci had stayed with me in Skopje for weeks at a time. I would come home after a long day at work and find him clipping his toenails on the sofa and watching *Psycho* from my collection of DVDs for the umpteenth time.

We always made noodles and butter for dinner, because Venci felt emasculated if I bought anything more extravagant. I supposed it had started to wear on both of us that I was always sneaking out and that when I came home—harried and exhausted after an agent meeting, neither one of us had anything to say. I supposed I'd found one too many hardened pellets of chewing gum, which Venci always saved for later use. And I supposed I'd wearied of his depressive silences and bitter smirks and the endless assortment of makeshift ashtrays that adorned every surface of my house.

Gradually, as the past winter had thawed into spring, I'd stopped telling Venci when I was coming to Sofia on the weekends. The last time I saw him was weeks before, the day we went to his father's tiny flat in Mladost—meaning "Youth." Venci's father was a *Picture of Dorian Gray* version of Venci himself, in whose eyes you could see a lifetime of wrong choices. A brawny uncle, minuscule grandmother, and Venci's bright-eyed little sister were there as well, each of them bustling about the apartment trying to find food or beverage for me, an obviously unexpected guest. I wondered if Venci had ever even told them about me.

Later, a cousin arrived: a total fixer-upper Brad Pitt lookalike who, as far as I could tell, had just come from fishing on the Danube. He stood in the doorway in huge rubber coveralls, a rod and reel in one hand and a big metal bucket in the other, his piercing blue eyes regarding me. At one point, I saw him wink at Venci and give him the thumbs-up.

The whole family, in fact, was beside themselves to be hosting an American, and rarely took their eyes from me. We all downed shot after shot of vodka from cracked teacups and ate unidentifiable lamb innards with thin, salty gravy poured on top. Later, the cousin fried up his catch, and while the rest of us picked it apart from a platter that was precariously balanced atop an overturned bucket, he produced a map of Bulgaria and started planning where he would take Venci and me for a fishing expedition upon my next visit.

At some point, I must have passed out in a drunken stupor on the couch. When Venci gently shook me awake, the whole gang shouted *"Nazdravey!"*—"To your health!"—in my face, raising their vodka-filled teacups to the ceiling.

It was then that I felt the walls closing in around me.

Venci's hopeless situation—poor, without prospects, and saddled with this totally dysfunctional, but somehow charming, family—had at one time seemed a little romantic. Now it all just seemed sad. As Venci's family members stared hopefully into my groggy eyes, I realized what they must be thinking: *She's his ticket* out!

Later, Venci and I shuffled wordlessly back to Emily's apartment, where he would leave me for the night. I felt like I could not take in enough air.

"You know, there is a joke about Bulgarians," Venci said suddenly, seeming to read my mind. "A Bulgarian guy goes to Hell and the Devil is showing him around. For every country, there is like a pit of burning flames—and at top, a guard to keep the people from climbing out. But when the Devil gets to the pit for Bulgaria, there is no guard there. 'Hey,' the Bulgarian guy says. 'Why is there no guard at Bulgaria's pit of burning flames?' 'Well,' the Devil answers, 'we don't need one here. When one guy starts to climb out, another Bulgarian will reach up and pull him down.'"

I chuckled in spite of the shudder in my heart. The telling of this joke was probably the most words Venci had ever said to me at one time. When he leaned in to kiss me in front of Emily's apartment building door, which—it occurred to me—Venci himself had never walked through, I think we both knew. I wasn't about to let myself be pulled down.

"Yeah, I am finished with the Bulgarian," I told Dr. Tuporkovski. At the end of my examination, she gave me a clean bill of health.

Appointment over, I walked out into Skopje. The day—September 11, 2001—was unusually lovely. I decided to leave my car in front of the doctor's building and stroll across the city toward the office, sucking in the scent of honeysuckles and enjoying the balmy breeze. I wanted to postpone my return to the tiny, windowless chamber where I would sit, writing up tedious correspondences to Headquarters, for the rest of the day.

Scott was waiting for me when I arrived. It was close to three in the afternoon.

"A plane flew into the World Trade Center," he said.

"Really?" I said, turning on my computer as I pictured a

small, four-person Cessna—the kind that my father and brother had flown recreationally when I was young—veering off course. "That's too bad. Was anybody killed?"

Later, I would look back on that moment and realize the absurdity of my question. How ridiculous even that Scott and I should be talking about this in such terms. We worked for the CIA, for chrissake. Shouldn't we have known?

I reached Emma—who had returned to New York City the week before—from my office phone minutes after I watched the second plane slam into the second tower on CNN. The moment of impact seemed unrealistically horrific, like something out of a video arcade game. Emma's line was busy and busy. I must have punched in the numbers twenty times before she finally answered the phone.

"Hullo?" she moaned weakly.

"Are you okay?"

As soon as Emma heard my voice, she burst into concerted sobbing.

"I can't believe you got through to me," she said, gasping for breaths between her words. "My phone hasn't worked. I can't call anyone. Linz, what am I supposed to do?"

"I don't know," I said.

"What the hell is going on," Emma wailed into the phone. She was clearly close to hysterics. "Did you guys *know*?"

Emma's question would haunt me for hours, days, weeks, months to come.

"No," I said. "We didn't know."

. . .

Emily took the Nedezhda (Hope!) bus from Sofia to Skopje later that day.

"I'd feel better if I were with you," she said over the phone. "And my parents said, 'Go stay with Lindsay.' They think you'll know what this is all about."

By evening, Emily and I were stationed in front of my television, watching CNN. It was a position we would take up night after night for a month, until mid-October, when Emily would fly to her parents' home in Kansas.

I woke up every morning for a week thinking, *Oh God, what a terrible dream I had last night,* and wondering why Emily was lying next to me. As my mind floated back to the image of a plane crashing, or a tower collapsing, or the Pentagon in flames, it took a few minutes to remember that none of it was a dream. In the evenings, Emily and I obsessively took turns on my computer, checking our e-mail for word from home. We kept the television on day and night.

Two nights after the attacks, a group of Macedonian ultra-nationalists hired a four-man band and rejoiced in front of the American Embassy.

The next day, I couldn't even look anyone in the eye. I kept my eyes straight ahead and my mouth fixed in a taut, angry frown, until I came home to Emily, who, like a wife, had straightened the house and prepared something for us to eat. We sustained ourselves on bottle after bottle of red wine. In the mornings, we poured Baileys Irish Cream into our coffee because neither one of us had the energy or inclination to go buy milk. Among the Macedonians, there lingered the inevitable impulse to gloat.

One night, my vile neighbor jauntily hauled a sack of groceries from her car. It looked to me as if she were planning some sort of celebratory feast.

"I am sorry for your country," Vassil called to say. "But only a little. Now you know how we feel."

Ahmet also called, but he was brimming with what seemed like sincere remorse.

"Where can we give our blood?" Ahmet asked, speaking not only for himself but his fellow Albanians. "We want to send our blood to New York. America is our brother." In addition to genuine sympathy, Ahmet probably felt panicky about the very real prospect that the events of September 11 would sour the United States' relationships with Muslims worldwide.

I couldn't focus at all on my work. Scott, trying to maintain some sense of normalcy, kept asking me if I'd met with Ahmet or Dimé or that suspect Russian intel guy whom I'd bumped into at a cocktail party a few weeks back. I didn't care. Who would care, I thought, when our whole world has been turned upside down? Now I truly felt exiled and useless in Macedonia, while the real work of the CIA would be getting under way in some other part of the world.

One gloriously sunny but crisp fall day, I stood outside the American Embassy. As I looked up at the half-mast flag, my mind wandered toward home. I thought about all the people I knew in New York and Washington—friends and colleagues—but, most of all, I thought about James.

I already knew he was okay. He'd been one of the first to respond to my widely distributed e-mail, whose subject line
read: *Please let me know you're safe.*

"I'm fine," James had written. "As a photographer, I guess
I'm supposed to run out to the Pentagon and take a bunch of
pictures. But somehow I can't bring myself to do it."

I wanted to write James and tell him that I knew how he felt,
but what could I say: *As a CIA agent, I guess I was supposed to
prevent things like this from happening. But somehow I couldn't
bring myself to do it.*

I stood staring at the flag that seemed to be waving for-
lornly, like a woman on a wharf waving good-bye to a ship as
it pulls out to sea. The nausea of a hangover—Emily and I
must have gone through three bottles of wine between the two
of us—combined with feelings of guilt, impotence, sorrow,
and above all, anger. I felt anger such as I'd never known myself capable of—anger at the terrorists (whoever they were), of
course, but, more than that, anger at myself and at the entire
CIA. My feelings of frustration suddenly coalesced into an unprecedented display of sobbing and an unstoppable flow of
tears. I wrapped my arms around my shaking body.

"Are you okay, ma'am?" asked an embassy guard, suddenly
standing beside me and proffering a tissue. "Ma'am, why don't
you take yourself on home now."

"Okay, yeah," I managed, refusing the tissue as I wiped my
face with my fists.

As my misfortune would have it, that day, the Screaming
Bible Lady was in the vicinity. An altogether mad Macedonian

woman who occasionally showed up at the U.S. Embassy, she would shake a Bible in her white-knuckled fist and shriek out condemnations of America. She'd apparently shown up about the same time as me.

"And another thing!" the Bible Lady now shouted to the embassy guards and small crowd that had gathered. "Look at this prostitute!" She shook her Bible at me. "PROSTITUTE! AMERICAN PROSTITUTE! AMERICAN PROSTITUTE! PROSTITUTE! PROSTITUTE! PROSTITUTE!"

She chanted at full volume until I had reached my car, where—once inside, with the tinted windows shielding me— I began to drive away, and also to laugh. I laughed and laughed—loud, hyena-style shrieks—and pounded my fist on the dashboard. I laughed until I cried again, when I reached the intersection where my favorite little Gypsy girl often stood begging. With her finely tuned radar, which always seemed to detect the approach of my car, she bounded over from the other side of the road. I opened my window to reveal her beaming, ever-optimistic face.

"*Kak si?*" she said, asking how I was and tilting her pretty head to one side.

"I'm okay," I said. "You know something bad happened in my country."

"I know," she said. She reached in and brushed a tear from my cheek. "Hey. Don't cry. It will be okay."

I thanked the Gypsy girl, gave her some change and a lipstick from my purse, and then drove off, marveling at this sly little street urchin.

"It *will* be okay," I told myself. "Now my job will have meaning. Now I really have something to do."

I will make it up to the Agency by relinquishing my misgivings and ambivalence, I thought. *And the Agency, in turn, will make it up to everyone else.*

ELEVEN

A slack-jawed teenager I assume to be the lifeguard stares at me in anticipation as I lower myself into the brackish water. My goggles prove useless since the pool water is nearly opaque. I end up smacking my face into the concrete wall as I come in for the turn. I complete two laps, twice down and back, the lifeguard watching me the whole time in evident disbelief.

If I'm going to get chlamydia *anywhere*, it's sure to be here, *I think as I pause at the ledge to swat away a floating hairball that seems to be pursuing me from one end of the pool to the other.* Great. I'll arrive home fat and angry and with an STD.

I am trying to get in shape, a few weeks before I return to Washington, D.C., for the first time in almost two years.

I start to swim again. With each breath, I glance out the enormous floor-to-ceiling windows that run the length of the building.

It's December, and in the distance, patches of snow coat Mount Vodno.

When I get home, I will see James. I'll talk to him about swimming. I'll tell him about this and the Soviet-style pool in Sofia, and the jumping trout in Lake Ohrid, and the crystal-clear blue waters of northern Greece where—before Macedonia went to hell in a handbasket—I occasionally took the girls in the summertime. Even when I travel in alias, I almost always manage to find some place to swim: in the baths of Budapest, along the shores of Cyprus, at some sports hall in Belgrade, next to a bombed-out building. (Truly, I have no excuse for being the lard-ass that I am today.) I will talk to James about swimming because swimming is one of the only parts of my life here that I can share with James.

I think about how many miles I've swum over the course of the past several months: lap after lap and stroke after stroke of planning surveillance-detection routes, rehashing agent meetings, worrying whether anyone has followed me, deciding upon the next lie I will tell Venci or my family or the girls.

One cupped handful at a time, I try to feel nothing but the water through which I move. I try to let the water wash away my troubled thoughts. I try to let it carry me somewhere, anywhere, but wherever I happen to be.

When Scott approved my leave request to attend my brother's wedding back in the States, I felt like a prisoner who'd just been granted furlough. Surprised and grateful, I started to plan my trip: Christmas shopping at the Albanian bazaar; a pedicure at Skopje's swankest salon; notices to all my agents and contacts that I would be gone for a whole month.

But as I began to pack my favorite outfits, it seemed that none of them fit. I struggled with buttons that popped off onto the floor like tiddlywinks, I yanked zippers that got stuck halfway up my crotch, I got my head caught in too-small sweaters and then lurched about the bedroom like a big blind bear. At last, I crumpled in front of the closet atop a heap of discarded items, where I began to come to grips with the depressing reality that being a spy—months of sitting in cars running interminable agent meetings, then sitting at desks writing countless cables back to Headquarters—had left me fat and angry.

Feeling a desperate urge to get in shape, and *fast*, I decided to brave Skopje's public swimming pool, which, from the outside, bore the look of an abandoned insane asylum. Once I'd paid my hundred-dinar entrance fee, a pool matron wrapped in a white laboratory coat grabbed my hand and yanked me into to the disconcertingly coed dressing room, which at that moment was occupied by a dozen teenage boys. The boys hurled a medley of what I could only assume to be derogatory slurs in my general direction.

I furtively changed into my bathing suit behind a wooden plank door, and then the lab-coated pool matron reappeared and dragged me through a small reservoir of some ankle-deep sludge.

"Must to disinfect feets," she said of the filthy footbath. She led me down a dark corridor to an Olympic-sized pool, which was more like an enormous algae-filled aquarium. The only other swimmer was got up in complete scuba gear.

I donned my cap and goggles and prepared, against all better judgment really, to submerge myself. *James would be proud of me*, I thought. And seconds later: *James is probably married by now.*

Although he hadn't *sounded* married when I spoke to him on the phone.

"I'll believe it when I see it," James had said when I called him on a whim, not expecting him to answer. When he did, I'd practically shouted, "I'm coming home for a month!"

He had sounded cheerful, and even hopeful, I thought. He'd said, "I guess we can finally go out for that beer you've been promising me for the past two years."

I'd dissected our three-minute phone conversation for hours. *What did he mean by he'll believe it when he sees it? Has my inability to come home made me seem like a flake? When had I promised him a beer? I don't recall a beer ever being discussed. Was this his way of asking me out for a beer? Had he really kept track of the time since I'd left?*

All I knew was that the thought of seeing James again filled me with a queasy sensation, somewhere between anticipation and dread.

In the aftermath of September 11, I should have felt motivated to be a better case officer. But the actions, or lack thereof, of the CIA had caused me to lose faith altogether. The attacks in New York and Washington had sent everyone at Headquarters into a tailspin: to view 9-11 as anything but a massive intelligence failure, we all knew, was sheer denial. Everybody at the Agency was wondering where we had gone wrong, and what the hell we were supposed to do now.

I could no longer perceive the value of the "intel" we received from the likes of Jasna the dour Bosniak, or Ahmet and his network of pesky Albanians, or Dimé and Tony and their circle of chauvinistic clowns. I argued to Scott, and also in cables back to Headquarters, that these cases ought to be terminated; that in light of the events of September 11, we should cut loose our less productive agents—to include my own— and focus on developing a network of terrorist-related targets. But it seemed that my arguments—as well as, I was sure, those of other similarly concerned case officers—fell on a conspiracy of deaf ears back at Langley.

"It's a good experience for you," Scott said when I balked about traveling again to meet Jasna, who I knew would have nothing of import to say.

"But she's useless," I said. "And we pay her a ton of money— for what?!"

"Headquarters wants you to keep running the case." Scott frequently blamed management back home.

And so I would continue to run Jasna, I realized, and a number of other second- and third-rate assets, because *someone* at the CIA thought it was good for my career. Privately, I conjectured what anybody who had lost a loved one in a terrorist attack would think of these pointless exercises. I felt that now, in addition to shortchanging myself, I was failing everyone else. The CIA, on the other hand, viewed me as one of their most promising junior officers.

One day, I was walking through Skopje when I got caught in the imaginary cross fire of a dozen young boys armed with plastic guns and rifles. They were playing "Macedonians and Albanians" like American boys used to play Cowboys and Indians. The boys ambushed one another from behind parked cars with a kind of maniacal zeal, and I thought, *I am someone who is caught in a game. A little boys' game that men continue to play as adults.*

September 11 had upset the CIA, I realized, because it meant someone was not playing by the rules of the game. If ever there were a chilling indication that the Cold War was over, and that the traditional spy-versus-spy tactics were not going to work anymore, it should have been then.

But the CIA was, and still is, made up of men who are loath to give up playing their game.

For a while, when my sense of dedication had been hovering around an idealistic peak, I'd started to pursue a developmental contact who I thought might have ties to regional Islamic extremists. The prospect both excited and motivated me. I met Fatos for the first time at a nightclub on the Albanian side of the River Vardar.

"I used to run with some of these guys," Fatos shouted to me over the Balkan version of Britney Spears. Fatos was referring to a group of *mujahedin*, about whom I'd inquired, who supposedly had infiltrated Kosovo during the Bosnian War and who now occupied themselves by spreading anti-American sentiment throughout the region.

My ears perked up when Fatos said, "I myself am not agreeing so much with the whole *jihad* thing."

"Go for it," Scott said later when I reported back to him about Fatos. "Just make sure you okay it with Headquarters."

I wrote up a lengthy cable, describing my introduction to Fatos and why I thought he might represent a worthwhile prospect, though I'd no doubt the cable would disappear into the netherworld of routinely ignored correspondences that we sent daily back to Headquarters. I described Fatos as "having extremist ties, but decidedly open to talking to an American such as C/O Hadley."

Meanwhile, I arranged to meet Fatos in Pristina, the capital of Kosovo. Kosovo, which remained an international protectorate, was divided into British, American, French, German, and Italian sectors, each one patrolled by soldiers from that particular country. The role of these NATO troops—aside from patronizing local whorehouses and thereby subsidizing the regional white slavery trade—was to keep the Serbs from killing the Albanians and vice versa. The latter case had become more and more prevalent in the late 1990s, since the fall of Milosevic and the tables had turned. Now it was the Serbs still residing in Kosovo who were afraid to leave their apartment buildings even to buy bread.

Given the few advantages that Skopje had to offer over Pristina, a renowned Balkan hellhole, many troops traveled frequently to FYROM for a taste of culture and diversion. It was unusual for a foreigner living in Skopje to venture in the opposite direction, though. Were I to be stopped and questioned as to why I was traveling to Kosovo, I would maintain that I wanted to pick up some souvenirs from the historically significant region before returning home for the holidays. Granted it was a lame excuse, but I also feared that in Macedonia itself, my cover—after almost two years of spying—might be wearing thin.

I set out from Skopje in the late afternoon, under cover of a heavy fog. The road to Kosovo was lined with the usual suspects: Macedonian soldiers who seemed baffled by their own weapons, and clusters of aimless Albanian men who would emerge from the mist like headless horsemen to scowl suspiciously at the passing cars.

Pristina, I perceived upon rolling within the city limits, would live up to its reputation as an exceptionally unaesthetic locale: satellite dishes on every decrepit balcony, trash-lined streets, posses of stray dogs roving the byways.

No sooner had I arrived in the city than I felt sort of desperate to get out. Congested with smog, dirt-caked vehicles, and an indisputably seedy-looking local population (it seemed almost entirely men), the main road through downtown ended abruptly at a gully of mud, in which I parked my car.

After some concerted plodding on foot through the mucky, chaotic streets, I found Pizzeria Fjala, where I was to meet Fatos. An overturned couch marked its entrance, next to a dumpster brimming with trash. Like so many other Balkan establishments where I'd met prospective agents, the restaurant itself was situated down a long flight of stairs in a dimly lit, windowless basement.

Fatos—an olive-skinned, prematurely balding man with one lazy eye—waited for me at a table for two near the front of the dining room. In an adjacent ballroom, a lively wedding reception was just getting under way.

Pizzeria Fjala, as it turned out, offered everything and anything to eat except pizza. I told Fatos to go ahead and order for the both of us. I'd learned, in these situations, it helped to give the man this small sense of having the upper hand.

While we waited to be served, several more guests arrived for the wedding, which proved to be an ongoing distraction. The Fjala's newly carpeted entrance must have possessed an indiscernible rumple in its material, causing more than a few of the decked-out Muslim women to topple headlong down the stairs. Fatos seemed completely unfazed every time one of these women tumbled to the floor in front of us like fruit dropped from a tree.

"Do you think you could reconnect with some of these guys you used to hang out with?" I asked Fatos, of the local *mujahedin*.

"I am not interested in their agenda." Fatos leaned back in his chair.

"But we are," I said, feeling compelled to cut to the chase. I figured Scott would be either horrified or proud.

"Who's *we*?" Fatos's eyes narrowed.

"Me," I said. "I mean America. Our government. Tracking extremists is a top priority for us."

"Ha!" Fatos laughed in an exaggerated manner. "You guys don't understand."

"What do you mean?"

"These people are not like, you know, just hanging out. You

want to be one of them? You have to be ready to sacrifice, to make some *jihad*."

"I get that," I said. "That's why we need someone like you, to get to know these guys, to keep an eye on them and to let us know if something major is going on." Even I was amazed by my own forthrightness. "Imagine how many innocent people we might have been able to save had we known in advance about, for instance, September 11."

"It's not so simple." Fatos ran his fingers through his sparse hair. "There are too many people who are hating the American these days."

"I know," I said. "And that's something we're trying to understand."

"I will think about these things." Fatos held up his shot glass over the bewildering platter of grilled meats, potatoes, and salads we were about to share. "But for now, we eat!" And with that, the two of us downed our *rakija* and dug into the "Albanian salad," which—as far as I could tell from the photo illustrations on the menu—was identical to the "Serbian salad."

"Look, I will call you," Fatos said later as we wended our way back to my car.

"Don't wait too long," I said, feeling like a woman about to get blown off after she'd failed to impress her first date. "I think that if you and I stay in touch, it will be well worth your while."

Minutes later, I'd cleared the last mud-encrusted median strip of Pristina and was engulfed in an utterly impenetrable fog. I couldn't see even a single foot in front of me. Alarmed that I might run off the road and into a ditch, where no doubt

I'd be left to die, I vaguely wondered how my demise would be reported back to my family and friends.

"What was she doing driving by herself at night?" I could hear my mother saying. "And where in God's name is *Kosovo*?"

For a short while, the driver of the vehicle in front of mine benevolently kept his hazards blinking so as to partially illuminate my way, or perhaps to prevent me from rear-ending him into the oblivion that lay ahead.

But that car eventually turned off the road, or maybe just disappeared off a cliff, and I found myself the unwilling leader of a caravan of cars heading into a wall of nothingness. I leaned forward, staving off impending panic, and squinted at the glass. My warm breath cleared a small peephole in the fogged-over windshield. At times, I wasn't sure if my car was even still on the road.

I was overcome by a wave of relief when, from out of the fog, a border guard appeared suddenly, *like the Grim Reaper*, I thought. He motioned me to stop. I rolled down the window and handed him my passport. I half hoped that the border guard would tell me that it was too dangerous to drive on, and invite me to stay at the frontier, in some insulated office next to a space heater, until the fog lifted.

But the border guard took a cursory glance at my passport and waved me on. The relief I'd been expecting to feel upon crossing back into Macedonia was obliterated by the swift and obvious realization that fog does not respect international boundaries. It was even worse on the other side.

By now, fairly convinced that I was unlikely to survive beyond the next few miles, my foremost regret was that I'd spent my last few hours alive eating dubious meat and sleazily trying to enlist the likes of Fatos. I felt an acute sense of having accomplished nothing in my life. By the time I finally arrived in Skopje—heralded by the golden arches of McDonald's—I could not help but interpret the fog as some kind of sign.

I'd been hell-bent on recruiting Fatos in a single meeting. I had neither the time nor the inclination to see through the charade of "becoming friends." I wanted to forgo the assessment and development stages of the relationship. I just wanted to get to the point. I realized that I was feeling what a lot of CIA case officers those days were probably feeling—useless and desperate. I didn't know much about Fatos at all, but he had seemed to me like a beacon.

Why, then, had our first real meeting coincided with this impenetrable fog?

As I drove through the engulfed valley of Skopje, trying to get myself back up the hill to where I lived, I felt like a fly wallowing in a vat of pea soup. *I need to get to higher ground,* I thought, *up and above this fog that, for the moment, offers no indication that it will ever lift.*

As it turned out, Headquarters would forbid me to pursue Fatos anyway.

"Our information suggests that Subject may at one time have had terrorist ties," the cable from Headquarters read. "We therefore recommend that C/O Hadley cease and desist from any further contact with Subject."

"This is ridiculous," I said to Scott on the day the cable arrived. "First of all, he already told me that! And how are we ever going to find anything out if we avoid all the people with terrorist ties?!"

"It doesn't make much sense to me either," Scott said. "But without Headquarters' support, you might as well give this one up. You've done well enough out here anyway. From here on out, everything is just gravy for you."

Later, I thought about how I didn't *want* gravy. And I also didn't want to keep stumbling through the corridors of the Agency, and the back alleys of unfamiliar cities, for the rest of my life, like a rat in a maze.

I wasn't the only one eager to prove I was doing my part in the war on terrorism. In March 2002, Ljube Boskovski, the whack-job interior minister—who incidentally lived in a heavily guarded salmon-colored mansion not far from my house, and more than once had implored me to "stop in for tea"— proudly informed Scott that Macedonian police had raided a terrorist cell and eliminated seven "Al-Qa'ida-linked" operatives. According to Boskovski, this terrorist group had been plotting to attack international embassies and diplomats in Macedonia.

Scott, who knew Boskovski to be an erratic nutcase, found the story completely implausible, as did the American ambassador. Two years later, it would emerge that Boskovski and five of his underlings in fact had smuggled in (from Bulgaria) one Indian and six Pakistani immigrants—with promises to the men of passage "to the West"—briefly housed them, and then coldly gunned the men down, a staged killing intended to prove that Macedonia was participating in the U.S.-led campaign against terrorism.

When Boskovski was formally accused of the crimes, he first denied the allegations, then told reporters that he and his associates had received a tip about the alleged terrorists from unidentified "American intelligence officers"—a claim that I feared only those of us on the inside would recognize as preposterous.

When James and I finally met for the beer, I wasn't entirely sure that we were on a date. Also, I felt somewhat ridiculous on account of my nails.

Two days before I left Macedonia, I'd visited Silhouette, Skopje's posh beauty salon, which occupied the entire sixth floor of a downtown apartment building. When I walked in, I was amazed by the level of activity in this warren of small curtained chambers. Macedonian women, who complained endlessly about not having enough money to buy bread, all seemed to possess ample funds to maintain every aspect of their outer appearance.

Seated on a black leather couch amid the whir of electrolysis gadgets, hum of hair dryers, and click-clack of high heels across the linoleum floor, I perused the menu of, in some cases, baffling services: vexing with depilation; con*gig*uring your body; climatic turbo solarium; lymphatic drainage; tuna masage; shirker and pedicure; superstructure of long-term euelashes and waving euelashes; American treatment with fruit acids; biology treatment with gristle from shark; caviar serum; ampulla with live ventricle; and, finally, vig's. I decided that this go-around, I would just get a manicure.

Aside from the Silhouette patrons, the place was packed with a battalion of manicurists, hairdressers, and masseuses. Little women in blue aprons with magenta hair, orange tans, and pink and purple makeup varnished all over their faces scurried from here to there operating the machinery to remove hair, cellulite, scars, moles, and blemishes. Every once in a while, a towering bleached blonde—obviously the owner—would strut around her domain barking out orders. When she noticed that I'd been waiting for more than five minutes, she snapped at one of the minions, who in turn snatched me up from the leather couch.

The beautician led me to a brightly lit room in which another customer lay facedown on an examining table that vibrated noisily and powerfully, causing the woman's flab to gyrate.

"What are we are doing for you today, sweetheart?" the beautician asked, setting me down in a cushioned chair.

"Just my nails," I replied. "I'm going home for my brother's wedding."

"Svatbah?" A stir of excitement passed through the salon like an electric current as she shouted to the others that I would be attending a wedding.

For the next two hours, two pedicurists devoted themselves to my feet while the manicurist attended to my hands. Not realizing that I could understand Macedonian perfectly well, the women cursed up a storm whenever the boss lady was not around, and also made great sport of the woman who'd been on the flab-gyrating machine as soon as she was out the door. I made a mental note never to take off my clothes. Then I reclined and closed my eyes and thought about going home.

When I woke, close to an hour later, I looked down at my hands and was alarmed to discover that the manicurist had shellacked, atop my own fingernails, two-inch-long fake nails, painted some kind of glittery pink and adorned with heart-shaped decals.

"*Super, ne li?*" The manicurist's voice brimmed with pride. "For your brother's *svatbah*!"

At home later, I made the even more discouraging discovery that the fake nails were too thick to cut, not to mention so strongly affixed that there'd be no way to remove them without ripping off my natural fingernails.

And so it was that I arrived for my first date with James looking like I was married to the mob.

We went to a Mexican restaurant near the pool where we used to swim and shared two pitchers of margaritas. I had a total of one piece of *ceviche*, because I was too nervous to eat and was trying to conceal my ridiculously manicured hands.

"Nice nails," James said, smiling, when at last I reached for a tortilla chip.

At some point during the course of the evening, during which we talked and laughed and leaned in toward each other until my head began to swim with ever-increasing hope and desire, it emerged that James's supermodel girlfriend was out of the picture. This was an actual *date*.

"I have to admit, I've been looking forward to you coming home," James said once we were outside.

When he leaned over to kiss me, I dug my spike nails into my thighs to prove to myself that it was really happening. When we finished kissing, I blurted out, "Don't you have some photographs you want to show me at home?"

In the next month, James and I went out on several real dates: giddy, stomach-churning occasions linked together by one after another all-night e-mail exchange, a flurry of phone calls, and a scary but exhilarating sense that something special, and unprecedented, was happening in my life.

At James's basement apartment, I would sit for hours leafing through piles of loose photographs that he had taken on his travels around the world. That old adage "the camera doesn't lie" kept coming to mind. There was a truth to his work that seemed to speak to me from sometime long before. His pictures calmed me, like the bedtime stories my father used to read aloud when we were young, or the way my mother always appeared with ginger ale and crackers when I felt sick.

James took photographs that somehow reflected joy amid the misery, richness in poverty, peace where there was war, and lightness through the dark. I could study those images for hours: the leathery faces of Indian women gazing coyly into his lens; two children walking hand in hand down a dusty village road; a Gypsy girl on a swing, her legs flying freely in protest against the dreary, darkened sky.

James had traveled the world as I had, I discovered, but touched people's lives in a wholly different way. While I'd been roving about plundering other people's privacy, he had been on a journey that gave as much as it took.

When he told me that he liked my writing and the particular way I had of looking at the world, I wondered what he would think if he knew I was a spy. I realized that I had written to him, and to others, the only things I could write: the small and honest observations that emerged like rare shining pebbles on the otherwise ravaged shore of untruths that had become my life.

The more time I spent with James, the more I liked him. I started to laugh out loud again. I dropped hints that maybe I was not entirely happy with the direction in which I'd taken my life. I even told him that, truth be told, I was no longer particularly proud to be American. And I mentioned that, yes, as a matter of fact, what I really loved was to write.

Each time I was with James, I felt like a snake shedding another layer of its skin.

Ordering dinner at an Indian restaurant, James and I cannot take our eyes from each other long enough to read the menu. I let him decide, and watch as his smile infects the hostess and the waiter and the boy who comes to refill our water, before he turns to me.

"I want to come visit you in Macedonia," James says.

In a few days, I'll be heading back to finish out my tour.

"You should," I say.

"I will," he says.

"Er . . . when?"

James laughs. "I guess as soon as I can."

I think about returning to Macedonia, loose ends, agents I have to turn over or—if I have my druthers—cut loose. I think about how now when I take that long, solitary bike ride up Mount Vodno, I will be fueled by the memory of these moments with James. And when I swim back and forth in the decrepit Skopje pool, I will have someone to take my mind off the polluted water, someone who isn't a developmental contact, a potential agent, or a recruited spy. I will have someone for whom I can care—not as a case officer or as an agent handler, but as a person, as a woman, as myself.

"You never finished telling me what it is that you do," James says, studying my face as he takes a long swig from his beer.

I laugh. In his eyes, I see compassion, humor, understanding, and—above all—truth.

"You know what James?" I take his hand in mine. "I never even started telling you what I do."

And with that, I slowly begin to lift my cover.

Epilogue

I was married to James Kegley in Vienna, Virginia, on September 21, 2003, four months after I officially resigned from the CIA.

Leaving the Agency, I was to discover, would be almost as difficult as getting in. For starters, my family—who had been dead set against my joining the CIA—was even more appalled by the thought that I might quit.

"What about your health insurance?" my mother kept saying. "You don't want to burn any bridges with 'the company,'" my father cautioned, cryptically, over the phone.

My brother never criticized my desire to leave, but I thought he must have been disappointed. We were about to go to war.

More accurately, *he* was about to go to war: stationed on the USS *Kitty Hawk,* which already was barreling its way toward Iraq. And there I was: on the verge of going AWOL.

I wanted out of the Agency for a number of reasons, not least of which was my conviction that invading Iraq was one of the most misguided courses of action our country could follow. The war, and the CIA's role in bringing it about, seemed to me a disgracefully concocted diversion, intended to obscure the fact that we still hadn't caught Usama bin Laden and that, truth be told, we'd accomplished precious little in our efforts to eradicate the terrorist networks that had caused September 11 in the first place.

Ironically, in early 2003, not long after my return from Macedonia, I was "surged" to the Near East (NE) Division in order to help gear up for the invasion of Iraq. During my short tenure in Iraqi Operations, I met one woman who had covered Iraq's weapons of mass destruction program for more than a decade. She admitted to me, unequivocally, that the CIA had no definitive evidence whatsoever that Saddam Hussein's regime possessed WMD, or that Iraq presented anything close to an imminent threat to the United States.

Another CIA analyst, whose opinion I'd solicited about the connection between Al-Qa'ida and Iraq, looked at me almost shamefacedly, shrugged, and said, "They both have the letter *q*?" And a colleague who worked in the office covering Iraqi counterproliferation reported to me that her mealy-mouthed pen pusher of a boss had gathered together his minions and announced, "Let's face it. The president wants us to go to war, and our job is to give him a reason to do it."

When I heard that, I'd been appalled. At that point, I knew I had to get out.

Meanwhile, I learned from cable traffic that Tornado Sally was at large in the Middle East, pitching Iraqis left and right, and though she didn't ever manage to recruit any of them, she garnered a tremendous amount of praise for her efforts from Headquarters.

One day, in the Agency cafeteria, I was surprised to run into Jin Suk, whom I'd not seen in three years. She sat upright, as if balancing a teacup on her head, and spoke of her desire to be on one of the advance teams that would march into Baghdad.

Ethan was also on his way to Baghdad, having somehow prevented the CIA medical examiners from discovering that he was afflicted with a crippling disease. He was eager to get to Iraq, where, like the multitude of other case officers being sent there daily, he would make gobs of money—hardship pay, danger pay, and overtime. *"Carpe per diem,"* he joked with me. Ethan and I didn't see the war the same way, but I knew that he was one of the few people whom I genuinely would miss.

I myself experienced the ultimate ethical mortification when I received an e-mail informing me that I was to receive an "Exceptional Performance Commendation" for my support of Operation Iraqi Freedom. I never went to the ceremony and decided the award was something I could live without.

In the months leading up to my resignation, the CIA seemed

to me, more and more with each passing day, like a ship with no one at its helm. One day, I ran into George Tenet in the Agency's underground gym. Once a confident and good-looking man, he now appeared overweight and overwrought. He stared dejectedly at his own reflection in the mirror as he struggled to complete one set of rather paltry weights.

Aside from the discouragement of my family and the uncertainty about my professional future, there was one other impediment to leaving: I quite simply didn't know where I was supposed to go in order to quit. Technically, my boss was the Chief of Iraqi Operations, an elusive balding bureaucrat who clearly had more important things to worry about than my personal misgivings about my career. I half wondered if I might be able to casually mention to him, "Hey, I quit," and then quietly slip out the door.

But I knew that eventually I would have to face the higher-ups in CE Division, to whom, I more than once had been reminded, I "belonged."

It was the Office of Security that ultimately provided me the courage to act. After two "conclusively inconclusive" polygraph exams during my routine reinvestigation, the Office of Security sent me to talk to an intra-Agency counselor, a sallow, poker-faced blonde who couldn't have been more than twenty-two years old. She warned me that I probably ought to "reconsider the value" of my out-of-Agency friends, as those relationships were likely to hinder my future career. I told her I'd much rather reconsider the value of my career, actually.

"That's a very telling remark," she said. "I'll have to record it in your file."

"Please do," I said, smiling.

When I finally quit, I was clutching a half-crumpled memo in my hand. The form—which would have required me to fill out details on James and his extended family on both sides, tracing back, it seemed, to the Civil War—represented to me the final straw.

"I'm not going to fill this out," I said to the security officer, who was leaning back in his chair and using a manila envelope stamped "Top Secret" to extricate a morsel of food lodged between his front teeth.

I turned on my heel, left the office, and walked so fast through the corridors that I could feel the breeze my body created in the otherwise still hallway. I stormed up four flights of stairs to the CE Division "Front Office."

Irene, CE Division's second-in-command, was a woman whom I'd met only once but had spotted many times as she anxiously paced back and forth, chain-smoking in the smokers' courtyard. She exuded a sense of power that at one time would have chilled me to the bone.

"I'm resigning," I said to Irene. "I'm leaving the Agency."

Impassive, Irene wheeled her swivel chair over to a computer and began furiously hacking away at the keyboard. I half expected some security goons to storm in, seize me, and haul me out. A painful silence ensued while Irene consulted whatever had appeared on her computer screen.

"We'll discuss this with the chief next week," she said when she finally returned her attention to me.

"There's nothing to discuss," I said. "I've made up my mind." I think it dawned on Irene and me at the same time that there was not really much she could do.

"We'd all be concerned for you . . . is the problem," Irene said, almost causing me to laugh out loud. "You may experience difficulty finding your way 'on the outside.' The Agency is your family now."

It's like the mob! I thought. "The Agency was never my family, Irene," I said. "In fact, I miss my real family."

Irene sighed when she said, "I suppose there's not much we can do."

"No," I said. "There's really not."

Irene rose, and I rose, and we awkwardly shook hands.

"There will be some paperwork for you to fill out before you leave," Irene said.

Of course there will, I thought. But I practically floated out of her office, and as Bill had cautioned me during training, I was careful on my way out, so that the door didn't hit me on the ass.

Outside, it was a gloriously windy day. Darkening clouds rolled over Headquarters but, in the distance, I could see the sun.

I would be going overseas again soon. This time, I was not going to ask anyone's permission. I would have no alias. I would have no mission. I wouldn't be under cover.

And I also wouldn't be alone. James and I had bought tickets to India. We were going on our honeymoon.

Acknowledgments

Thanks to my agent, Douglas Stewart, who believed in this project from its inception and without whose dedication and encouragement it never would have happened. Thanks also to my editor, Jennifer Hershey, who is as caring as she is exacting, and to everyone else at Putnam who helped make this book come about. I would like also to thank the late Harvard professor Richard Marius, who, many years ago when I asked him if I should enter public service, said, "Yes . . . you should write." Thanks to my family, keepers of my secrets and manuscripts; to Annie Ward and Amy Gorin Chapman, incomparable women and invaluable friends; and to all of the people whom I can't thank by name—you know who you are. Most of all, I would like to thank my husband, James Kegley, my love and my life's inspiration.

Lindsay Moran is a freelance writer whose articles have appeared in the *New York Times,* the *Washington Post,* and *USA Today*. From 1998 to 2003, she worked as a case officer for the CIA. She lives in Washington, D.C.